Seeking Virtue in Finance

Since the Global Financial Crisis, a surge of interest in the use of finance as a tool to address social and economic problems suggests the potential for a generational shift in how the finance industry operates and is perceived. JC de Swaan seeks to channel the forces of well-intentioned finance professionals to improve finance from within and help restore its focus on serving society. Drawing from inspiring individuals in the field, de Swaan proposes a framework for pursuing a viable career in finance while benefiting society and upholding humanistic values. In doing so, he challenges traditional concepts of success in the industry. This will also engage readers outside of finance who are concerned about the industry's impact on society.

JC DE SWAAN is a lecturer in the economics department at Princeton University, where he is affiliated with the Bendheim Center for Finance, and a partner at Cornwall Capital, a New York-based investment fund. He also teaches at the University of Cambridge and is a member of the Council on Foreign Relations.

Advance Praise for *Seeking Virtue in Finance*

"In his unique and important book, JC de Swaan applies Aristotle's virtue ethics to modern finance. The result is a highly sophisticated account of how the finance industry contributes both good and ill to the economy and society. De Swaan knows the evidence, and presents it with care, objectivity, and moral purpose – to help make modern finance a force for good in the world. Kudos for a major contribution to the debate on reforming business for the common good."

Jeffrey D. Sachs, University Professor at Columbia University, and Director of the United Nations Sustainable Development Solutions Network

"The words 'virtue' and 'finance' do not often appear in the same sentence – unless there is a negative in between them. Finance has earned its bad name. This remarkably original book points would-be financiers in a starkly different direction. Through both general principles and specific examples, JC de Swaan shows how the twain can – and should – meet, how the financial industry can become more virtuous and contribute more to society. Every Wall Street executive should read this book."

Alan S. Blinder, Gordon S. Rentschler Memorial Professor of Economics and Public Affairs, Princeton University

"JC de Swaan applies the concept of mindfulness to the untilled field of finance in his new book *Seeking Virtue in Finance*. De Swaan deconstructs the complexity and opacity of the financial industry, laying bare the conflicting and often self-serving incentives that motivate many of its professionals. In doing so, he provides a vocabulary and framework for the next generation of well-intentioned financial leaders to be able to better assess and navigate their way through the industry and advance the common good."

Janet Cowell, CEO, Girls Who Invest

"I've been waiting a long time for someone to write this book, and it couldn't come at a better time. JC de Swaan examines how finance careers can be more socially responsible and the industry can add more value to the world. He makes a convincing case that people and companies don't need to be ruthless to be successful."

Adam Grant, New York Times *bestselling author of* Originals *and* Give and Take, *and host of the chart-topping TED podcast* WorkLife

"In today's world, it has become all too common for individuals to believe that markets and competition are inconsistent with humanistic values. In Seeking Virtue in Finance, JC de Swaan demonstrates how finance professionals can successfully operate within the industry to improve the collective interests of society through moral character, practical wisdom, and moderation. In doing so, financial professions not only make us better off – they make us better."

Arthur C. Brooks, author of Love Your Enemies; *President Emeritus, American Enterprise Institute; and Professor of Practice, Harvard Kennedy School, and Faculty Fellow, Harvard Business School*

"A thoughtful book at a very appropriate time. Can the worlds of finance also be worlds of societal good? JC de Swaan explores this idea in a considered but provocative way. Definitely an important read, especially for leaders of financial firms and leaders of financial functions – as well as younger people considering such careers."

D. Ronald Daniel, former Managing Partner, McKinsey & Company

Seeking Virtue in Finance

Contributing to Society in a Conflicted Industry

JC de Swaan
Princeton University, New Jersey

CAMBRIDGE
UNIVERSITY PRESS

University Printing House, Cambridge CB2 8BS, United Kingdom

One Liberty Plaza, 20th Floor, New York, NY 10006, USA

477 Williamstown Road, Port Melbourne, VIC 3207, Australia

314–321, 3rd Floor, Plot 3, Splendor Forum, Jasola District Centre, New Delhi – 110025, India

79 Anson Road, #06–04/06, Singapore 079906

Cambridge University Press is part of the University of Cambridge.

It furthers the University's mission by disseminating knowledge in the pursuit of education, learning, and research at the highest international levels of excellence.

www.cambridge.org
Information on this title: www.cambridge.org/9781108473132
DOI: 10.1017/9781108561815

First published 2020
Reprinted 2020

Printed in the United Kingdom by TJ Books Limited, Padstow Cornwall

A catalogue record for this publication is available from the British Library.

ISBN 978-1-108-47313-2 Hardback

CONTENTS

PREFACE

One moment [this] herd of graduates of the nation's best universities are young people ... with young people's ideals and hopes to live a meaningful life. The next they are essentially old people, at work gaming ratings companies, and designing securities to fail so they might make a killing off the investors they dupe into buying them, and rigging various markets at the expense of the wider society, and encouraging all sorts of people to do stuff with their capital and their companies that they never should do.[1]

Michael Lewis

This book is written for my students. Many of them intend to pursue a career in finance but are concerned about being corrupted the minute they walk into their first job, be it at an investment bank, hedge fund, or other financial institution. The fundamental question I seek to address is how, given the existing structures and set of incentives in the finance industry, a finance professional can pursue a viable career while benefiting society and upholding humanistic values. To do so, I shine a light on remarkable individuals in the industry, to inform what a self-interested yet virtuous path in finance might look like, and to counter the daily onslaught of stories about badly behaving, self-serving finance professionals. The insights I developed from researching these issues, debating them with my students, and writing this book apply just as much to me, having been involved in the industry for some time, as to my audience.

I recognize that individual behavior is largely driven by incentives which, in turn, are shaped by market forces and regulation. Yet, the surge of interest in the use of finance as a tool to address social and economic problems, particularly among students and young profession-als, suggests the potential for a generational shift in the approach to finance. This book seeks to channel the forces of well-intentioned finance professionals to improve finance from within and help restore its focus on serving society. Its ultimate aspiration is to make a modest contribution to the debate about how to advance society via finance.

INTRODUCTION

Working at a successful hedge fund bestows upon members of the team not only attractive compensation but often a stream of perks from brokers eager to sway trading business their way: dinners in high-end restaurants, open bar tabs, and the occasional round of golf or outing at sought-after sporting events. Not so at Watermark Group, a long-standing Princeton-based hedge fund. When an investment analyst broke an internal rule against broker favors by accepting US Open tickets from Lehman Brothers, co-founder Andy Okun insisted that the analyst pay back not simply the ticket's face value, but its (much greater) scalp value. It took months of prodding for Lehman to cash the check.[1]

Okun, an energetic intellectual who would more naturally fit in an academic setting than a hedge fund, quietly rages at the extent to which the finance industry has entangled itself into conflicts of interest and become increasingly self-serving. Coming out of Salomon Brothers' famed fixed-income arbitrage group, Okun and his co-founder Stephen Modzelewski wrote their client terms on a blank sheet of paper based on first principles rather than industry standards. Their terms were skewed in favor of their clients, even in the fine print. They cared about creating reciprocity between the fund manager and its clients. For close to twenty years, this meant for Okun and his partners not simply retaining a share of clients' profits in good years but *paying back* to clients a portion of losses in unprofitable years from their own savings – a complete outlier in the industry. Okun, who now runs the fund on his own, would come across as eccentric, and perhaps even self-indulgent, to many hedge fund managers.

For an industry whose hallmark traits include being nimble and creative, there is a noticeable homogeneity across hedge fund fee structures, with few outliers. I queried on separate occasions the heads of the two leading prime brokerage departments in New York, who both have a commanding view of the hedge fund industry since they act as the gate-keepers for all the services their banks provide to hedge funds, if they could point out fiduciary leaders in the universe of hedge funds. Both drew blanks. Whether in the hedge fund industry, investment banking, or most other parts of the finance industry, the trend has been toward obsessive short-term profit maximization, often at the expense of clients.

Why is it worth pausing on Okun's client terms, a technical and pedestrian aspect of his fund? Because they carry meaning by deviating from the norm. Vulnerable to conflicts of interests, hedge funds are often characterized by complexity, opacity, and information asymmetry between fund managers and their own investors. Terms and the accompanying fine print typically embed a bias in favor of the fund manager rather than the client.

Most hedge fund managers would agree on several characteristics that would enhance returns to their clients, including, at the top of the list, lower fees and a cap on assets under management. Yet, successful hedge funds almost always end up eventually disregarding these best-practice guidelines. What distinguishes those who breach them from those who don't is often simply the fact that they can: the temptation is too great, the rewards too outsized to resist.

Okun obsesses about serving his clients faithfully, even in areas where the client might not notice. His motivation to offer terms favorable to his customers is not driven by commercial considerations – he is convinced that clients are not swayed by better terms, at least in his narrow field. Rather, he took a stand against industry norms to express his values, at the cost of leaving money on the table.

Okun's departure from the crowd raises the question of what makes a finance professional virtuous. At a minimum, his claim to virtue as a finance professional stems from carrying out his professional mandate to serve his customers purposefully, by prioritizing their interests. And while the earnest and diligent fulfillment of that client responsibility is critical, and arguably the most important way in which a finance professional can contribute to society, being a virtuous finance professional can be defined more broadly.

Consider Frédéric Samama, a manager at Amundi, a large French asset manager, who became convinced that the forces of commercial finance deployed to serve his bank's clients could be harnessed to address social and economic problems, in conjunction with the bank's client mandate.[2] In the late 2000s, he took it upon himself to convene financiers and academics to reflect on ways in which long-term capital holders could solve various market failures, including climate change.

In partnership with Patrick Bolton, an economist at Columbia Business School, and Mats Andersson, the then head of Swedish national pension fund AP4, Samama and his team became pioneers in embedding environmental, social, and governance (ESG) factors in investments. They developed the first mainstream low-carbon equity index, in partnership with MSCI, paving the way for a new market in low-carbon or "decarbonized" exchange-traded funds (ETFs). That market has gained considerable traction, under the premise that capital allocators can make passive investments that will apply pressure on listed companies to lower their carbon footprint, with either no or a positive impact on their investment returns.

Erin Godard illustrates yet another approach to contributing to society as a finance professional. Early in her career as an accountant in Toronto, she became convinced of the linkages between accounting and economic development after spending a summer volunteering in Kigali.[3] In a developing economy such as Rwanda, many firms and not-for-profits founder because of the pervasive lack of financial training and experience. Having a weak or non-existent accounting system creates permanent managerial confusion, preventing organizations from functioning sustainably. With only about 400 Certified Public Accountants (CPAs) in a country of twelve million, few Rwandan organizations can be managed efficiently. At the age of twenty-eight and with only five years of professional accounting experience, Godard moved to Rwanda, partnering up with another Canadian accountant to create an accounting training institute. In doing so, she is helping address a gaping hole holding back Rwandan firms, while contributing in a small but tangible way to the development of Rwanda's middle class by creating a path for young men and women to become accountants.

As finance professionals, Okun, Samama, and Godard have distinguished themselves in the way they contribute to society, yet they have done so taking completely different paths. They share a willingness to challenge industry standards and traditional definitions of success. To new entrants into the industry, they don't fit any recognizable patterns, because no parameters have been developed to assess how, in today's finance industry, individuals can pursue enduring careers that contribute to society and reflect humanistic values. Practitioners seldom question whether industry norms reasonably serve customers. They rarely stray outside of their increasingly narrow silos to question the impact of their work. In a variation on an old saying, what is good for Goldman Sachs or Citadel is assumed to be good for society. But that is not systematically the case.

In this book, I propose a simple framework to assess in a structured manner how finance professionals affect others, and I illustrate it with the stories of remarkable individuals. The framework can be reduced to simple messages: Serve your customers faithfully. Do not extract value from others. Treat colleagues with dignity. And, as much as possible, apply your finance skills and resources toward the collective interest. By evaluating personal impact along these four dimensions, the framework addresses how a finance professional can contribute to society, suggesting models of behavior and career paths to do so.

A Piece of the Puzzle

This book does not offer a comprehensive solution to the role of finance in society. It complements the continuous debate on how best to regulate the industry and channel financial institutions to set employee incentives in a manner that can both motivate individual performance and be consistent with collective interests. The framework I propose seeks to influence the behavior of well-intentioned practitioners, while acknowledging that their decisions are largely shaped by standard incentives to maximize short-term profits and tend to be clouded by cognitive biases. Within these constraints, the framework aspires to guide a subset of finance professionals away from self-serving ends toward serving clients and society more earnestly. It intends to spur greater mindfulness of what might constitute virtuous, yet self-interested behavior and an Aristotelian "good life" in the finance industry.

A fundamental context for the proposed framework is that individual behavior is swayed by incentives, which, in turn, are shaped by structural factors – for instance, the legal structure of financial institutions, the contractual agreements between financial institutions and their customers, and the regulations in place. Incentives evolve as these structural factors evolve. Conflicts of interest have proliferated as a result of structural changes experienced by the industry over the past four decades, particularly in the United States and the United Kingdom. A clear example is that of US and British banks and the extent to which their transition from unlimited liability private partnerships up to the mid nineteenth century to limited liability public companies post-1990s has led to a fundamental change in incentives and behaviors.[4]

No longer on the hook for potential losses incurred by their firms, CEOs and their senior colleagues have been Q incentivized to manage them more aggressively, often translating into greater leverage and a potential personal upside that vastly exceeds potential downside, even accounting for situations in which a bank goes bankrupt. The lure of ever-larger bonuses and the prevalence of stock option-based compensation have fueled a drive to boost their firms' share price over short time horizons and to crystallize gains quickly. Angelo Mozillo and Dick Fuld respectively led Countrywide Financial and Lehman Brothers into bankruptcy but still emerged dynastically rich, albeit reputationally impaired.

To be clear, the premise of this book is that finance is a force for good. Popular culture has traditionally portrayed finance as a value-extracting activity, from the historical linkages with usury[5] to the more recent depiction of Goldman Sachs as a "vampire squid wrapped around the face of humanity."[6] But finance underpins economic processes in fundamental ways – by, for instance, facilitating payments, enabling savers to preserve and grow their capital, channeling capital toward productive uses, and creating insurance mechanisms to mitigate the risk of a large loss. Going back at least to the Dutch Republic's establishment of the first modern financial system in the seventeenth century, finance has been a critical driver of economic development.[7] Since the 1990s, empirical research has identified multiple channels through which finance helps society. It spurs economic growth (up to a certain point), promotes entrepreneurship, accelerates the rate of innovation, improves corporate governance, and increases opportunities for low-income individuals, to name a few of its benefits.[8]

At the same time, the impact of structural and behavioral changes on the finance industry's client-serving mission over the past few decades appears to have been resoundingly negative. Wall Street has strayed far from its original mission aimed at supporting the real economy. Its objectives have become increasingly self-serving. Excess risk-taking, a by-product of that shift, led to a crisis that devastated our financial system and felled several of its largest institutions. After years of extolling the benefits of finance, research has shifted its attention to the limits of finance.

It is futile to try to pinpoint a single reason for the industry's turn. One can't bemoan the vanishing culture of stewardship on Wall Street without acknowledging that the financial system has structurally changed. It is not simply a matter of practitioners opting to act in a more narrowly self-interested manner or the industry attracting more self-interested individuals. And the institutional shifts that drove these changes in behavior were justifiable at every step of the way. Starting with Donaldson, Lufkin & Jenrette in 1970, the dominant investment banks publicly listed in order to raise capital and expand the scope of their business.[9] After the first few competitors went public, others were pressured to follow suit in order to remain competitive, especially in capital-intensive businesses such as underwriting.

Does this mean that addressing the industry's ills should entirely concentrate on regulatory solutions in order to fine-tune the industry's structure and incentives? Hardly. Even if regulation is critical, it is simply not enough. In fact, the more precise the rules and regulations, the more they tend to induce a gaming approach – a license to identify ways to skirt the rules or to circumvent them.[10]

The example of "manufactured defaults" induced by owners of credit default swaps (CDS) – a security that provides insurance against the default of a firm's bonds – is a case in point. In one of the most controversial iterations of this trade, Blackstone-owned hedge fund GSO Capital Partners purchased $330 million of CDS on Hovnanian, an American construction company, and extended attractive financing to Hovnanian, contingent on the company voluntarily missing a debt payment in order to trigger a payout from the CDS to GSO.[11] In order to shield Hovnanian from the negative brand effects of a default, GSO asked the company to miss the payment on specific bonds held by a subsidiary, thereby engineering a bespoke default, highly customized to GSO's interests.

To justify previous versions of the trade, GSO effectively argued that we need to see past its manipulation – the net result is that the recipient company ultimately benefits by receiving a cheap loan from

GSO, subsidized by the losses of the sophisticated financial firms who sold the CDS to GSO. This trade elicited awe from those who see beauty in the technical virtuosity of sophisticated finance professionals concocting bold, path-breaking mechanisms to extract profits from other sophisticated practitioners.[12]

But how can we not conclude that this type of market manipulation impairs the integrity of the financial instruments at stake and their fundamental purpose? Or that it treats in a cavalier manner the duty of good faith and fair dealing which underpins the good functioning of markets?[13] As many have observed, this is not far afield from burning down your own house after taking out insurance on it.[14] Going back to its first foray into inducing a manufactured default with Spanish gaming company Codere in 2013, GSO implicitly took the position that since no rule had considered the possibility that a company would voluntarily default, it was permissible to ask a company to do so as a condition to another loan.

This is by no means an outlier example of ruthless tactics adopted by financiers at the mercenary edge of the industry. As George Akerlof and Robert Shiller have argued in *Phishing for Phools*, deception and manipulation are intrinsic features of our free-market system (which, they recognize, has created unparalleled prosperity in the contemporary world).[15] If GSO had not come up with this clever trade, eventually someone else would have, since any weakness or loophole tends to be exploited given the pervasive pressure to generate excess profits.

Hovnanian's manufactured default triggered an even greater firestorm of criticism than previous examples of the trade such as Codere, because the company was asked to default despite not being financially stressed. In response, an industry group proposed new rules to prevent that particular trade from being deployed again. They stipulate that there should be a relationship between a company's failure to meet interest payments and its financial health. But as Bloomberg columnist Matthew Levine has observed, the new rules narrowly target the particular tactic used by GSO with Hovnanian, leaving the door open to multiple other derivatives of that trade – for instance, the "orphaned" CDS, when a provider of new financing makes it a condition for the recipient to transfer its debt to a new subsidiary, benefiting the sellers of CDS on the old debt, who are left insuring CDS owners against the default of bonds which have now vanished.[16] To the extent that aggressive, sophisticated groups like GSO consider technical loopholes fair game, even if they go against the spirit of fair play, regulation will not stamp out this form of gaming of finance on its own. A broader toolkit is necessary.

Since the time when the industry was dominated by private partnerships, the boundaries of permissible behavior have continuously been pushed toward shorter-term, profit-oriented tactics. As it is shaped by the industry's prevailing structure, set of incentives, and norms, the behavior of finance professionals at any given point in time tends to be broadly consistent. Still, behavior is not entirely uniform. Even if it is affected by incentives, it is not fully determined by them nor is it systematically swayed by the norms set by the most aggressive firms. Presented with the possibility of generating substantial profits from inducing a manufactured default, many practitioners would forgo that opportunity on the premise that it crosses a line.

Along a spectrum, some approach their professional activities with siloed focus and intensity that can easily devolve into self-serving behavior, often unwittingly so – the result is that they "grab what they can when they can," while others endeavor to serve their customers, are mindful of their impact on other stakeholders, take interest in mentoring junior colleagues, and care about contributing to society. This book's proposed framework seeks to inform the behavior of a subset of well-intentioned finance professionals, over the long arc of a career in the industry.[17]

Bounded Awareness

The potential value of such a framework stems from the observation that well-intentioned people can end up making bad decisions. By simply following the rules of the game and emulating successful peers, finance professionals can unwittingly slide into self-serving mode, with little attention devoted to the moral dimension of their decisions and their impact on others. Behavioral ethics, a vibrant area of research, helps explain these dynamics.[18] Cognitive biases influence people's decision-making process. Situational factors have a considerable impact on these biases. Finance professionals may be particularly vulnerable because the industry offers unusually fertile grounds for these biases.

Consider, for instance, the finding that time pressure and stress – hallmarks of a large portion of the finance industry in which deal or market dynamics predominate – tend to impair people's ability to act ethically.[19] More broadly, finance can accommodate and even fuel people's propensity to self-serve because of its complexity, opacity, and the frequent asymmetry of knowledge base between finance professionals and their customers.

Finance professionals are also susceptible to slippery slope biases, which lead well-meaning people to incrementally cut ethical corners and, at times, not notice for extended periods of time that they have allowed themselves to slip from initially pedestrian ethical lapses to major breaches of trust.[20] Companies beset by accounting misstatements often start by adjusting their numbers to manage earnings within the confines of accepted norms in order to meet earnings expectations or other benchmarks and eventually creep into more aggressive, intentional actions that are fraudulent.[21]

Motivated blindness, or the tendency to screen out others' unethical behavior when acting upon it would impair the interest of the observer, especially affects auditing firms and rating agencies. Both are hired and paid by the firms they are mandated to monitor and evaluate. Auditors may find it to be in their interest to disregard anomalies and turn a blind eye to small transgressions. In doing so, they are at risk of becoming captured by their customers and assimilating their clients' cognitive biases.[22]

This tendency helps explain why Arthur Andersen failed to take action on Enron's fraudulent accounting – leading to one of the most spectacular corporate collapses of the past decades in the United States, or why PricewaterhouseCoopers didn't identify Satyam Computer Services' massive accounting manipulation, signing off on the reporting of a fictitious USD 1 billion in cash on its balance sheet, in a fraud that spanned a decade and shattered one of India's most prominent corporate champions. In the same vein, feeder funds channeling capital to be managed by Bernie Madoff were highly incentivized by lucrative management and incentive fees to remain oblivious to the implausibly consistent high returns and low volatility of Madoff's portfolio.[23]

In many instances, sophisticated, well-meaning professionals end up making decisions which an outsider with the same level of financial sophistication and ethical proclivity would find indefensible – and yet, they often ardently rationalize those decisions. In the run-up to the Global Financial Crisis, Goldman Sachs professionals marketed to clients long exposure to the US subprime mortgage market via Abacus, a synthetic collateralized debt obligation (CDO), without disclosing to them that the security had been primarily designed by a fund whose intention was to short it, meaning that its value would decline, nor that Goldman Sachs as an institution was massively shorting that market. After several of its clients were wiped out soon after gaining exposure to either Abacus or similar securities structured and marketed by Goldman Sachs, Goldman executives vigorously defended their actions as well within the bounds of what is not only permissible but expected of an investment bank in that situation.

Finance professionals are also prone to conformity bias and the tendency to be overly obedient to authority. Unethical behavior can be "contagious."[24] An employee may feel that as long as management is pushing for a certain approach and colleagues or peers are adopting it, then there is little need to question the activity's underlying premise. At Wells Fargo, unrealistic cross-selling goals which were aggressively pushed through the retail business led to the creation of 3.5 million fake accounts by customer representatives who were driven to meet institutional objectives and avoid running afoul of an unforgiving corporate culture. The few employees who sought to ring alarm bells were either ignored or fired.

Finance creates conditions that facilitate bounded awareness, which occurs when people fail to incorporate into their decision-making process critical information that is available to them, due to blind spots.[25] The web of incentives, conflicts of interest, and pressure under which finance professionals operate often prevents them from being able to objectively evaluate their actions.

Much attention in behavioral ethics research is now devoted to identifying how best to utilize the considerable insights developed on cognitive biases to improve decision-making. Important channels include applying this understanding to nudge decisions toward desirable personal or social outcomes with the use of "choice architecture," which carefully calibrates how choices are presented and questions are asked – a concept popularized by Richard Thaler, Cass Sunstein, and John Balz.[26] Checklists can be helpful in explicitly raising issues that might otherwise be glossed over by cognitive limitations.[27]

Many of the behavioral solutions to improving finance's capacity to serve society work toward creating greater awareness among practitioners. This book's framework is one tool in that arsenal. It will not resonate with those who are well aware of their transgressions – the fund manager who bribes a corporate executive to reveal inside information will find little value in clarifying how to embed humanistic values in his professional conduct. Rather, the framework targets those well-intentioned, thoughtful professionals who may not be aware of the potential self-serving nature of their behavior and the extent to which it may be at odds with the client-service orientation of their professed mission. It clarifies the distinction between acting in a self-interested manner to serve customers and self-serving – or nominally acting to serve customers while extracting value from them or anyone else under the cloak of the industry's opacity and complexity. The book's framework creates a frame of reference that can, at a minimum, spur awareness in those who intend to serve others earnestly.

Virtue and Success

Won't the pursuit of a virtuous approach to a career in finance inevitably lead to less professional success? It may. As much as I wish it were the case, I am not professing that being virtuous will make a finance professional more successful over time, at least defined according to the industry's prevailing norms. In fact, odds are that incorporating the collective interest in decision-making will make a finance professional less competitive in the short term and vulnerable to negative feedback and pressure from superiors and colleagues. The junior member of an investment banking team calling attention to the moral dimension of daily professional decisions, when, say, raising capital to fund the growth of a cigarette brand targeting youth in developing economies or concocting a sophisticated financial engineering mechanism to mask the overall indebtedness of a client, may be perceived by colleagues as detracting from the team's goals. Stanford behavioralist Jeffrey Pfeffer argues compellingly (and depressingly) that those who rise to the top of organizations often exhibit deeply self-interested, and at times self-serving, behavior.[28]

As Cambridge ethicist John Hendry has pointed out, finance is experienced by practitioners as a sophisticated game whose own rules are the only ones that matter.[29] Financial theory explicitly assumes that people are opportunistic wealth maximizers, leaving no role for moral norms or consideration for the interests of a broader set of stakeholders. What many sitting outside of the financial industry perceive to be unethical behavior is often seen by industry professionals as simply following the rules of the game. To the extent that they believe finance helps the economy in the most generalized manner, they typically do not question the usefulness or morality of their everyday actions. From this standpoint, the only ethics that are relevant are those that are confined to their role – performing their defined tasks as well as possible. This unquestioning agnosticism is often traced back to Adam Smith's invisible hand, or, rather, a caricature of it.[30] The obsessive pursuit of profit, and the lack of debate around the means to achieve profit goals as long as they are within the industry's own guidelines, validate my students' concerns regarding the risk of being corrupted as soon as they enter the industry.

This book is not about day-to-day decision-making and short-term effects – it is about repetitive, long-term behavior. And while it doesn't purport to enhance a finance professional's earning power, it can provide a useful roadmap for long-term success, defined in broader than conventional terms, for those who are inclined to have a positive impact on society. The book's framework can also help assess the culture of a financial firm by providing a benchmark against which to evaluate senior professionals.

While a bent toward the collective interest may not be the shortest path to conventional success, the trade-off between the two is not etched in stone. For instance, there is some evidence that "playing the long game," which often converges with virtuous behavior, can be beneficial to an individual. Wharton professor Adam Grant shows that givers – those who give without expecting something in return (albeit with some boundaries) – tend to be more successful than takers, who try to extract more than they contribute, and matchers, who give only to the extent that they can expect something in return.[31]

Some may even develop over time a professional distinctiveness by explicitly embracing deeply held values – for instance, a commitment to pursuing the client's interests above all or reluctance to engage in activities that are profitable but have a negative impact on society. These values are often publicly espoused by financial firms but only followed when they happen to coincide with profit-generating activities. A finance professional who emphasizes these values is likely to do so successfully only to the extent that he or she has achieved credibility along the industry's traditional norms, by demonstrating a sharp professional skill set and the ability to contribute to the firm's profit generation.

Individual Stories

When I first taught a course on ethics in finance, halfway through the semester, one student asked why our discussions put so much emphasis on unethical behavior and none on laudable decisions and inspiring people. She was right. A theme of this book is to discuss a few outstanding individuals in the industry to illustrate the saliency and applicability of each aspect of the framework and to counter the daily noise emanating from badly behaving, self-serving finance professionals. Some are finance professionals who innovated or set a new standard in their ability to contribute to society via their particular area of finance. Others simply endeavored to cut their own fees while maintaining the quality of their service in order to deliver greater value to their customers. Almost none of them went into finance primarily to help others – few ever do. These leaders and innovators are typically self-interested, ambitious, and successful, each in their own way. However, they also tend to take into consideration more than just their own bottom line, or at least did so at important decision points.

I hesitate to call them ethical role models. None of them is perfect. And the role model characterization inevitably invites broad scrutiny that few finance leaders could withstand given the industry's web of conflicts of interests. Glorifying any individual in finance can quickly turn into embarrassment as this or that allegation surfaces.

Some of the accomplishments to which I draw attention might strike readers as pedestrian. After all, isn't cutting customer fees, or promoting a corporate culture that embraces diversity, what finance professionals should endeavor to do regardless? Aren't these part and parcel of a strategy to remain competitive? In other words, do I risk projecting virtue on a finance professional who is simply positioning for commercial success? In some instances, that may be the case – they may have found a path that happens to both bestow conventional success and contribute to society, whether intentionally or not. But in most of the specific situations discussed in this book, the decisions made by the portrayed individuals reflect a lifelong pattern of eschewing the type of self-serving behavior prevalent in parts of the industry. These decisions typically involve what many would consider personal trade-offs, even if the individuals I discuss might not perceive them as such. In all cases, they clearly stand out from the crowds – at times, in dramatic and unique fashion. They merit our attention because they signal the possibility for deviating from the norm to carve thoughtful, virtuous paths in the industry.

Although the temptation is to focus on the highest-profile individuals, contribution to society as a finance professional doesn't necessitate being in a senior position, being an innovator, or performing heroic feats. By extolling the achievements of selected individuals, we run the risk of over-emphasizing them relative to the many other finance professionals who anonymously contribute to the common good on a daily basis. By virtue of operating in a corner of the finance industry that directly supports the real economy, and by fulfilling their fiduciary commitment to their clients, finance professionals at all levels of an organization can contribute positively to society – be it the bank teller, the back-office specialist, or the first-year analyst. They may also help advance some of the beneficial trends we discuss in this book – for instance, the passive investment revolution or the surge of activity in ESG investments.

The Good Life

Economist and philosopher Amartya Sen argues that the divorce between modern economics and moral philosophy is a contemporary phenomenon that should be considered unnatural:

> [T]here is nevertheless something quite extraordinary in the
> fact that economics has in fact evolved in this way, characterizing
> human motivation in such spectacularly narrow terms. One reason
> why this is extraordinary is that economics is supposed to be
> concerned with real people. It is hard to believe that real people
> could be completely unaffected by the reach of the self-examination
> induced by the Socratic question, "How should one live?"[32]

Responding to that exhortation, the central question addressed by this book is how to work in finance and live the "good life." The underlying premise is that all individuals are self-interested but that self-interest doesn't necessarily have to be narrowly defined as the pursuit of material wealth. It links to the moral theory of Adam Smith, who, despite being widely perceived as the father of modern economics, perceived human beings to be motivated not by purely selfish motives, as is often erroneously asserted, but by a combination of self-interest and interest in the welfare of others, because we are social beings who care both about others and how we are perceived by them.[33]

It also harkens back to the philosophy of Shibusawa Eiichi, who is considered to be the father of Japanese capitalism. At a time when business activities were perceived in Japan to be inferior to the work of the government bureaucracy, he advocated on behalf of their inherent morality and their necessity for the country to develop economically. He perceived banks, in particular, as playing an important role in contributing to the collective good by investing in new businesses (as the founder of Japan's first joint-stock bank in 1873, he supported or seeded over five hundred businesses during his tenure).[34] He argued that economic activities should be underpinned by the same Confucian principles that supported samurai ethics.[35] In his writings, he invoked the image of the abacus, symbolizing business, and the Analects of Confucius to project the harmony between morality and the economy, two spheres that are inseparable and necessitate balancing.[36] According to Shibusawa, not only are profit and wealth generation moral as long as they are generated ethically and benefit society, but they are critical in achieving individual morality – his interpretation of what a virtuous career would entail.[37]

At various points, I will refer to the book's object as "well-intentioned" or "well-meaning" finance professionals. By this, I mean individuals who seek to be successful but embed as a fundamental aspect of their definition of success contributing to the common good rather than extracting from it. I frame this as an aspiration to lead the good life and thrive as a virtuous human being.

Rooted in Aristotelian philosophy and virtue ethics, the concept of *eudaimonia*, often translated as either "flourishing" or "happiness," calls for living in accordance with the virtues and exercising practical wisdom in the face of conflicts and dilemmas, all of which lead an individual to flourish and live the good life.[38] Its optimistic outlook resonates – Aristotle believed that anyone could find happiness by living virtuously and could thus fulfill their own potential as human beings.[39]

I did not set out to write this book with an explicit objective to apply virtue ethics to finance, but I draw from its tradition – in particular, its emphasis on moral character and practical wisdom, its aspiration to achieve both moral and skill-based excellence as intertwined concepts, and the importance accorded to leading by example – all in contrast to a consequentialist approach, which would solely care about outcomes, or a Kantian approach, which would emphasize rules and principles.[40]

Character is emphasized with a view that context matters – in this case, the rules and dynamics of the finance industry, which can be highly idiosyncratic. The details of specific circumstances can materially affect what a virtuous person would do. Not everyone would agree – virtue theorist Alasdair MacIntyre has argued that a finance professional is intrinsically at odds with the virtues in the same way that a thief would be. In my mind, this reflects a misunderstanding of the fundamental social value of finance.[41]

I do not systematically characterize the individuals portrayed in this book according to the virtues but I find that the virtues' inclination toward self-restraint suffuses many of these individuals' narratives. In the Aristotelian tradition, virtues are desirable character traits, which are defined in accordance with moderation: they characterize the mean in between extremes.[42] Courage stands between cowardice – a deficiency, and recklessness – an excess. The virtues might include honesty, integrity, prudence, loyalty, kindness, and generosity – traits that would serve practitioners well in pursuing thoughtful careers that benefit the common good. While they may be informed by cultural differences, they apply consistently across social communities.[43] Virtues relevant to commercial bankers should be no different than those relevant to investment bankers or traders.

The virtues have intrinsic benefits not only for the finance professional, who might value them for their capacity to lead to the good life, but also for society, by bolstering finance's capacity to act as a force for good. In particular, their bias toward temperance could help mitigate greed and other behavioral excesses that often lead finance to stray away from the common good.

This book's approach challenges traditional concepts of success, even if it recognizes that many finance professionals will continue to be motivated by conventional markers of success such as compensation and promotion. A junior insurance professional may find great fulfillment by steadfastly delivering on her mandate to assist in the underwriting of small insurance contracts, and be confident that those contracts genuinely help the families that own them, while exhibiting honesty, integrity, temperance, and other virtues – more so than the fast-rising hedge fund manager who may be compensated many times more and may have attained the exalted social status that tends to be associated with material success, but might act in bad faith with counter-parties whenever doing so can yield additional returns, exploit the fund's limited partners with poorly disclosed terms, display hubris and recklessness in managing the portfolio, and treat colleagues disrespectfully. Along the parameters of this book's framework, that junior insurance professional would be much closer to fulfilling her potential as a human being than the hedge fund manager.

To fully understand whether she is leading the good life, she would have to contemplate whether her underlying professional activity has goals which advance the common good.[44] In finance, this is not always a given. While much of finance remains true to its fundamental objective of helping people achieve their objectives and enabling society to prosper (and insurance may largely belong to that category), we will consider evidence suggesting that various corners of finance fail that test.

Going beyond the purview of this book, she would need to examine herself holistically, including her conduct as a family member, as a neighbor, and as a citizen, rather than simply focusing on her professional role and skill set.

The Framework

The simple framework I propose can, at a minimum, make finance professionals mindful of what markers of a virtuous, responsible approach to finance might be. This could be particularly valuable to the many finance professionals who are well-intentioned but unwittingly oblivious to their impact on others. The framework channels their attention toward four separate sets of considerations, or, at the risk of sounding glib, the Four Pillars of the Good Life for finance professionals, each of which is addressed in subsequent chapters. It adopts a longer-term perspective, over a career and a life. As Hendry puts it, "To judge how ethical a fictional character is, we need to read the whole novel, not just a few pages."[45]

Customer Mandate: Serving Customers' Interest Faithfully

Finance professionals are naturally incentivized to do well by their customers. To be successful, they need to create demand for their financial services or products. However, the complexity and frequent opacity of the finance industry create numerous opportunities to obfuscate the terms of financial services and their true value. A financial service that ostensibly delivers value to customers can be corrupted by faltering integrity: the fine print that enables a bank to impose additional fees on unsuspecting customers for superfluous add-on services; the lenders that pass on sloppily underwritten loans to securitizers; the insurers that are less than straightforward about the constraints on the definition of an insurable event; the private equity manager that imposes hidden fees on his investors.

The framework's first pillar, serving customers' interest faithfully, ranks highest in the hierarchy because it embodies the core mandate of financial professionals. To the extent that the fundamental value of finance is to help customers achieve their goals, no objective should be more important to a finance professional. Indeed, conscientious finance professionals have traditionally aspired foremost to be good fiduciaries.

This chapter highlights empirical research that has unearthed specific ways in which financial institutions are taking advantage of their customers, reflecting the extent to which breaches in the relationship of trust with customers are rife in the industry. We contrast these behaviors with models of distinctive customer-oriented conduct.

No discussion of virtue in prioritizing customers' interest can take place without the towering figure of Jack Bogle, the founder of pioneer low-cost fund manager Vanguard, who arguably created more social value than just about anyone in finance over the past several decades. His impact has been profound, having been instrumental in convincing a large and growing subset of individual savers to shift their capital from high-priced actively managed funds to low-cost index funds and in pressuring the asset management industry to cut fees. We will also examine Dodge & Cox, a San Francisco-based active asset management firm which has prioritized customers and shown unfashionable restraint since its founding in the 1930s, as well as the Japanese "herbivores" – Haruhiro Nakano, Ken Shibusawa, and Hideto Fujino – who seek to achieve similar goals in Japan.

In addition to Andy Okun's outlier take on the hedge fund model, we will explore other corners of the alternative asset industry, with examples illustrating how new models are chipping away at some of the old standards of private equity – from Vincent Mai, who structured Cranemere to specifically address some of the industry's more questionable practices, to Ryan Williams, a young serial entrepreneur whose real estate private equity platform significantly revamps that industry's fee structure and investor participation model.

This chapter also discusses finance professionals whose sense of mission and loyalty to their clients have led them to forgo significantly higher-paying jobs, including the stewards of university endowment capital whose passion for their university has clearly swayed their career decisions – Yale's David Swensen, Notre Dame's Scott Malpass, and Princeton's Andy Golden as prime examples. Finally, we consider those who exhibit a heroic form of fiduciary duty by whistleblowing on the wrongdoings of their own firms, endangering, in the process, their employment, reputation, and ability to work in the industry – including Alayne Fleischmann, who incarnates the plight of many earnest whistleblowers by having paid a high personal cost for acting according to her values, and Eric Ben-Artzi, who stands out for not only having lost his livelihood as a result of calling out his former employer Deutsche Bank on malpractice, but having subsequently declined on moral grounds a multimillion-dollar payout from the US Securities and Exchange Commission (SEC) for which he was eligible.

Social Wealth Creation: Contributing to Society beyond the Customer Mandate

The second pillar of the framework, social wealth creation, asks whether financial professionals benefit anyone besides themselves and their customers. It addresses a conundrum – a finance professional can be a great fiduciary, serve his or her customers with distinction, and yet not contribute to society because many financial activities tend to extract rather than create value for society. In some instances, negative social returns are a by-product of the service to a client, while in others, they are a more direct result of the client's mandate. We will consider, for instance, how investment banks helped Italy and Greece obfuscate their national levels of indebtedness in official European Union reports.

Finance professionals are often oblivious to the distinction between the value delivered to a client via a financial activity and that activity's incidental impact on society, as well as to the potential tension between the two concepts. This stems from the primacy of achieving client satisfaction, or, in some cases, simply generating revenues from clients, in the evaluation of their performance. It also reflects a practical constraint: Evaluating performance in serving clients tends to be a clear-cut exercise, whereas evaluating impact on other stakeholders can be a murky, ill-defined process that lacks a standard approach.

This pillar of the framework speaks to the virtue of justice – a finance professional who generates gains, even on behalf of their client, by extracting value from others would be acting unjustly. Aristotle associated injustice with, among other defects, greed, or the desire to have more than what should be rightfully ours.[46] Adam Smith considered justice to be the most basic virtue and criticized the economic actors who made improper excess profits.[47]

Of the four pillars of the framework, social wealth creation has the broadest ramifications and, yet, is the most difficult to define precisely. In its prevailing definition drawn from marginal utility theory, value is a relative concept, derived from individual preferences. Accordingly, towering CEO or fund manager compensation and skyrocketing specialized drug prices are socially justifiable because they result from a market process driven by supply-and-demand dynamics.

That definition of value relies on assumptions that have been increasingly called into question since the Global Financial Crisis. Drawing on recent work by economist Mariana Mazzucato, I argue in favor of a concept of value which is consistent with the production of goods and services that promotes the long-term capacity of the economy in a sustainable manner, and takes into consideration whether the activity contributes to promoting or reducing inequality – a concept that has been long overlooked in the field of economics until recently.

Using the investment management industry as a case study, we consider the social value of major investment strategies. Curiously for a group that tends to be cerebral, investment managers often appear stumped when asked whether they create social value, at least in my experience. In assessing social impact, a first line of inquiry should be whether an investment strategy fulfills its client mandate in generating attractive financial returns over time. Absent this, an investment strategy becomes a conduit for an unproductive and unsustainable allocation of capital.

Assuming that bar is cleared, I propose two channels by which an investment strategy can contribute to society. First, by simply fulfilling a role in supporting the sustainable functioning of the real economy, which can be reflected in positive contributions to certain economic indicators, such as growth, employment, productivity, research & development, and innovation, even if the effect is small and indirect. Second, by actively improving an investment's underlying business or asset – the domain of activist strategies, in particular venture capital, private equity, and shareholder activism in public markets. We will review the empirical data for these three strategies, and several others, including public equity (non-activist), global macro, and trading and derivative strategies. We will also delve into the surge of interest in embedding ESG factors in investment decisions, as well as the early promise shown by impact investing, which explicitly targets both financial returns and social impact.

Humanistic Leadership within the Organization: Treating Colleagues with Dignity, Empowering Them, and Fostering a Responsible Culture

How should we consider a manager who effectively serves customers with their interests at heart, creates positive social value in the process, and yet conducts himself as a tyrant at work, hogs all of the credit, and manipulates, harasses, and humiliates colleagues, to paint an extreme scenario? The framework's third pillar looks inside the organization: It tests whether financial professionals who have managerial roles treat employees with dignity and help develop them, while fostering a culture of service to customers and responsibility toward other stakeholders. Recognizing one of social psychology's core ideas that situation and environment tend to drive behavior, organizational culture warrants emphasis, particularly in the context of the industry's engrossing incentives and its vulnerability to cognitive biases. Accordingly, this pillar of the framework can be used as a screen to assess the culture of a potential employer.

Because institutional culture and management processes are critical in achieving the goals embodied by the framework's first two pillars, managers have an implicit duty to develop a culture of responsibility. In an Aristotelian framework, a fundamental role of firm leaders is to provide guidance to more junior colleagues in developing the virtues and applying them to their daily professional activities.

In finding the right balance between the pursuit of personal and collective goals at work, we will examine competing behavioral models, including the servant leadership model, Jeffrey Pfeffer's self-proclaimed realist approach, and Adam Grant's framework of reciprocity.

We will seek to learn from individuals who were able to strike the right balance. In this respect, examples from the era of Wall Street partnerships can continue to illuminate contemporary dynamics. We will discuss how John Whitehead inculcated a culture of responsibility at Goldman Sachs – one that has been under intense fire in recent years for having deviated from its original aspiration, how Warren Hellman instilled a forward-looking team culture at Hellman & Friedman, and how Bridgeway Capital Partners explicitly addresses the issue of inequity within its ranks.

Diversity merits attention on its own, particularly for an industry that stands out for its lack of diversity. Yet the reason for including diversity in the framework has little to do with its beneficial impact on performance, even if it makes the case for diversity stronger.[48] Absent an explicit policy, passive discrimination can all too easily become the norm, as even well-intentioned individuals have cognitive limitations that lead them to unwittingly discriminate – whether in the hiring of employees or the evaluation and promotion of colleagues.

We will discuss Arjuna Capital's Natasha Lamb, who has gained traction in persuading listed companies with large gender pay gaps to address that disparity by filing shareholder proposals; Dame Helena Morrissey, a prominent asset manager, who channels her high profile in the British media to pressure boards to reach a minimum level of gender diversity; and Halla Tomasdottir and Kristin Petursdottir, who sought to instill what they consider to be feminine values into their asset management firm.

Engaged Citizenship: Contributing Expertise, Time, and Wealth to the Common Good

Finance can be a noble enterprise. At its best, it enables customers to achieve their goals and helps society generate greater prosperity than otherwise might be achieved. Yet the individual impact of finance professionals is inherently limited by the fact that they are intermediaries. Their direct, personal effect on society cannot compare to, say, that of a nurse who compassionately cares for sick patients, a public school teacher who endeavors to help students learn and develop in the context of overcrowded classrooms in under-funded schools, or a firefighter who takes physical risks to save lives. The impact of finance professionals is also muddled by the fact that their compensation appears unhinged relative to many other professions and that the aggressive, narrowly self-interested pursuit of financial gains by large segments of the industry is widely perceived to have set the stage for the Global Financial Crisis.

For these reasons, finance professionals may be unusually motivated to contribute to society outside of the confines of their professional role in the industry. The framework's fourth pillar assesses whether finance professionals utilize their skills, experience, and network, as well as capital for those who have generated wealth, to act as responsible, engaged citizens.

We will discuss models of philanthropy, particularly for those professionals who have created wealth, as one channel to contribute to society. This speaks to generosity, and in some situations, magnificence, the virtue of generosity for the common good on a large scale. We will reflect on a range of approaches, from the thoughtful, thematic giving of George Soros and Michael Bloomberg, to the secretive giving of hedge fund managers Andrew Schechtel, David Gelbaum, and C. Frederick Taylor. We will also address the thornier case of Denny Sanford, who has donated generously over decades to pediatric care and other causes, but built his wealth controversially.

This chapter will also portray distinct models for financial professionals to contribute their skill set and experience to public causes, either in the context of a new professional endeavor, or as a parallel effort to their main professional occupation. Robert Lovett, a prominent member of a group of leading US public servants who helped build the post-World War II order, embodies the public spirit of Wall Street bankers who decided to serve their country (since his era, a well-worn, and at times, controversial path) and illustrates the benefits of applying financial analytical skills to the public sector.[49] One of the first female partners on Wall Street, Michaela Walsh utilized her finance experience to create and develop Women's World Banking, a pioneer institution providing women access to credit.

We will also consider the travails of Nicholas Benes, a long-time US expatriate in Japan trained in finance and law, who has selflessly advocated for better corporate governance and has become a critical, albeit unheralded, behind-the-scenes architect of the seminal reforms implemented by the Shinzo Abe administration since 2014. David Webb, a former investment banker turned investor and corporate governance activist in Hong Kong, has also had disproportionate impact by the sheer power of his dogged campaigns targeting cronyism, breaches of minority shareholder rights, and threats to Hong Kong's democratic process, underpinning his cases with detailed, rigorous analysis made freely available to the public.

We will end the book by discussing the timeless example of Alexander Hamilton, the US founding father who is credited with having built the country's modern financial system. For our purposes, we will concentrate on what he did not do – the restraint he exercised in his role as Secretary of Treasury in the context of a rapidly expanding financial system.

The framework I propose implies that a finance professional can lead the good life by serving their customers faithfully and by being mindful of their responsibility and impact on the rest of the world – other stakeholders, local and extended communities, as well as colleagues and employees. This call for mindfulness is meant to act as a safeguard against doing harm, but falls short of exhorting every financial professional to explicitly pursue positive social impact through their professional activity in finance. Even if a growing sector of finance seeks to target social impact, few go into finance in order to have a positive impact on society. Because of the beneficial effects of much of finance, professionals who deliver on their fiduciary mandate, exhibit a sense of responsibility regarding their impact on others, and cultivate that responsibility among their colleagues, are likely to impact the world in a positive way.

1 CUSTOMER MANDATE
Serving Customers' Interest Faithfully

The Wells Fargo Case

In my research for this book, I spent many months trying to identify ethical role models in finance. One name that repeatedly came up in the context of the US banking industry was John Stumpf.

One of eleven children, he was raised on a dairy and poultry farm in Pierz, Minnesota. He first worked in a local bakery before enrolling in college and becoming a community banker. Industry analysts I interviewed in 2013–2014 were uniformly impressed by his civility and no-nonsense approach. Articles on Stumpf consistently highlighted his Mid-Western rural upbringing and values. In its 2013 Banker of the Year profile of Stumpf, industry publication *American Banker* noted the frugality of his office and the pervasive folksiness of his senior managers as the self-conscious marks of a values-based bank.[1]

After many years in senior management roles, Stumpf became CEO of Wells Fargo in 2007. Wells Fargo was a trusted, community-oriented bank, founded in 1852 in San Francisco as a bank and express delivery service. It had deftly navigated the real estate bubble of the 2000s, largely eschewing the sirens of subprime mortgages. Stumpf's steady leadership enabled Wells Fargo to emerge stronger from the financial crisis than most other large US commercial banks. He was widely praised for his ability to implement one of the largest bank mergers in history, integrating Charlotte-based Wachovia, the fourth largest bank in the United States, on the verge of collapse at the time of its acquisition. Under Stumpf's watch, Wells Fargo became the largest US bank by market capitalization and the largest bank employer in the country. By 2015, it reached number seven in *Barron's* "World's Most Respected Companies" list.[2] Stumpf could do no wrong. I was pleased to have found a titan of the banking industry to portray as an ethical role model.

And of course, a colossal scandal surfaced in September 2016. It emerged that 5,300 Wells Fargo brokers had created 2.1 million checking and credit card bank accounts – a number later re-appraised at 3.5 million, without the consent of their customers. An investigative report dating back to 2013 had already uncovered evidence of this fraud, but few would have anticipated its magnitude.[3] Besides, it didn't fit the prevailing narrative on Wells Fargo.

This scandal was all the more confounding because it came out of a commercial bank that was portraying itself as having deep roots in its communities – not from your typical aggressive New York- or London-based investment bank. And it wasn't a case of complex finance which required industry specialists to parse out whether a true breach of trust had taken place between finance professionals dealing in esoteric capital markets instruments. Employees had created fake accounts for their unsuspecting retail customers. For some of the duped customers, this represented no more than a nuisance. For others, the fraud had real implications. Unsolicited credit card accounts could negatively affect credit ratings or even place customers into collections when unauthorized fees went unpaid.[4]

While Stumpf initially tried to frame the breach of trust as the work of rogue employees, it quickly became apparent that it spawned from deep inside the company's culture. For years, intense pressure had been put on employees to sell as many products as possible to their existing clients. In Wells Fargo's 2015 annual report, Stumpf wrote that cross-selling enabled the bank to develop "deep and long-lasting relationships" with customers.[5] It is also more profitable to sell additional products to existing customers than to acquire new customers. The emphasis on cross-selling was initiated by Dick Kovacevich, Stumpf's widely admired predecessor. Kovacevich perceived financial products as being no different than consumer products, calling Wells Fargo branches "stores."

On the surface, Stumpf accepted responsibility for the scandal but effectively directed the blame toward low-level employees. He resigned in the face of overwhelming criticism in October 2016. Wells Fargo paid $185 million for the fraud to regulators, including the US Consumer Financial Protection Bureau (CFPB), and another $575 million in a settlement with attorney generals of all fifty US states. It also paid hundreds of millions of dollars in refunds, settlements, and legal fees related to the fraud (and a $ billion fine in late 2018 related to its auto and mortgage lending practices).[6] In an unprecedented move, Janet Yellen imposed an unusual penalty on Wells Fargo on her last working day as Fed Chairwoman, capping the bank's assets at their 2017 year-end level, until the bank shows sufficient improvement in its governance. The bank has struggled to regain its footing with retail customers as the scandal has eroded the perception of its value proposition, although its valuation is consistent with that of other large US banks as of early 2020, albeit no longer at a premium.[7]

How could such a cancer be allowed to spread within an organization that touts itself as a main-street bank dedicated to consumer and small businesses? The factors at play all reflect industry-wide challenges. The first is that over the last decades, the finance industry has increasingly become a minefield of conflicts of interest. The fact that most large banks such as Wells Fargo are publicly listed creates a tension. The relentless pressure to deliver short-term results to boost shareholder value can too easily divert management away from the patient, solicitous handling of customers that is necessary to foster long-term relationships. Maximizing shareholder value, the mantra of listed companies for the past few decades in the United States and many other advanced economies, conflicts with putting customers' interest first if shareholder value is constantly measured on a short-term basis. The internal goals at Wells Fargo had little to do with its customers' interests and everything to do with shareholder value. These goals were pursued via an unforgiving incentive system, or punishment system depending on how one looks at it, that fetishized target numbers, to the exclusion of other considerations.

In theory, the goal of selling multiple financial products to existing customers was not nefarious in and of itself. Underlying that goal is the desire to create deeper relationships and a more loyal, stickier customer base, which is encouraged to source most, if not all, of its financial products from one trusted bank. As Stumpf insisted, "there was no incentive to do bad things."[8] In fact, the disciplined use of targets has become standard across the finance industry. Since the

1990s, management consulting firms have converted their clients to "value-based management." Accordingly, all resources should be channeled toward increasing the value of the firm and its share price. Discipline toward that overarching goal is imposed by tying incentives to departmental-level targets on metrics that management deems to have the greatest potential impact on the firm's value. Where Wells Fargo stood out was in its uniquely aggressive cross-selling targets, and the relentless pressure on low-level employees to achieve these often unrealistic, short-term goals, no matter how they got there. Prior to the scandal erupting, a petition signed by 5,000 employees had called on management to lower sales quotas, to no avail.[9]

As of 2013, employees were reportedly asked to sell at least four financial products to 80% of their customers, while the stretch goal was the "Gr-Eight," meaning eight financial products per retail banking household.[10] That practice had been carried over by Kovacevich from his days as CEO of Norwest Corporation, prior to its merger with Wells Fargo. The intensity of Wells Fargo's targets was an outlier in the industry. For instance, a former Chase employee reported that she was given daily sales goals at Wells Fargo versus monthly ones at Chase.[11] Wells Fargo managers met with employees several times a day to report on their progress.[12]

These unrealistic goals spurred a culture of permissiveness – results at all costs, that led to fraud. Former bankers reported being pressured by their managers to invoke spurious reasons to convince customers to open new accounts – for instance, stating that it was unsafe to travel without separate checking and debit cards – or opening and closing new accounts for customers by claiming there had been fraud in the existing account.[13] Managers encouraged employees to order credit cards for pre-approved customers without their knowledge, filling forms using their name and contact information, and at times moving money away from existing accounts. Specific directives to open unrequested accounts came from branch as well as district managers, the very people who would have been expected to exercise oversight over the integrity of customer interactions.[14] In a staggering display of cynicism, Wells Fargo fired employees who reported abuses via the bank's formal internal whistleblower channel.[15] When it fired employees prior to the scandal becoming public, Wells Fargo would not inform its customers of the fraud or refund fees that had been illegally extracted from them.[16]

A culture of results at all costs – and results not being inherently defined in ways that are consistent with serving the customer's best interest – necessarily stems from the top of the organization. As Stumpf stated during congressional testimonies, "I care about outcomes, not process."[17]

The fraud could be interpreted as the unintended consequence of poorly designed incentives – unintended because these fake accounts created no tangible value to the bank. Wells Fargo extracted approximately $2 million in fees from 85,000 of the more than 1.5 million unauthorized deposit accounts opened, and a bit above $400,000 in fees from 14,000 credit card accounts of the more than 565,000 that may have been unauthorized – a pittance in the context of a bank that generated revenues of over $88 billion in 2016.[18] It is implausible to think that Stumpf would have wanted these results to occur.[19]

Narrowly defined reward systems can lead employees to lose sight of their broader purpose. A 1990 study showed that when students were asked to proofread a paragraph for a marketing brochure that had both grammatical and obvious content errors, they were more likely to highlight both content and grammatical errors when asked to "do your best" than when they were specifically asked to focus on one or the other.[20] Examples abound of well-intentioned but narrowly defined reward systems gone awry. In the early 1990s, Sears set a sales goal of $147 an hour for its auto mechanics. This led to widespread overcharging and delivery of unnecessary services.[21] When goals are too challenging, they induce employees to adopt riskier and, at times, unethical practices.[22] A better approach at Wells Fargo might have been either to widen the reward system to incorporate targets that were aligned with their customers' interests or to shift the financial resources used to incentivize employees toward improving their customer value proposition – for instance, by reducing prices or creating new customer incentives.

While poorly designed incentives can promote self-serving behavior at the expense of customers, the personal judgment of employees should act as a safeguard. However, cognitive biases often prevent the exercise of independent judgment. Blind spots lead people to make unethical decisions without being mindful of the lack of moral consideration in their decision-making. Traditional approaches to ethics assume that most people recognize an ethical dilemma when they encounter one. In practice, they often don't.[23] Environmental and situational factors hold great sway on decision-making. Certain aspects of the finance industry – its complexity and opacity, the prevalence of information asymmetry between service providers and customers, and the pervasiveness of conflicts of interest – make finance professionals particularly vulnerable to cognitive biases. They are so deeply enmeshed in a complex web of engrossing incentives and high pressure that they can easily succumb to bounded awareness, the tendency to artificially bound the information they take into account in making decisions, favoring their self-interest at the expense of others. As Cambridge ethicist John Hendry has argued, finance is experienced by practitioners as a sophisticated game whose own complex rules tend to make them oblivious to any other considerations.[24]

Another cognitive bias, motivated blindness, can help explain why Wells Fargo's senior management and board failed to exercise oversight. Motivated blindness refers to people's propensity to not recognize other people's unethical behavior when that behavior furthers their own interest.[25] That pattern is often ascribed to rating agencies that extended high credit ratings to firms right before they collapsed, and to auditing firms that vouched for the financial numbers of firms that turned out to be fraudulent. In both cases, the presence of a strong vested interest not to highlight information that would endanger their lucrative contracts can stem from a bias, at times unwitting, to make generous assumptions that known problems are immaterial or bounded and thus not worth investigating further, or to avoid digging too deep.

In the Wells Fargo scandal, Stumpf and his senior management were arguably most at fault for the informal culture they engendered across the organization. Informal culture often trumps an organization's publicly espoused values. The "true values" of an organization tend to be internally disseminated through the behavior of managers and colleagues, stories they emphasize, and behaviors that are rewarded.[26] In its literature, Wells Fargo touted its honesty, trust, and integrity and emphasized its focus on defining its customer relationships along the customer's own definition of "financial success."[27] By contrast, many employees were rewarded for pushing, and at times imposing, products onto their customers that often did not respond to their needs. The Wells Fargo scandal illustrates how an inordinate focus on narrow goals can overtake and define an organization's culture.

For lower-level employees, behavior likely didn't turn egregiously unethical in one swoop. Patterns of deep breaches of trust often start with small ethical compromises which escalate along a slippery slope. Marketing experts Andris Zoltners, P. K. Sinha, and Sally Lorimer posit that the first step might be minor – perhaps advising a customer to take on a product that's not in their interest as a way to relieve pressure from unrealistic goals.[28] With goals still unattained, additional steps might include asking friends and family members to open new accounts, another incremental step. At this point, an employee might justify to him or herself opening a new account without authorization as yet another small incremental compromise, perhaps making the assumption that the new product won't generate additional costs for the customer and could be closed soon thereafter.

There are likely thousands of other Wells Fargo employees who swayed their customers to open new accounts for products that may not have been in these customers' interest, without resorting to deception. These employees might have considered themselves good soldiers for having successfully cross-sold products, and would have been rewarded for it by management. It's plausible that these employees advised their customers to take on additional products without devoting much, if any, thought to whether these products would be helpful to their customers. In such cases, bounded awareness and other cognitive biases can go a long way in explaining why good people can end up unwittingly breaching the trust of customers.

Are the 5,300 Wells Fargo employees who opened fake accounts good people who unwittingly made bad decisions? That is probably taking the argument a step too far. They were pressured, and in many cases bullied, into a pattern of deception for fear of losing their job by a dogmatic management group. While cognitive biases could have facilitated a slippery slope toward an increasingly self-serving relationship with one's customers, it is hard to imagine an employee opening an account behind the customer's back, at times creating fake email addresses to complete the application without alerting the customer, and doing so without ever thinking that this could represent a breach of trust.

Individual character plays a role and, in some instances, did act as a safeguard against immoral behavior. In the Wells Fargo scandal, the whistleblowers stand out for having made that judgment call and intervened, at great risk to their careers (and often, as it turned out, at the cost of their job). Another commendable, albeit less conspicuous, group of employees would have left on their own, perhaps quietly, because they felt uncomfortable committing breaches of trust, or would have been fired because they were not seen as performing given their unwillingness to cut ethical corners, as others were.

An Unfulfilled Responsibility

On the heels of the Global Financial Crisis, numerous scandals have come to light, from Bernard Madoff's Ponzi scheme to the Wells Fargo scandal. The creation of fake accounts at Wells Fargo symbolizes how the industry has increasingly deviated away from prioritizing its customers' interests. It is no surprise that trust in the industry is collapsing. In early 2020, the Edelman Trust Barometer, an annual global survey, showed financial services to be once again the least trusted industry amongst fifteen major industries, a position it has comfortably held for years.[29] As of June 2018, a Gallup poll showed that only 30% of Americans had confidence in their banks (to be fair, a significant uptick from June 2016, and still ahead of US Congress).[30] Simply put, many people now assume that their financial service providers intend to fleece them when they can, rather than serve their best interest.

This context of repeated scandals and eroding trust raises the question: What is the industry's responsibility toward its customers? And what is the standard to which it should be held?

The industry's duties and obligations toward its customers can be murky, certainly from the point of view of customers, due to a combination of overlapping regulations, intentional obfuscation, and, at times, the inherent difficulty in defining the exact role a finance professional takes on in serving a customer. In the United States, finance professionals recommending investments are not systematically held to a fiduciary standard. In some situations, they can breach a customer's trust while adhering to the rules and regulations technically applicable to their function.

The definition of who should be held as a fiduciary has constantly evolved. The term fiduciary stems from the Latin word for trust. The concept of fiduciary duty can be traced back to the Code of Hammurabi in Babylon, circa 1790 BC.[31] It appears in one form or another in the Old and New Testaments, Chinese historical texts, and Roman law, which articulated under Cicero the relationship of trust between an agent and principal.[32]

The entry in *Black's Law Dictionary*, the standard American legal dictionary, acknowledges that "fiduciary is a vague term, and it has been pressed into service for a number of ends."[33] To complicate matters, the legal recognition of a fiduciary duty in the United States varies from state to state. Fiduciary principles typically apply to professionals that have some discretionary authority and whose customers show some degree of dependence on these professionals' advice. In some instances, the definition simply emphasizes a relationship of trust and confidence. As a result, there is not one set of clearly identified roles that are held to that standard but a spectrum of functions that call for varying levels of fiduciary care. For example, while most brokers are not legally held to a fiduciary standard, some brokers with discretion or effective control over a customer's investment account have been considered to be fiduciaries.

The evidence suggests that explicitly extending a fiduciary duty affects behavior – in a study of large financial service firms selling annuities, brokers operating in US states where broker-dealers have a fiduciary duty to clients tend to sell simpler, lower-cost products and fewer variable annuities (which are often seen as carrying high fees and generating low yields) compared to brokers from states that do not impose that duty.[34]

Over time, courts in the United States have applied a fiduciary standard to an increasing universe of relationships, including investment bankers and clients, priests and parishioners, and even teachers and students.[35] A similar pattern is observable across markets, raising the bar in the duty of care of financial professionals, and particularly investment professionals. In the United Kingdom, the Kay Review of 2012, an independent review commissioned by the UK government in the wake of the Global Financial Crisis, argued that restoring trust in equity markets requires applying fiduciary standards across the investment value chain, and that contractual terms should never override this duty of care.[36]

But progress toward applying higher standards of care is not linear. Some seemingly straightforward applications of a fiduciary standard of care have generated fierce industry pushback. Consider the US Department of Labor's proposed Fiduciary Rule, which was to deem all professionals making investment recommendations or solicitations on retirement assets to be fiduciaries, not just those who charge a fee for service. This would have required all advisors to act in the best interests of their clients and disclose conflicts of interest. Implementation that was initially planned for 2017 was scuttled, under a Trump administration loath to impose new regulations, leading to a diluted version.[37]

Going back to the example of a universal bank serving large numbers of retail customers, only a subset of Wells Fargo professionals is subject to a fiduciary duty in the traditional sense of the word. Wells Fargo's management and board of directors owe a fiduciary duty to shareholders. Some professionals in specific roles are also deemed to owe a fiduciary duty to their customers: for instance, investment advisors, trustees in wealth management, and investment bankers when they perform "fairness opinions" to provide an objective perspective on the valuation of a business. But brokers and the bulk of professionals interacting with customers on a daily basis at Wells Fargo branches are not technically held to a fiduciary standard of care.

Yet banks such as Wells Fargo clearly aspire to become trusted advisors across their client-facing functions and exert influence. John Stumpf wrote in his 2015 letter to shareholders: "our highest honor is the trust that customers place in us. And trust is best built through relationships," adding that "we put our customers first" and that "we are committed to our customers' satisfaction and financial success and to work in their best interest."[38] *The Vision and Values of Wells Fargo*, the closest Wells Fargo has to a constitutional document, states that "We want our customers to see us as a trusted financial advisor, for outstanding service and sound advice."[39] Even though Wells Fargo is not technically a fiduciary for its customers in most aspects of its business, it is positioned as one, at least in its marketing. Customer representatives and brokers strive to become trusted advisors, but since the rules treat them as mere salespeople, they are afforded discretion to recommend to their customers products that may be reasonable but not ideal and to encourage behavior that may not be in their customers' long-term interest.

The image of trusted advisor or trusted partner that finance professionals seek to convey often conflicts with the predatory, at times even extortionary, nature of some of the products sold to retail customers. Credit cards are a case in point. Credit cards offer a critical service by facilitating payments and providing to consumers readily available credit to purchase goods and services. The popularization of credit cards in the 1960s ushered in a new era in consumer finance. They remain ubiquitous, facilitating the lives of millions of consumers. Some 44% of US households have credit card debt and 33% of Americans who have ever had credit card debt report having run up credit card debt from paying for basic necessities like health care.[40] Absent credit cards, they would have to turn to less institutionalized forms of funding, with potentially higher costs. Yet, the ease of access to credit cards can be too much of a good thing for consumers with limited self-discipline. Two out of five Americans with credit card debt report having built up their debt balance from unnecessary purchases. By charging what are arguably usurious rates on credit – an average of 14.9% in 2017[41] at a time when short-term US interest rates were close to 0 – as well as exorbitant fees on overdrafts, card companies can benefit from customers behaving in ways that are counter to their own interests.

Already in the early days of credit cards, a pattern of abuse emerged. Credit cards were simply mass mailed to bank customers considered to have good credit risks, without their requesting one. Many of these cards found their way to customers that were prone to overusing them. During the Lyndon Johnson US administration, Special Assistant Betty Furness likened that process to "giving sugar to diabetics."[42] Today, credit card companies continue to systematically encourage profligate spending on credit – the kind of behavior that senior executives of these card companies would discourage their own children from adopting. For instance, credit card companies tend to emphasize payment options that postpone full payments by using credit and don't warn debit card holders when they are about to trigger an overdraft – all subtle cues toward the less responsible behavior.[43]

They also tend to obfuscate the costs associated with building up debt. The average credit card agreement has 4,900 words and requires an 11th grade reading level, despite the 2009 Credit Card Accountability, Responsibility, and Disclosure Act and the simplification guidelines recommended by the US CFPB in 2011.[44] While readability has improved in recent years, these agreements remain unreadable to a majority of Americans as most Americans read at a level two or three grades below the highest grade they completed.

In open competitive markets, we would expect competition to channel customers toward those financial service providers that offer the most attractive terms and services. After all, customers can shop around, read customer reports, and compare notes with friends. But financial institutions tend to be aligned in their service offerings and research points to the fact that these institutions are often able to obfuscate the value of their products through complexity. Since the Global Financial Crisis, much of the input into the theory of competition has moved away from the notion that the equilibrium point tends to lead toward a Pareto optimal outcome, where resource allocation is such that any change could not make any individual better off without making another one worse off. In particular, Robert Shiller and George Akerlof, two Nobel prize winners, have argued that the equilibrium tends to be swayed toward whatever opportunity there is to fleece or manipulate customers.[45]

Financial innovation offers insight into this dynamic. Some financial innovation clearly benefits customers. The most beneficial new products are often those that create greater transparency, simplify things, and lower costs – passive index funds, for example. Even well-intentioned innovation – meaning innovation primarily designed to benefit customers, can backfire. For instance, peer-to-peer loans, once lauded as a way to disintermediate banks and reach an under-served population, have developed the allure of predatory lending. Recent data points to increasing delinquencies, a downward trend in credit scores for borrowers, and use of these loans to increase overall debt levels rather than substitute for high-rate credit card debt.[46]

However, in recent decades, innovation appears to have often been designed to benefit financial institutions more than their customers. For instance, innovation has driven greater retail product complexity, yet research shows that the more complex the product, the greater the profit for financial institutions and the lower the performance for households.[47] In a landmark study of retail structured products offered in European countries, where these products are more lightly regulated than in the United States, Claire Celerier and Boris Vallee showed that the most complex retail products tend to be targeted at households that are least likely to understand them.[48] For instance, they found that savings banks, which largely service lower-income households, offer more complex products than commercial banks. To illustrate the finding, they highlight the following product marketed by Banque Postale in 2010:

> Vivango is a 6-year maturity product whose final payoff is linked to a basket of 18 shares (largest companies by market capitalization within the Eurostoxx 50). Every year, the average performance of the three best-performing shares in the basket, compared to their initial

levels is recorded. These three shares are then removed from the basket for subsequent calculations. At maturity, the product offers guaranteed capital of 100%, plus 70% of the average of these performances recorded annually throughout the investment period.[49]

With a product of that complexity, whose evaluation calls for the skill set of an investment professional steeped in exotic options, retail customers need to entirely rely on the advice of the financial professionals with whom they interact. Yet these professionals are comfortable recommending products that tend to benefit the provider more than the customer.

A Fiduciary-Like Universal Principle

At the core, finance professionals are in the business of serving customers. By debating the finer points of who is a fiduciary and who is an agent or intermediary, and what the minimum standard should be for counter-parties, we can lose sight of the underlying principle that should be applied to all finance activities, which is that all finance professionals should serve their customer's interests faithfully. Even finance professionals who have a more narrowly defined role than traditional fiduciaries, such as customer service representatives and branch managers, should be held to a fiduciary-like standard, i.e. a fiduciary standard in spirit if not legally, because they render a socially important service to customers, who are in turn highly dependent on their financial professionals for sound advice. Retail customers of banking, lending, and investment services are especially vulnerable to self-serving behavior by finance professionals because of the technicality of financial products, the high potential for information asymmetry between them and their finance service provider, and the significant potential consequences of misguided decisions. Used-car dealers also endeavor to be perceived as trusted advisors but the ramifications of overpaying for a car once every several years are more benign than biased influence over relatively frequent and consequential financial decisions.[50]

In some instances, the dilemma faced by Purdue Pharma in marketing OxyContin, a powerful painkiller that has been prone to abuse and dependency, is the better analogy.[51] When brokers aggressively marketed subprime mortgages in the run-up to the financial crisis, they responded to a customer need but masked or at least glossed over the risks involved, and at times irresponsibly extended mortgages such as the infamous NINJAs, which required no jobs and no assets. At issue is a lack of self-regulation in the marketing of these products to a group of customers particularly vulnerable to dependency – an unemployed couple that gets a NINJA mortgage to purchase a house is at high risk of needing more debt down the road to service their mortgage.

Of course, there are limits to the analogy. Users of OxyContin often desperately need medication to alleviate their pain in a way that low-income households do not desperately need to buy a house. And while the opioid crisis primarily affects opioid users (with some indirect effects on the rest of the population), the subprime crisis triggered a collapse in home prices across the country, massive job losses, and a global economic slowdown. Still, the manner in which abuse of the availability of subprime loans contributed to a nationwide crisis in the United States has parallels to how the over-prescription and abuse of OxyContin and other powerful painkillers have led to a national opioid crisis.

In a world of increasingly complex products and relationships, simple principles can offer useful guidance. Serving your customers' interests faithfully is a simple and versatile articulation of that spirit. It echoes one of the three daily questions of self-examination that is attributed to Confucius: "In acting on behalf of others, have I always been loyal to their interests?"[52]

Should this universal principle equally apply to serving sophisticated institutional customers? Are there circumstances when the *caveat emptor* concept, which entails that the buyer alone is responsible for checking the quality of the purchase, should hold sway? Absent a traditional fiduciary relationship in which an institutional customer has entrusted a financial firm to make decisions on its behalf, the degree to which a fiduciary-like standard of care should apply depends on the extent to which the financial service provider is positioned as a trusted advisor in the context of a significant information, and at times knowledge, asymmetry. A pure market intermediary, for instance a market-maker who matches offers to buy and sell specific securities, should be held to a lower standard of care since he or she is not positioned as a trusted advisor. He or she should have a duty to share buy and sell quotes and to provide best execution with competence, diligence, and care.[53]

But many roles in capital markets call for a combination of execution and advice. One of the best-documented examples of conflicts of interest in serving sophisticated institutional customers relates to Abacus, a $2 billion synthetic collateralized debt obligation (CDO) Goldman Sachs helped structure and sold to customers in 2007. This complex security was created in response to the desire of John Paulson, who led a large hedge fund, to gain short exposure to the subprime mortgage sector in the United States, which he expected to collapse. The synthetic CDO referenced specific residential mortgage-backed securities, which John Paulson helped select based on his view that they were poised to perform poorly or fail.

Abacus was structured as a zero-sum instrument, which required customers on both sides of the trade: long (betting that the underlying mortgages would increase in value) and short (betting that they would decline). On the short side, Paulson & Co. bought a credit default swap (CDS), paying a premium to the CDS writers, who took the long side of the trade, in exchange for a payout from the CDS writers if a credit event occurred in the reference assets (in the event the underlying mortgages referenced by the CDS went unpaid). Although Goldman Sachs hired ACA Management as a third-party portfolio selection agent, forty-nine out of the ninety securities that ended up in the portfolio of reference were selected by John Paulson.[54] Having coordinated the structuring of the security to suit Paulson & Co.'s interest in shorting it, Goldman Sachs successfully marketed the long side of the Abacus securities to three customers, including German bank IKB and ACA, which claimed it did not realize that Paulson & Co. would take the short side of the trade. Signs of deterioration in the financial health of the underlying mortgages surfaced soon after the deal was completed. In a span of a few months, the three investors lost more than $1 billion, while Paulson & Co. generated a similar amount in profit.[55]

Of the several aspects of misconduct Goldman Sachs stood accused of, failure to disclose material information loomed largest. In marketing Abacus, it omitted to mention that its one customer on the short side of the trade had picked a majority of the referenced securities to maximize the probability that the portfolio would fail. Presenting ACA as a third party ostensibly responsible for the selection of these securities masked John Paulson's role in structuring a security that was customized to his interests. Goldman Sachs omitted to disclose to clients it was soliciting for Abacus that as a firm, Goldman Sachs was also significantly net short the subprime mortgage market, meaning that it would benefit from a fall in prices, with views aligned with those of Paulson & Co.

At first, Lloyd Blankfein, CEO of Goldman Sachs, argued that the firm was not significantly net short the subprime mortgage market and, furthermore, that it did not bet against its clients.[56] Fabrice Tourre, the Goldman Sachs salesperson identified in the SEC claim, made the point that his clients were highly sophisticated institutions, implying that they should be expected to develop their own views and not rely solely on Goldman Sachs' marketing pitch.[57] He also argued that Goldman Sachs had acted in this case as a market-maker, meaning a simple conduit bringing together buyers and sellers without soliciting them, rather than an underwriter, thereby lowering the firm's duty to share material information.

These claims were debunked by testimonies under oath and internal Goldman Sachs emails.[58] Goldman Sachs had acted as an underwriter since it had created Abacus. It later surfaced that the firm was substantially net short the subprime mortgage market (a credit to its investment savvy since so few firms were prescient enough to anticipate the imminent meltdown), while actively marketing several securities such as Abacus to get some of its customers to take the long side of those trades.[59] In three synthetic CDOs similar to Abacus, Goldman Sachs took a substantial portion of the short side of the trade, without telling its customers on the long side.[60] At best, Goldman Sachs misled its customers on the long side, whether intentionally or not. In its settlement with the Securities and Exchange Commission (SEC), Goldman Sachs eventually recognized that it had been a mistake to omit disclosing the role of Paulson & Co. in Abacus's portfolio selection process, agreeing to pay a record fine of $550 million.[61]

The debate over the distinction between being a market-maker and an underwriter obfuscates the fundamental necessity to serve customers faithfully. In this case, it would not have necessarily entailed that Goldman Sachs disclose its own proprietary analysis supporting the negative view on the sector, or endeavor to convince customers that they shouldn't take the long side of Abacus, and thereby ensure that the security would never be taken up. There were still customers at that point in time that were interested in getting long exposure to the subprime mortgage market. Serving customers faithfully would have entailed disclosing all material facts related to the transaction and conflicts of interest while still offering them the possibility, once they had all this knowledge, to take on the long side of the trade because these customers explicitly wanted to express a long view, even if they understood it was diametrically opposed to that of the de facto portfolio selection agent, John Paulson, and of the underwriter, Goldman Sachs.

Holding yourself to serving your customers' interests faithfully is a guiding principle that requires adaptation to specific roles in finance. For a customer service representative, whose main role is to facilitate retail customer transactions, market products and services, and provide guidance to customers, being faithful to a customer's interest doesn't mean advising them to find a better, cheaper product at a competing bank. It means channeling them toward the products and services that are best aligned with their profile and interest, being transparent with the trade-offs involved, and refraining from pushing hard other products and services that are not ideally suited. For a sell-side trader who executes trades on behalf of institutional investors, it entails, for instance, not using the information to benefit the broker or another of the broker's clients. Evidence abounds that this breach of trust occurs frequently – a study showed, for example, that in the United States, clients of a broker employed by an activist investor to execute its trades tend to buy the same stocks as the activist prior to the activist's filing of a 13D form, which is required when an investor accumulates more than 5% of a company's shares and at times spurs a positive share price reaction.[62] Other studies suggest that brokers tend to share with selected clients order-flow information when they are liquidating large portfolios, enabling them to benefit from the information.[63]

This type of universal duty of care applied to a broad range of finance professionals is in the spirit of the principles of fiduciary duty released in draft form by Japan's Financial Services Agency (FSA), in 2017.[64] The FSA articulated seven principles, including foremost the duty to pursue the best interest of the client. Neither a rule nor a law, the duty underpinning these principles is meant to be freely adopted by financial service firms.[65] However, if financial service firms operating in Japan do not comply with these principles, they are required to explain why they don't, potentially putting them at a competitive disadvantage to peers that are compliant by shedding some light on areas in which they may not be systematically acting in the best interest of their customers. By targeting all "Financial Business Operators" that engage in customer service, and intentionally keeping vague the definition of who should be held to that standard, they are promoting a universal duty of care to be adopted by all finance professionals, consistent with the principle of serving one's customers faithfully.

Serving Customers' Interests Faithfully: Models of Fiduciary Leadership

How can finance professionals become fiduciary champions? The asset management industry offers a useful case study. For years, the industry's focal point was the heroic fund manager, striving to beat the market year after year. However, fund managers that beat the market in any given year are unlikely to do so consistently. The attention devoted to short-term outperformance obscured for a long time a problematic data point: The vast majority of asset managers underperform the market. According to S&P Dow Jones, over a fifteen-year investment horizon, 90% of US large-cap managers underperformed their benchmark index.[66] Extolling the exploits of the few outperforming fund managers has tended to divert attention away from the fact that persistence in returns tends to be low across the industry. S&P Dow Jones found that of the US equity mutual funds that were in the top-performing 25% of their peer group in the five-year period to March 2012, only 22.4% performed in the top quartile in the following five-year period to March 2017. In fact, a greater proportion of that top-performing quartile of funds in the five years up to March 2012 ended up in the bottom quartile over the following five years.[67]

The steep increase in assets invested in markets, the proliferation of funds, the draw of talent, and the application of new technologies have made it increasingly difficult for fund managers to find inefficiencies and capture alpha – returns in excess of the systemic risk they take on. A more sustainable approach for asset managers to faithfully serve customers is to reduce the cost of their intermediation. Research on asset managers suggests that the level of management fees and operating expenses that are charged to clients are the best predictor of future fund performance.[68] Advertising, marketing, and distribution are examples of expenses that are funded by management fees, but not supporting activities that are helpful to existing clients. In the United

States, no one has done more to reduce the industry's costs than John ("Jack") Bogle, the founder of low-cost mutual fund company Vanguard.

The Returns of a Lifetime: Jack Bogle's Moment

Right up until his death in early 2019 at age 89, Jack Bogle lost no opportunity to make his case.[69] Every time the Vanguard Group founder came to visit my first-year students at Princeton University, as he did for the last several years no matter what physical shape he was in, he was quick to blast the asset management industry. "Too much costs, not enough value" – his deep voice and high energy would startle the students. He bemoaned the eroding sense of professionalism – managing money had become a "business." He lamented the rise of "speculation" over "investment." He extolled the value of hard work.

Those tenets could form a roadmap to Bogle's career as one of the most important figures in American finance over the past century. He epitomizes how finance can be a force for good by genuinely focusing on the interest of customers rather than those of the intermediary.

When he came to meet with my students at Princeton, he would talk about how he had stumbled upon a *Fortune* article on the nascent mutual fund industry in the Firestone Library reading room, almost seventy years prior. Up to that point, he had struggled to find his footing academically. A scholarship student at Princeton, he worked long hours in between classes. The article triggered his interest. He wrote his senior thesis on the ethical shortcomings of the mutual fund industry. His central argument: "Mutual funds can make no claim to superiority over the market averages." Decades later, his ideas around indexing finally caught fire. Vanguard, the asset management firm he founded in 1975 to address the very issues he had highlighted in his undergraduate thesis, is draining assets away from traditional asset management firms at a record pace. The Fidelitys and Franklin Templetons have reluctantly brought down their fees over time.

Academic studies have proven Bogle's point for over four decades. In 1974, Nobel Prize winner Paul Samuelson published "Challenge to Judgment," arguing that there was no evidence that fund managers could systematically outperform the S&P 500 on a sustained basis.[70] Around the same time, Charles Ellis published "The Loser's

Game,"[71] which found similar evidence, while Princeton professor Burt Malkiel called for the creation of a mutual fund that mirrors the market in his seminal book *A Random Walk Down Wall Street*, first published in 1973.[72]

Retail investors are better off putting their savings into passive, indexed funds, which simply replicate the performance of a stock index, rather than "active" fund managers that pick stocks. Why pay for expensive fund managers when the index they are supposed to beat outperforms them? The more vexing question is why did it take so long for Bogle's idea to become mainstream? "Too much salesmanship, not enough stewardship," according to Bogle: Marketing, rather than investment management, has become the asset management industry's core strength.

Empirical research suggests that a large proportion of the compensation differential between the finance sector and the rest of the economy comes from rent extraction, or the act of obtaining economic gain by extracting value from society rather than creating new wealth.[73] Value extraction can appear in various forms, including excess fees. One of the most thoroughly documented examples comes from the asset management industry. Bogle stood out in his zeal to buck that trend.

Not everyone was enamored. From the time he launched his first index funds and was denounced as "un-American" on posters sponsored by a competitor firm, he never had a particularly warm relationship with finance industry leaders. That's not surprising, considering that his life's mission has been to call the industry's bluff on fees. A relentless champion of small investors against the system, he publicized the self-serving interests of active managers.

Some simply resented the "holier than thou" tone of his message. His energy and missionary zeal tended to translate into a tyrannical disposition at work, by his own admission. Perhaps this explains the frosty relationship he had with some of his successors at the helm of Vanguard. Clashes mounted when he came back to work after a heart transplant at age 67, implausibly reinvigorated after years of diminishing health. Boardroom drama forced him off the board, after which he was exiled in a corner of the executive building on Vanguard's campus. From there, he proceeded to push his industry agenda.

Bogle gave away his equity to his customers when he created Vanguard as a mutual company. This means that all of Vanguard's profits go back to its customers, the owners of Vanguard funds, thereby reducing their fees and ensuring that no traditional Wall Street firm could sustainably challenge Vanguard on a cost basis. By doing so, Bogle also effectively forwent vast wealth. He insisted that never in his wildest dreams could he have imagined Vanguard managing over $5 trillion as it does today. He was very wealthy by any absolute standard, but his wealth was very modest by the standards of the finance industry for someone who founded and managed one of the industry's behemoth institutions. That fit his character. In discussing his lifestyle during lunch right before talking to my students, he pointed out how he had owned the blazer he was wearing for more than thirty years. "Why buy another one?" Bogle asked. He systematically gave away a large chunk of his compensation, funding scores of Blair Academy and Princeton students over the years.

Bogle cringed whenever he was asked whether setting up Vanguard as a mutual company owned by its customers, and focusing on low-cost index funds were meant as acts of public service. He typically retorted that they were tactical decisions, made purely to avoid triggering a non-compete clause with his former employer and to quickly gain market share. Yet Bogle's pattern of decisions throughout his career and his lifelong crusade on behalf of individual investors point to broader motivation. At times, he described himself as an academic masquerading as a businessman. A better description might have been a public servant masquerading as a businessman.

A sub-theme of the course I teach on ethics in finance explores role models in the finance industry. They are few and far between. The challenge in discussing Bogle lies in the scale of his impact. By so effectively pressuring the asset management industry to lower its fees, he created more social good than perhaps any contemporary in the finance industry. He makes comparisons with other potential role models daunting.

The emphasis in this chapter on pioneers and change-makers such as Bogle should not create the impression that only those finance professionals that can have large-scale impact are worth emulating. In practice, most finance professionals, including those in entry-level and mid-level positions that do the bulk of the day-to-day work and interact with customers, can act virtuously and be helpful to society. Just about all employees of Vanguard, or "crew-members" as they are referred to internally, would do so, simply by enabling, in whatever small or large way, Vanguard's mission as a transparent, deeply customer-oriented and customer-biased financial institution.

A Spartan Active Asset Manager: Dodge & Cox

Vanguard is a benchmark for the asset management industry that is difficult to replicate given its mutual structure and its enormous scale, which both contribute to lowering its costs. Still, other asset management firms have managed to exhibit fiduciary leadership. San Francisco-based Dodge & Cox is a rare asset management firm which forgoes all marketing and broker expenses in order to focus its resources on stock-picking activities and offer lower fees to its clients. Typically described as disciplined, sober, and long-term oriented, the firm has maintained a bare-bones structure, with no sales force and no overseas offices.[74] As a result, its fees are on average about 50% lower than its active asset management peers. Since its founding in 1930, the firm has shown unfashionable restraint, offering a very small array of mutual funds – six at last count, and closing some of its funds to new investors. It has steadfastly avoided the temptation to launch new funds to capture demand for the hot investment trend of the moment.

Entirely owned by its current employees, the firm has remained independent and private, allowing it to minimize conflicts of interests. Shareholder employees who reach 65 years of age are asked to start selling back their shares, in a structure that is reminiscent of Wall Street partnerships of a bygone era.

Its strong fiduciary culture has fostered employee turnover that is among the lowest in the industry. Perhaps to prove the point, co-founder of the firm Morris Cox came to the office until he was 95 years old.[75] Dodge & Cox hires only one or two new research analysts a year and once hired, they tend to stay. In fact, every member of the firm's Investment Policy Committee has started at Dodge & Cox as an analyst. CEO Dana Emery has spent her entire career at the asset manager, coming in as an analyst thirty-four years ago after being a varsity swimmer at Stanford. Among her priorities as CEO are to maintain the culture that emphasizes client focus, frugality, a low profile, and a long-term approach. She and Chairman of the firm Charles Pohl speak with reverence of the firm's co-founders, referring to them as Mr. Dodge and Mr. Cox, in a nod to the firm's explicit positioning as an old-fashioned, values-driven organization.[76]

Dodge & Cox stands out as a fiduciary leader in an industry that has increasingly played defense, as widespread underperformance relative to benchmarks has driven massive flows of funds from active to passive asset management. Asset managers are typically compensated on the basis of fixed annual management fees, at times in addition to an upfront sales fee. The emphasis on a fixed management fee implies that fund managers are rewarded for being asset gatherers. Of course, performance plays a critical role in a manager's ability to attract funds, but with many asset management funds acting as "closet indexers," deviating little from their benchmarks, marketing takes on a significant role in the vast majority of funds, Dodge & Cox being a rare exception.

In order to differentiate themselves, a very small but growing number of funds have experimented with so-called fulcrum fees, which reward managers when they beat their benchmarks and penalize them when they underperform it. San Francisco-based Orbis Investment Management has introduced an investor-friendly performance fee on several of its flagship funds. It charges a 0.45% annual management fee and a 25% fee on any profits generated above the MSCI World Index, but if it underperforms that benchmark, it will reimburse 25% of that underperformance from the fees it generated from the prior outperformance. It does so by putting into a reserve fund most of the fees it generates from outperformance since they can be clawed back. Founded in 1989 out of South Africa's largest private asset manager, it manages $35 billion as of mid 2019. The fulcrum fees it offers fit well the firm's positioning as a fundamental, long-term, contrarian investment manager. Anecdotal evidence suggests that its clients have been stickier during periods of underperformance as a result of this mechanism.[77]

Fidelity and AllianceBernstein have recently offered similar fee structures on selected funds. Fidelity has structured its fulcrum fees on three-year performance relative to the benchmark in order to address the concern that excessive risk may be taken if a fund manager focuses too much on annual outperformance. Still, these innovative fee structures remain a small niche of the industry – an estimated $1 trillion out of a total of about $14 trillion of assets under management for the US mutual fund industry as a whole.[78]

Japan's Herbivores: Haruhiro Nakano, Ken Shibusawa, and Hideto Fujino

The dynamics in Japan are altogether different, with many Japanese reluctant to invest in a stock market that has yet to recover to its peak of the late 1980s. Over the last two decades, a group of three mission-driven fund managers have taken on the fight to convince Japanese individuals to invest in equities for the long term and focus on costs. They articulated their philosophy in a book titled *Herbivore Investing – Taught by Professional Asset Managers*, which they published in 2010. The herbivore moniker is meant to facetiously invoke the passive nature of certain Japanese men, referred to as "herbivore males," in the presence of women, and symbolize the opportunity represented by long-term, low-cost, buy-and-hold strategies, even if they are not particularly fashionable.

Similar to the experience in the United States, the push toward lower fees has faced strong resistance within the Japanese asset management industry. Haruhiro Nakano endured years of setbacks at financial firm Credit Saison in his attempt to get the company to offer a product that emulated what Vanguard offered in the United States. A former high-yield bond and derivatives trader, he experienced a conversion of sorts, coming to the view after more than a decade working in capital markets that his job created little if any social value.[79] By age 40, he became driven by the need to "do an honest form of asset management."[80]

Japan's herbivores found critical support from Atsuto Sawakami, a highly respected investor who offered Japan's first low-cost independent mutual fund in the mid 1990s. One of the highest-profile investors in the country, Sawakami has acted as a mentor to the three members of the group. At age 70, he continues to give numerous seminars on the benefits of long-term investing, railing against the short-term biases of the investment industry. When Nakano found himself once again overruled by a new boss at Credit Saison, Sawakami met on several occasions with Credit Saison's board members and CEO to extol Nakano's project.[81] After years of rejection, Nakano finally prevailed and convinced his firm to offer the Saison Vanguard Global Balance Fund, starting in March 2007.[82] With no sales commission and 0.47% management fee, the fund's cost is less than half the average for the industry. He also offers an actively managed fund, the Saison Asset Building Tatsujin Fund, with no sales commissions and 0.54% management fee. By comparison, its peer funds average 2.6% in sales commission and 1.4% in management fees. Both of Nakano's funds have outperformed the vast majority of retail funds offered in Japan.

A similar mid-life pivot led Ken Shibusawa, the former Japan head of global macro fund Moore Capital, to work toward helping retail investors manage their savings with their best interest in mind.

With no sales commission and 1.15% management fee, his Commons 30 fund also has a significantly lower cost than its peers. Shibusawa admits that his commitment to offer a low-cost, long-term-oriented fund has taken a toll on his personal financial standing.[83] The sense of mission runs strong in his family – his great-great grandfather, Shibusawa Eiichi, was a pioneer in the establishment of Japan's financial system, discussed in the introduction of this book.[84]

The third herbivore, Hideto Fujino, also had a pedigree background in asset management – with stints at Nomura, Jardine Fleming, and Goldman Sachs – before launching his own company, which more clearly reflected his values. That entrepreneurial streak leading successful investment professionals to leave well-established firms is much rarer in Japan than in the United States or the United Kingdom, making Shibusawa and Fujino true stand-outs, particularly since their purpose was to establish low-cost, values-based organizations.

These fiduciary leaders have found strong support from the Abe government. Nobuchika Mori, head of the powerful FSA between 2015 and 2018, took on as a mission the battle to sway individual investors toward longer-term, low-cost investing. He worried about the toll of having too much of Japanese household savings parked in cash and deposits – 51.7% versus 13.7% for US households, which goes a long way toward explaining why US household savings grew 3.3× in 1995–2016 versus only 1.5× for Japanese households.[85]

He was also appalled by the self-serving nature of the asset management industry in Japan. He asked rhetorically whether asset management businesses reliant on high fees "deserve to be preserved in our society" and whether they are "providing their employees with worthwhile jobs."[86] In a country feeling vulnerable about the plight of its aging population, he also questioned what "financial institutions selling unsuitable products to the elderly look like in the eyes of their children."

In 2017, he announced an investment program that allows individuals to invest tax-free up to ¥400,000 (about US$37,000) in equities and bonds for their retirement. The catch for the asset management industry is that only those funds that are low cost, unlevered, and with a long-term horizon can participate. He made his point clearly: as of November 2017, only 50 out of 5,400 funds were deemed eligible by the FSA. That number rose to 141 as of early 2018, as traditional asset managers introduced new funds to meet the criteria.[87] The end goal for the Japanese government is not only to bring down fees which have been charged, in Mori's words, "with little regard for customers' interests," but also to sway households to move their dormant $8.0 trillion in cash and bank deposits into more productive uses.[88]

A Rare Beacon in an Industry in Need of Fiduciary Leadership: The Watermark Group

Hedge fund management has been commonly referred to as the most overpaid profession in the history of the world, and it's hard to find many people outside of the industry that would disagree. The press regularly reports on the seemingly obscene amounts made by the leading hedge fund managers, often denominated in hundreds of millions of dollars, if not billions. These numbers reflect a business model that combines a relatively inflexible fee structure linked to assets under management (AUM) and the ability of a small group of investment professionals to benefit from gigantic scale effects. The typical fee structure pays fund managers an annual management fee of 1% to 2% of assets under management and 15% to 20% of all annual profits.

As a hedge fund's AUMs scale up, its management fees tend to increase linearly, while the costs of running the fund's operations typically don't come close to increasing commensurately. Potential incentive fees also increase with AUMs, although not in a linear way, as increased scale tends to have a negative effect on investment returns. A hedge fund typically revolves around a central figure who has developed an ability to generate alpha, i.e. returns in excess of the portfolio's market risk. A firm is created around the talented investor or group of investors, by encapsulating in a pithy manner the alpha-generating investment approach in its marketing message and by building a supporting group of analysts, traders, finance, back-office, marketing, and investor relations professionals. For many hedge funds, ramping up assets under management from, say, $1 billion to $3 billion triples management fees and greatly increases potential incentive fees, without requiring a massive increase in infrastructure and personnel. This can lead to large excess management fees at the end of the year, regardless of performance, since downward adjustments to management fee terms are seldom proactively offered, unless performance deteriorates to the point where fee discounts can be used to entice investors to stay.

Why are investors in hedge funds willing to pay such steep fees? Various reasons have been proffered. One theory goes that the mandate of hedge funds – to generate excess risk-adjusted returns that are uncorrelated – plays a critical role in the management of a pool of savings, and pursuing that objective requires a specialized and rare skill set for which institutions and wealthy individuals are willing to pay. Yet hedge funds failed to perform when they were most needed. During the market meltdown of 2008, they generated 23% of losses on average, while global equity markets declined by 40%. Even putting aside the financial crisis, the hedge fund industry has had increasing difficulty in generating alpha over the years, perhaps not surprising given the more than eighty-fold increase in the industry's assets under management between 1990 and 2017. Contrary to expectations, fees have only declined from an estimated average of 1.6% management fee and 20% incentive fee in 2008 to 1.5% management fee and 17% incentive fee – far from the 1% management fee and 10% incentive fee that *The Economist* predicted in early 2009.[89] One reason may be that hedge fund investors decided to apply their increased bargaining power to secure better liquidity from hedge funds as a condition of investing, having been burned in the aftermath of the financial crisis by a wave of hedge funds "pulling up the gate," or ceasing to honor redemption requests to wait for better markets, because the fine print in their foundational documents allowed them to do that.

The slight improvement in fees doesn't make up for the fundamental asymmetry that underpins the compensation of hedge fund managers. Every year, they keep an average 15% to 20% of profits on the assets they manage. When they lose money, the losses must be recouped before they can earn incentive fees again. The asymmetry stems from the fact that fund managers earn, without recourse, incentive fees on gains in any given year, but provide an IOU to their investors when the returns are negative. Theoretically, if an investor stays in a fund that has generated losses, the fund manager should be able to steer the fund to climb back to its "high-water mark" over time. In practice, however, that is often not the case as hedge fund managers may not reach their high-water mark again and may decide to shut down their fund in light of the lack of prospects for generating incentive fees. Alternatively, their investors may decide to redeem from the funds, despite the fact that they have paid incentive fees over the life of their investment in the fund that are much greater than the nominal incentive fee as a percentage of profits that was advertised.

Other aspects of hedge fund terms point to a skewed relationship. While hedge fund investors are willing to pay high fees for alpha, much of the returns hedge funds generate are in the form of beta, or market risk, to which investors can gain exposure for minimal fees via index funds or exchange-traded funds (ETF).[90]

One constraint that is easy to dismiss from outside of the industry is the organizational effect of fee-related decisions made by a firm's leader or its senior partners. By making a decision to charge lower than standard fees, a hedge fund manager reduces the available pool of compensation in a way that is highly transparent to the rest of the employees. The lower fee may benefit the organization in the long term by creating better alignment with its investors and more goodwill and trust, but the most direct near-term effect will be a reduction in the compensation pool. The challenge is to attract and retain employees who were not recruited under the premise that their fund would innovate with non-standard fees but whose value to the organization tends to increase along with their ability to move to other, potentially better-paying funds.

One of the few hedge funds that has survived for more than three decades, the Princeton, New Jersey-based Watermark Group discussed in the first pages of this book, happens to be the only true fiduciary leader I have encountered in the industry.[91] It was co-founded in 1988 by Andy Okun and Stephen Modzelewski, who had both worked at Salomon Brothers' fixed-income arbitrage group in its heyday. Intent on creating a hedge fund fundamentally aligned with the interests of its clients, they did what just about no one else in the industry does: create a structure that is purely about ensuring symmetry between the fund manager and its clients, rather than referencing what is standard or acceptable in the industry.

That structure echoed the fulcrum fees seen in a small number of funds in the mutual fund industry, which we discussed above. A meaningful difference, however, is that US securities laws require mutual funds to create that symmetry if they want to charge a performance fee in addition to their management fee, while no such regulation affects the hedge fund industry – the likely reason why Watermark remains the only hedge fund manager I have found that offered such symmetric structure. A very small number of hedge funds have offered "first loss" terms – for instance, the Singapore-based investment manager for the Vulpus Kit Trading Fund will absorb up to an annual 2% of losses before the client experiences any losses.[92] But none of them offer the unadulterated reciprocity that Watermark used to offer.

Between 1990 and 2009, the vast majority of Watermark's incentive fees went toward building a reserve fund. If and when Watermark incurred a loss relative to a hurdle, it would pay out to its clients a percentage of the losses equal to the percentage used to calculate the incentive fee, with the capital coming out of the reserve fund. In the event the reserve fund was entirely used up to pay fees on losses, Watermark's funds would revert to a traditional high-water mark mechanism, according to which Watermark would not earn an incentive fee until its clients were made whole again. Watermark reluctantly gave up its symmetric incentive fee terms in 2009 when a change in the US tax code prevented a fund manager's incentive compensation from being kept in the fund with deferred taxation. The mechanism to ensure symmetry no longer worked once the fund manager had to pay personal taxes on newly crystallized incentive fees slated for the reserve fund.

Still, Watermark, which today manages in excess of $1.5 billion, continues to stand out from a fiduciary perspective in several important ways, including in its unusual level of transparency – with the fund's daily net asset value shared with clients, its commitment to prevent unintended value transfers among investors by establishing a mechanism to fairly share across investors the costs of the portfolio's large bid-ask spread (for each position, the difference between the highest price at which buyers are willing to purchase and the lowest price at which sellers are willing to sell them), and its decision to cap its assets for close to a decade and even return capital when there was a lack of attractive opportunities at various times. It has also charged its clients a lower than average management fee, reflecting Okun's and Modzelewski's conviction that management fees should simply support the business and not become a source of profits.

Watermark's singularity comes across even in the fine print of its legal documents, the very place where its peers tend to pack terms detrimental to its investors. Look closely and you'll find that Watermark's high-water mark actually grows with interest or that it can't "gate" clients in the event of a market crash.[93] Almost none of these investor-friendly terms were requested by investors, who tend to have an ingrained bias in favor of standard terms.

Since the firm's founding, one of Okun's golden rules has been that no one on his team should accept any of the benefits that brokers commonly extend to their hedge fund clients – whether a concert ticket, a round of golf, or an invitation to a benefit event. The incident discussed in the opening of this book, in which Okun asked an analyst to repay not only the face value but the scalp value of a US Open ticket he accepted from Lehman Brothers, reflects the intensity of Okun's personal insurgency against accepted industry practices and ways in which, one might argue, Watermark simply doesn't fit its own industry. It takes committed leadership at the top of a hedge fund organization to impose this kind of discipline, and a strong culture to attract and retain a high-quality team that is willing to accept lower pay, at least in the short term, and fewer perks, rather than move to another, higher-paying fund.

At Watermark, Andy Okun and his partners have built a team that appears to embrace the group's core values. Watermark's relatively uncommercial approach stems from Okun's visceral dislike of the industry's in-built rapaciousness. By making his and his co-founder's values central to the way Watermark's client relationships are structured, Okun has built a group in his image – distrustful of Wall Street and remote from it, deeply analytical, and academic in orientation, with many scientists among its employees, and a large proportion of PhDs. A consequence of the strength of those shared values has been unusually low turnover since 1988.

Could Watermark become a model for other hedge funds? The answer up to now has been: not unless they have to. Watermark is also an unlikely trend setter, simply because Okun shuns the spotlight (deeply averse to the limelight, he only agreed to sharing information for the purpose of this book once I convinced him that the book will barely sell).

Mission-Driven Fiduciary Leaders: Endowments and Pension Funds

The spirit behind the Watermark Group's fiduciary discipline is rare among hedge funds but common among endowments, pension funds, and other tax-exempt investment funds. The gap in fiduciary commitment between hedge funds and tax-exempt funds is notably pronounced in their cost discipline. The Commonfund Institute estimates that well-diversified endowments are typically run on a cost basis of between

1.00% and 1.75% of assets under management.[94] Since endowments typically allocate their capital to outside investment managers, much of these costs go toward compensating these managers. An analysis of the cost structure of nine diverse US university endowments based on data requested by Congressional committees in 2016 showed an average 0.20% of AUMs in internal costs and 1.24% of AUMs in external costs (largely fees to outsider investment managers), for a total of 1.43% in total average costs.[95] It suggests a significantly leaner cost structure than for hedge funds, even if the comparison is not apples to apples, since hedge funds have a direct investment model.

A critical difference is the fact that tax-exempt institutions are spending their own money when running their operations and are thus naturally disciplined, as opposed to hedge funds, which, by and large, manage "other people's money." Visiting a pension fund in Missouri, I was impressed by the fact that it had an internal process to approve the purchase of sandwiches for a working lunch – a far cry from the typical culture at hedge funds. The bureaucracy may be tedious on a day-to-day basis, but these types of cost controls instill discipline, align employee behavior with the organization's mission, and ultimately reflect a strong fiduciary culture.

The lower costs to run large pools of capital in the tax-exempt sector can also be ascribed to greater transparency and oversight relative to for-profit funds. That translates into lower compensation for key personnel, including their investment professionals. A common anecdotal observation about investment managers in the tax-exempt sector, particularly with endowments of universities and foundations, is the prevailing sense of mission. The clear linkage between investment returns and their use toward socially beneficial activities helps attract individuals who are not predominantly motivated by building up the size of their net worth.

As arguably the most respected and heralded chief investment officer (CIO) in the endowment industry, David Swensen epitomizes the mission-driven character of many of the professionals in the tax-exempt investment world. After six years on Wall Street, Swensen was tapped at the young age of 31 to manage Yale University's endowment in 1985. Over the past thirty-three years, he has developed in partnership with long-standing colleague Dean Takahashi the widely emulated Yale Endowment Model and has achieved a stellar investment track record. His Endowment Model consists of a structured approach to asset allocation with broad diversification. Critically, he was a pioneer in shifting his portfolio composition toward illiquid and alternative assets because he considers them to be less efficiently priced and to fit well an endowment's long-term horizon. That investment model has become the standard in the endowment world. Swensen and his team have delivered for Yale an industry-leading 12.5% average return per year over the past thirty years.[96]

In the age of compensation maximization, Swensen stands out for having steadfastly stuck with his position at Yale for more than three decades, despite his ability to make significantly more money managing private sector capital. He took an 80% pay cut when he moved from Wall Street to Yale and has since then turned down offers that would have generated multiples of his compensation, reflecting his enduring sense of mission.[97] Still, he makes a very comfortable living and acknowledges that he is paid very well for what he does, even if his compensation is but a fraction of his for-profit peers.[98]

Swensen appears to be motivated by a deep belief in Yale's mission, while harboring an emotional attachment to the school, having completed his PhD there, worked for two years as a freshman counselor, and lived on Old Campus, the heart of Yale College. He has taught full semester classes since 1980, and frequently gives one-off lectures or student talks. Two-thirds of his team have degrees from Yale, some of whom he recruited from his undergraduate seminar.[99] He has become a hero to the Yale Community, which is clear-eyed about the unique value he has delivered to the institution. In 2005, the Yale president at the time, Richard Levin, unveiled a chart at a party marking Swensen's twentieth anniversary at the university. It showed a list of those who had contributed the most to Yale going back to the school's founding, with names such as Beinecke and Harkness, which adorn some of Yale's most prominent landmarks on campus. On top of the list was Swensen's name. By that point, the university estimated that he had contributed $7.8 billion, based on his outperformance relative to other university endowments (that number had grown to $28 billion by the middle of 2017).[100] In the late 2000s, a campaign by a group of alumni sought to have Yale name a residential college after him to memorialize his contribution to the university. A full-page ad in the *Yale Daily News* asked "What Man Gives Up at Least $100M a Year to Work for Yale?"[101]

Swensen's sense of mission may also stem from his mother having had a strong influence on him. A mother of six, Grace Swensen became a Lutheran minister after all of her children went through college. Swensen considered the ministry when he attended college at the University of Wisconsin-River Falls.[102]

In turn, Swensen invests in investment managers that have, in his words, a "loose screw," in the sense that they define success as generating the greatest possible returns rather than maximizing their own compensation.[103] He considers that group to be only a small subset of the industry. He has had a disproportionate influence on endowment management in the United States, not only through the proliferation of his investing model but also by having trained and mentored many of the industry's leading CIOs who started as part of his team at Yale – prominent examples include Andy Golden at Princeton, Seth Alexander at MIT, Peter Ammon at Penn, and Donna Dean at the Rockefeller Foundation, to name a few.

While Swensen stands out for his long-term performance and his influence on the industry, other CIOs share some of the same attributes. Scott Malpass has managed the University of Notre Dame endowment since 1989, generating over 10% average returns over the past two decades, helping grow the endowment from $425 million when he took over to $13 billion.[104] Under Malpass, the endowment has climbed from the 23rd largest in the United States to the 10th largest, enabling Notre Dame to transform itself into a highly competitive national research university. Like many other university endowment professionals, Malpass is deeply dedicated to his alma mater and, in his case, to the school's mission as a Catholic university. There is a significant religious dimension to Malpass' management, with close attention paid to the social responsibility guidelines of the US Conference of Catholic Bishops and monthly investment office masses.[105] The Notre Dame investment team is almost entirely comprised of alumni and has experienced very little turnover through the years. Malpass is also highly involved on campus, having created and taught several investment classes over the years.

Princeton's CIO, Andy Golden, also stands out for his longevity at the helm of one of the major university endowments and for his stellar track record. A philosophy major as an undergraduate, he first tried his hand as a professional photographer until he pursued a management degree at Yale, where he was hired by David Swensen and Dean Takahashi. Since 1995, Golden's skilled investment management has helped grow the Princeton endowment from $3 billion to

$26 billion. Like Swensen, Malpass, and other supremely talented endowment and pension fund managers, he lacks no opportunity to earn multiples of his compensation in the private sector. Golden exhibits the strong commitment to nurturing talent – both among his external managers and his staff – that seems prominent among those at the top of the endowment field. Clearly passionate about the linkages between his work and the school's mission, he has been a highly engaged participant in my freshman seminar on ethics in finance for almost a decade.

As a result of Golden's distinctive long-term investment performance and generous giving by the university's fiercely loyal alumni, Princeton's endowment towers as the largest among US universities on a per-student basis. In recent years, the endowment has enabled students from families earning less than $65,000 to receive grants to cover full tuition, room and board, and for more than 80% of seniors to graduate debt-free.[106]

Emerging Fiduciary Structures in Private Equity: Cranemere and Cadre

Fiduciary concerns related to the private equity industry have been well documented. Over the years, private equity funds have introduced and made standard a slew of fees that are additional to their fixed management fee – typically 2% of assets under management – and their carried interest, the 20% of profits they typically take upon exiting an investment. Those additional fees can include transaction fees once an acquisition has been completed, investment banking fees when additional acquisitions are made on behalf of the portfolio company, monitoring fees that are meant to compensate private equity funds for the work they perform to improve operational efficiency, director fees to sit on their boards, and advisory fees to help secure new loans. For small funds that manage assets below a critical mass, these fees can enable investment professionals to sustain themselves. However, investors in private equity, also referred to as limited partners (LPs), generally consider them to be superfluous. For most funds, the standard management fees comfortably compensate ongoing operations, regardless of performance. These additional fees raise concerns about investment professionals receiving generous compensation even when they generate mediocre returns.

Disclosures around these fees have been discreet at best, leading to a perception that private equity funds are self-serving, in contrast to their stated goals and the long-term nature of their investment approach. An academic study estimated that as much as $20 billion in additional fees were charged to US portfolio companies by private equity firms between 1995 and 2014.[107] These fees are described in this study as "hidden" because they generally did not appear in the agreements that specify the fees charged by the general partner to LPs. They are typically defined once an acquisition is made, in a negotiation between the general partner of the private equity fund and the executives of the acquired company, who are by then quasi-employees of the private equity fund.[108]

The four largest leveraged buyout (LBO) firms (Carlyle, KKR, Blackstone, and Apollo) are estimated to have generated $2.5 billion in monitoring and transaction fees from portfolio companies between 2008 and 2014, in addition to $27.3 billion in management and performance fees. To provide a sense of scale, these incremental fees charged to portfolio companies were estimated to total 1.75% of these companies' enterprise value and 3.6% of their earnings[109] – not inconsequential numbers.

Given the large fees paid to private equity funds, some large US pension funds are contemplating building their own private equity teams to save on costs. Among those are the California Public Employees' Retirement System (CalPERS), the largest public pension fund in the United States, which paid close to $700 million in fees to private equity funds in the year ending June 2016.[110] A fraction of that cost could help build a private equity team with distinctive experience. Some Canadian pension funds have been managing internal private equity teams for two decades, resulting in a two-third cost reduction.[111] It is not yet clear whether they can perform at the level of the well-established private equity funds and whether the right model is to perform direct investments independently or, as is more often the case today, pursue primarily co-investments with the private equity funds in which they are invested as another way to reduce management fees, since co-investments typically require far lower fees than the traditional 2% of management fees and 20% of profits.

Not all private equity funds charge these additional portfolio company fees. Hellman & Friedman, a San Francisco-based private equity fund created in 1984, prides itself on having a strong fiduciary culture that stems from Warren Hellman, a co-founder. The firm's private equity funds forgo all fees incremental to their management fees and carried interest.

Warburg Pincus is another example of a highly successful, long-established firm which has a policy of not charging deal, transaction, or monitoring fees. The firm has a large investment support team that provides consulting services to portfolio companies at no charge. The advice can pertain to capital markets, external communications, government relations, or shared services such as employee benefits. Since its founding in 1966, the firm has put significant emphasis on alignment of interests with its investors. By keeping things simple – having one line of business, market-based management fees to run the firm, and incentive fees to share gains, it can more easily maintain that alignment. The firm doesn't boast about its culture or about higher morality. By remaining private, it isn't swayed by the argument that capital markets put a higher valuation multiple on recurring fee streams, which has incentivized many of its successful peers to seek market listings and to add fee-generating businesses. The firm's roots in venture and growth equity also made it unnatural for it to assess fees on its portfolio companies in its initial phase. It has maintained that discipline, even as late-stage control deals have come to represent a significant portion of the portfolio. When Warburg Pincus partners on specific deals with other private equity funds that impose monitoring and other fees on their portfolio companies, it has negotiated a larger equity piece from its partner rather than impose the same fees on the portfolio company.

An innovative approach to private equity structure and fees was developed by Vincent Mai, a leading figure in the private equity world for several decades (and, for full disclosure, the co-founder of the family office that seeded the fund I work in). Mai was profoundly affected in the initial phase of his career by his mentor, Sir Siegmund Warburg, the founder of the London-based investment bank S.G. Warburg & Company. According to Mai, Warburg passionately believed that one's reputation was everything and that money should always be a secondary concern.[112] Mai went on to become a partner at Lehman Brothers, when the firm was private, and led for more than two decades AEA Investors, one of the early private equity funds, backed by S.G. Warburg & Co. and the Rockefeller, Mellon, and Harriman families.

In 2011, he created Cranemere as a long-term fiduciary that seeks to address some of the structural weaknesses of the private equity model by adopting a "buy, build and hold" strategy for its portfolio companies. This model eschews the value destruction inherent in prematurely selling companies in order to conform to the time constraint of traditional private equity vehicles. Research by Bain & Company suggests that a long-term-hold model can generate almost twice the performance of a traditional private equity fund structure based on the theoretical difference between holding a company for twenty-four years and buying and selling out of four successive, equally performing companies over the same time horizon.[113] The delta in performance stems from the elimination of the frictional costs of constantly buying and selling companies, deferred taxation of capital gains, a more fully invested portfolio, and greater flexibility in exiting at the opportune time rather than when investor terms dictate it. With Cranemere's unusual model, Mai seeks to acquire good companies "forever," letting his investors sell their Cranemere shares to others if and when they decide to leave.

While the model incorporates Mai's beliefs regarding how to achieve better performance, it also explicitly embeds fiduciary values at the core of the organization by, among other things, extending governance rights to the shareholders.[114] Rather than the standard structure separating the investment management company from the fund, Cranemere was formed as a holding company, in which investors are shareholders rather than LPs, and are invested side-by-side with the management team.

The model also reflects Mai's deeply ingrained view that there is value in moderation. In a marked departure from the rest of the industry, the firm operates on a cost basis, meaning that the board must approve a budget annually on behalf of the shareholders, leaving no room for unwarranted compensation from excess management fees or undisclosed fees. This implies that Cranemere professionals can do well financially but over a longer horizon than would be the case at more traditional private equity funds.[115] Still, Cranemere has attracted high-quality talent, likely due to the combination of strong fiduciary values at the core of its model and the distinguished pedigree of its founder and top managers.

Other innovative models have emerged to help lower fees. Ryan Williams, a 31-year-old African American entrepreneur, created Cadre, a "fintech" platform that seeks to upend the real estate private equity industry by offering a US real estate investment product of similar quality to the leading private equity funds at lower fees and with greater transparency and flexibility. During his time working at Goldman Sachs and Blackstone, Williams noted the private equity industry's pronounced inefficiencies resulting from its clubby, relationship-driven deal-making environment and its multiple layers of fees, notably those of the private equity investment manager and of the operating partner. He believed that the industry was ripe for a new model, to be enabled by technology.

Cadre creates for its investors transparency and accessibility by offering them the ability to purchase a slice of any of the commercial real estate opportunities it offers on its online platform. It provides investors all the necessary data to make an informed decision, including extensive statistics, qualitative information on each building for sale, and drone videos of the properties and their amenities.[116] Investors can pick and choose on a deal-by-deal basis. Cadre offers this product at fees that are more than 30% lower than standard real estate funds, by charging a lower than market reporting and asset management fee (typically between 1% and 2% of net asset value), an upfront transaction fee typically 1% or lower of the cost of purchasing the building spread across all the investors that decide to buy a piece of it, and an incentive fee for its operating partners (which doesn't go to Cadre) of between 15% and 25%, rather than the standard duplicate 20% incentive fees for the investment manager and the operating partner.[117]

For a venture led by a young entrepreneur in an industry that has been dominated by the same set of companies for decades, Cadre has managed to attract highly established industry leaders, including the former CEO of Vornado Realty Trust, who also serves as Chairman of Cadre's investment committee. The value proposition of a new, flexible, transparent and lower-fee model has driven Cadre's rapid success in attracting investors. The early backing of a few high-profile industry leaders gave it enough credibility to overcome investors' bias for standard private equity models.

Cadre also offers investors the ability to exit their investments earlier than the five- to ten-year horizon of the traditional private equity model. It does so by creating an internal secondary market with an option to exit starting at year two. Over time, the resilience of an innovative illiquid asset platform such as Cadre that relies on a secondary market will need to be tested against the vagaries of a sharp economic slowdown. Early indications are that the combination of Cadre's innovative platform and Williams' ability to assemble a group of world-class real estate investment and technology professionals and backers could present a real competitive threat to traditional real estate private equity funds.

While Cranemere and Cadre signal a growing trend in the private equity industry, lower-fee models are still few and far between. One noteworthy development has been the extent to which the private equity industry has cut back on undisclosed fees after complaints by investors and increased involvement by the SEC. Following the Dodd-Frank Act, the SEC created a private equity unit in 2012 to monitor the industry more closely. Its initial targets included undisclosed fees and expenses, the misallocation of "broken deal" expenses, and the failure to disclose conflicts of interest. Some of the largest private equity firms, including KKR and Blackstone, ran afoul of the SEC's effort to create more transparency. This has spurred more stringent standards. Blackstone, for instance, announced in 2014 that it would no longer take accelerated monitoring fees when it completely exits a portfolio company in a private sale.[118] Close to 75% of North American buyout funds now offset most or all undisclosed fees against management fees.[119] While these fees are increasingly being offset, they remain popular because they help reduce stated fees and thus boost reported performance.

A Heroic Form of Fiduciary Leadership: Alayne Fleischmann, Paul Moore, Eric Ben-Artzi, and the Lonely Path of Whistleblowers

Whistleblowers often risk their careers, reputations, and livelihoods in order to alert authorities about wrongdoing at their firm, typically after having failed to trigger remedial action via internal channels of communication. Once they uncover malfeasance and try to capture the attention of senior managers, they often get either ignored or reprimanded. Once they go public, they are often ostracized by their former colleagues and the rest of the industry. For most whistleblowers, it is a thankless path.

Alayne Fleischmann fits the mold. She provided US federal prosecutors evidence that led to a $9 billion settlement by JP Morgan Chase. Fleischmann's early career interests leaned toward human rights and public international law but she decided to enter the securities industry after graduating from Cornell Law School in order to pay back her student loans.[120] She soon developed an affinity for the work and was hired by JP Morgan Chase in 2006 as a transaction manager. At the peak of the mortgage market at the time, US banks were frantically buying mortgages in order to repackage them into securities whose senior tranches routinely garnered AAA ratings, signaling their lack of risk, at least in theory. Fleischmann's role was to control the quality of the mortgages that JP Morgan Chase purchased for securitization.

Things started unravelling when the bank hired a new diligence manager in charge of approving loans. That manager asked Fleischmann and her colleagues to stop communicating with him by email, a red flag in an industry subject to heavy compliance requirements. By late 2006, Fleischmann and her colleagues were asked to audit a $900 million package of mortgages that Chase was contemplating acquiring from GreenPoint, a mortgage originator. It quickly became apparent that many of the loans were problematic. The mortgages were unusually old – many of them seven to eight months rather than the typical two to three months, as mortgage originators typically look to pass on their mortgages as quickly as possible. Fleischmann took it as a likely sign of defective loans – loans that had been rejected by other banks or in early default. Delving deeper into a subset of mortgages to check their quality, Fleischmann and her colleagues found that 40% of them were based on overstated incomes. Although the threshold of acceptable error rate for Chase was typically 5%, the loans were cleared.[121] Fleischmann approached a managing director to have the purchase reconsidered but she was ignored. She sent a letter to another managing director detailing the situation. Despite her objections, the loans were bought, repackaged, and sold to investors without appropriate disclosures on their likely impairment.

A 2011 lawsuit by a group of credit unions against Chase provides some color on how defective the GreenPoint loans turned out to be. One credit union had invested $135 million in a pool of mortgage-backed securities, 40% of which came from the GreenPoint loans. According to the lawsuit, losses amounted to $51 million in the first year, almost fifty times its projected losses.[122] While it's impossible to say how much of these losses stemmed from the GreenPoint pool, it is not a stretch to imagine that it was an important driver.

Fleischmann was laid off in early 2008. She was contacted by the SEC in 2012 regarding an investigation targeting another Chase deal. Keen to expose the financial misconduct surrounding the Green-Point case, she enabled the government to pursue JP Morgan Chase. In November 2013, the bank reached a $9 billion settlement. While the face value was large, Fleischmann was at a loss. No executives were criminally pursued, the bank did not admit to wrongdoing, and the fine extracted value from the shareholders, not from the perpetrators. That prompted her to go public with her story by reaching out to a journalist from *Rolling Stone* Magazine.

Since being laid off, Fleischmann has struggled to regain her footing, as is typical for whistleblowers. Several law firms turned her down after she disclosed that she could be a witness against Chase. Her situation was compounded by the fact that she lost her job in the middle of the Global Financial Crisis. She went back to Canada and worked as a legal intern at a law firm in Calgary as part of the process to qualify as a lawyer in Canada.

She is part of a cohort of whistleblowers who reacted to malfeasance in the run-up to the financial crisis, often related to the willful misrepresentation of mortgage securities. Her experience of being shunned by the industry and her related professional and personal struggles are common. Richard Bowen is Fleischmann's parallel at Citigroup. Convinced that Citigroup was misrepresenting bad loans, he repeatedly shared his concerns with the most senior levels of management and the board out of frustration and got fired. Michael Winston was a whistleblower at Countrywide Financial, one of the most aggressive mortgage originators. A managing director prior to being fired, he has talked about being "punished, isolated, tormented, financially harmed and ultimately dismissed."[123]

Similar dynamics linked to mortgage businesses in the run-up to the financial crisis occurred in financial institutions outside of the United States. Paul Moore was a high-profile whistleblower at Halifax Bank of Scotland (HBOS), one of the largest British banks. As Head of Group Regulatory Risk, he became an agitator internally to stop what he deemed to be irresponsible sales tactics. He was fired in 2004 and wrote a detailed memorandum to the UK Treasury Select Committee in 2009 to blow the whistle. He was partly vindicated when James Crosby, the HBOS CEO who had fired him, had to resign as Deputy Chairman of the UK's Financial Services Authority and give up his knighthood. However, Moore's story since his own firing has been one of addiction, depression, and suicidal thoughts, as he revealed in his 2015 memoirs.[124]

Fleischmann, Bowen, Winston, and Moore's fates are typical: A study showed that 82% of named corporate whistleblowers end up being fired, leaving the firm under pressure, or finding their responsibilities altered.[125] Why do whistleblowers decide to pursue this path despite being cognizant of the limbo most whistleblowers have to settle for? Academic studies have shown that whistleblowers tend to be driven by moral considerations rather than personal gain.[126] In cases like Alayne Fleischmann's, that characterization resonates. She credits her upbringing: "I actually think it was because I came from a small town – Terrace, British Columbia... I just grew up with a value that a lot of people have – and that is, it's okay to do well, but you can't do that at other people's expense."[127]

The introduction of the SEC Whistleblower Reward Program under the Dodd-Frank Act of 2011 has brought in a significant potential financial reward. Whistleblowers can receive a financial award equal to 10% to 30% of the monetary sanctions collected in cases where they provide the SEC with information that leads to a successful enforcement action. Since its introduction, the program has led to $1.6 billion in financial sanctions and more than $387 million in awards to whistleblowers, as of the beginning of 2020.[128] Some awards have been enormous, peaking at $50 million for two former Merrill Lynch employees who exposed that the bank was misusing customer cash. Given its large awards, the program can eliminate for would-be whistleblowers the financial risk of being unemployable. It also enables them to enlist the help of expensive lawyers who can work for a percentage of a potential award. Yet studies of the motivation of whistleblowers in the pharmaceutical industry, which has awarded large financial rewards to whistleblowers for a longer period of time than the securities industry, suggest that even when they qualified for a potential financial reward, the ethical motivation was the most significant driver of their decision to blow the whistle.[129]

One awardee stands out for having turned down his compensation on the grounds that it was immoral to take the money. Eric Ben-Artzi was one of three whistleblowers who exposed improper accounting at Deutsche Bank in 2010–2011. A PhD in mathematics, Ben-Artzi was hired from Goldman Sachs as a risk manager. In assessing the risk in Deutsche's exposure to credit derivatives, Ben-Artzi gradually developed a view that the bank had inflated valuations by $12 billion at the peak of the Global Financial Crisis (the SEC estimated the overvaluation at $1.5 billion at the settlement with Deutsche in 2015). After actively raising the issue internally, Ben-Artzi was fired. He brought his case to the SEC and found out that at least one other whistleblower from Deutsche had gone to the SEC on the same issue. After Ben-Artzi got wind that the investigation might be shut down, he went public, sharing information with *Financial Times* journalists and writing an op-ed. The SEC eventually pushed forward the case and settled with Deutsche Bank for $55 million in 2015.

Ben-Artzi decided to turn down his share of the settlement between the SEC and Deutsche Bank, which amounted to $3.5 million (after deducting the share of the award to his lawyers and his ex-wife),[130] because it was taken from shareholders, who he perceived to be victims of a financial crime, rather than the managers who perpetrated the crime.[131]

Not everyone sees Ben-Artzi as a moral exemplar. Some have argued that his claims of fraud are far-fetched because the losses were paper losses which eventually went away and that there is a legitimate debate as to how to value the exotic derivatives at play.[132] They also perceive an attitude of moral superiority that they find grating. Still, Ben-Artzi is an intriguing, and even refreshing outlier. Examples of financial professionals who turn down large sums of money with no strings attached out of moral reasoning are rare, to say the least. He did not turn down his award because he didn't need the money. After getting fired, he could no longer afford his rent or his children's private school and moved to Israel after failing to find work in the United States.[133] He acted out of moral conviction, at a significant personal cost.

These examples point to various paths finance professionals can take to prioritize their customer mandate, which at times entail departing from the norm and forgoing some incremental compensation. In doing so, they fulfill their most important responsibility as professionals. But while that measure of contribution to society is critical, and arguably the most important, it does not capture comprehensively the impact of a finance professional on society. In the next chapter, we expand our definition of contribution to the collective good.

2 SOCIAL WEALTH CREATION
Contributing to Society beyond the Customer Mandate

Being a Good Fiduciary Is No Panacea

A traditional perspective on the responsibility of finance professionals would hold that being a diligent fiduciary fulfills all of one's professional and moral obligations since those are inherently intertwined. The industrious practice of a profession, trade, or art embodies moral behavior. Consequently, for a finance professional, as for any type of professional service provider, being a good fiduciary *is* the fulfillment of professional responsibility. However, I will contend that being a good fiduciary doesn't automatically lead one to contribute to society. It simply entails faithfully delivering on the set of responsibilities entrusted by a client. The underlying financial activity matters because it can have a positive or negative impact on other people, independent of its impact on the client.

As discussed in the previous chapter, a finance professional who fails to deliver on his or her fiduciary mandate not only destroys value for the client but is also likely to have a negative social impact. Yet, being a good fiduciary is not enough to generate a positive social impact or even prevent harmful impact. An investment professional may generate high investment returns on behalf of investors by, for instance, trading complex derivatives, but in the process not contribute to any aspect of the real economy while unwittingly increasing risk in the financial system because of the complexity and opacity of the traded instruments. A conundrum is that a finance professional can be a great fiduciary, deliver on his or her mandate, be vastly successful and highly rewarded, and yet not serve society.[1] At its extreme, Alasdair MacIntyre, a contemporary moral philosopher, argues that financial market professionals are engaged in a profession that is antithetical to virtue – not unlike burglars who, no matter how skilled they are at their craft, will never achieve virtue.[2] While that view raises useful questions, it lacks nuance and understanding of the role of finance in society.

In my experience, most professional investors, taking that subset of the finance industry as an example, think almost exclusively about their mandate in terms of financial returns, and thus in the framework of their fiduciary responsibility, because financial returns drive the assessment of their performance and their compensation. I have frequently asked investment managers who were guest speakers in my courses over the past decade whether they believe that they create social value and if so, how. Surprisingly for a group that tends to be cerebral, few seem to have thought about this. They generally invoke their ability to generate attractive returns on behalf of institutions that help society, such as university and research hospital endowments, or on behalf of "main-street" savers via pension funds, as the main channel through which they contribute to society. They also typically highlight their philanthropy. At times, they argue that they help make markets more efficient.

My objective in this chapter is to draw attention to the concept of economic and social wealth creation as one that is separate from, and at times in conflict with, the management of a client relationship. This distinction is often overlooked by finance professionals given the primacy of achieving client satisfaction, or, more simply, generating revenues from clients in the evaluation of their performance. The "narrow" goal of focusing exclusively on client satisfaction is all but inevitable given how finance professionals' incentives are set. But finance professionals can pursue activities that generate high private gains, for both their client and themselves, and negative social returns. While the social impact of any individual finance professional pursuing his siloed interests defined by his fiduciary responsibility may be negligible, the collective impact can be disastrous if incentives are defined without any regard to effects outside of the client relationship and finance professionals remain oblivious to the indirect impact of their activities.

In some situations, serving a client's interest can slip into complicity between a financial service provider and a client to skirt rules.

Consider the case of JP Morgan's use of derivatives to allow Italy to mask the fact that it had breached its European Union budget guidelines in 1996. By entering into a cross-currency swap agreement with the government, JP Morgan was able to effectively extend a loan to the Italian government to retire debt, without Italy having to report the cash injection as new debt given the prevailing weak reporting requirements of Eurostat, the European statistical agency. In essence, JP Morgan helped Italy take advantage of a reporting loophole to engage in "window dressing," as described by Gustavo Piga, an academic who wrote an early report uncovering the stratagem.[3] A similar approach was taken by Goldman Sachs in 2000 and 2001 to help Greece report a lower debt to GDP ratio that was within the mandated EU guidelines, a practice that was widely adopted by many other European member states, as the bank pointed out.[4] In some ways, these transactions showcased the reason why clients are willing to pay these pre-eminent banks enormous fees: They solved a critical problem for their client and did so by exhibiting financial savviness and creativity.[5] Despite what comes across as pure deception, these trades were not illegal. They were permissible under Eurostat rules, and EU officials reportedly knew at the time that various countries were pursuing these tactics (even if, in hindsight, there are indications that EU officials did not fully understand the implications of these trades).

Did JP Morgan and Goldman Sachs act unethically? Several observers have argued that they acted ethically because these transactions were permissible, were understood to take place, and were agreed to freely by both parties.[6] I disagree – while they served their clients' interest and followed the letter of the law, there was a tangible probability that their action would generate negative economic spillover effects. Enabling a country to maintain more debt than it has pledged to seems socially dangerous, if not reckless. The Eurozone crisis that emerged in the early 2010s was largely driven by a surplus of debt in countries such as Greece and Italy.

The Concept of Value

One significant challenge in assessing the social value of financial activities is to define what we mean by value. In this book, I refer interchangeably to the concepts of social and economic value creation and wealth creation. I use them in relation to *indirect* social outcomes.

Direct outcomes pertain to performance relative to a specific mandate – for instance, whether an asset manager delivers on his or her return benchmark with the capital invested on behalf of a client. Indirect outcomes relate to how anyone outside of the asset manager and its client might be affected by the manager's investments.

Economist Mariana Mazzucato has argued that the lack of explicit debate amongst economists regarding the proper definition of value has left its neo-classical economic interpretation as the prevailing norm.[7] Prior to the advent of the marginal utility theory in the second half of the nineteenth century, economic activities were typically defined as either productive or unproductive. Activities considered to be outside of a conceptual production boundary were either value-extracting activities or explicit transfers of wealth following social welfare policies.[8] The marginal utility theory shifted the emphasis to concepts of supply and demand in the context of scarce resources. Value was now derived from a subjective assessment by individuals based on their preferences.[9] In that framework, prices inherently reflect value: Activities are valuable and productive to society to the extent that a buyer and a seller have agreed on a price. The market becomes the final and only arbiter of value.[10]

Mazzucato argues that the correspondence between price and value made by modern economics has obfuscated any differentiation between value-creating and value-extracting activities in finance.[11] Recklessly lending to individuals with no income or assets, and thereby fueling a property bubble, or overcharging retail savers via the fine print are all productive activities because they each stem from a transaction and generate income. This conceptual framework underpins modern finance and pervades our national accounting: All of these activities register as boosts to the GDP.

Mazzucato invokes the ability of pharmaceutical companies to increase the price of a drug a thousand-fold as another example of an activity that is considered intrinsically valuable in the neo-classical economic paradigm. According to the prevailing logic, competition creates a market mechanism to prevent the possibility of excessive prices for goods and services, or unearned income. By definition, prices cannot be excessive as long as the market bears them.

By the same token, CEO compensation that is more than a hundred-fold median pay is justifiable because the very fact that the CEO was able to negotiate that price implies that the market validates its commensurate value to society. The mere existence of a market mechanism to generate compensation levels justifies the resulting distribution of income across the economy, no matter how skewed.[12]

Unintended consequences of the unconditional support for these market mechanisms have come to the fore. French economist Thomas Piketty ascribes the significant increase in inequality experienced in recent decades to an unprecedented surge in the top wages, particularly in the United States and the United Kingdom, where the share of income going to the top 1% grew from about 8% in both countries in the 1970s to 20% in the United States and close to 15% in the United Kingdom by 2010.[13] As a result of the neo-classical framework's widespread acceptance, distribution of income became neglected in both economics and policy research up to the financial crisis, based on the premise that, in efficient and competitive markets, factors of production should get compensated by their marginal contribution to output, leaving little room for debate.[14] As Adair Turner has argued, given the evidence that inequality is an inevitable by-product of free markets, and inequality can have a substantially negative effect on human welfare and happiness which is not necessarily remedied by growth, there is now a greater question mark regarding the wisdom of long-term economic growth as the overarching policy goal in advanced economies.[15]

Philosopher Michael Sandel argues compellingly that "market triumphalism" has transformed us into a market society where almost everything has a price, corrupting activities that were not historically transacted and allowing wealth to influence increasingly large parts of society.[16] In the prevailing neo-classical economic narrative, more finance leads to more complete and efficient markets, which, in turn, drive efficient allocation of resources across the economy. The market's pervasive influence has supported the rampant financialization of the economy experienced in recent decades, leading to the surge of the finance sector's weight in the overall economy.

The general equilibrium of neo-classical economics makes assumptions about the efficiency of markets that have been increasingly called into question, particularly since the Global Financial Crisis. In practice, economic activities can generate either positive or negative externalities. British economist Roger Bootle argues that rather than entirely falling into one or the other category, all business activities lie somewhere on the spectrum between having a social wealth-creating effect and having a distributive or extractive effect.[17] Those externalities can lead to large gaps between the private costs and returns of a financial activity and its costs and returns to society as a whole. The classic example of a negative externality is that of a polluting firm. The firm makes decisions solely based on the direct, near-term costs of production, without taking into account the indirect costs to those harmed by the pollution. As a result, bystanders can see their quality of life and healthcare costs affected, leading to changes in consumption and production patterns.

A Spectrum of Social Outcomes in the Finance Industry

At the heart of the concept of value is the production of goods and services which promote the long-term capacity of the economy.[18] In this respect, much of finance is a force for good. Finance provides critical services to the economy, from facilitating the allocation of capital from savers to users, to facilitating payments, to creating mechanisms to manage risk. In practice, many of these activities lead to positive externalities. The benefits of some areas of finance are readily apparent: The lender to small and mid-size enterprises might allow these firms to grow, generate new employment, boost consumption through new products and services they offer, employees they pay, and profits they generate. The venture capitalist invests in a firm that might develop new drugs and help solve a healthcare issue, and in so doing generate new knowledge or novel approaches which other firms might seek to build upon, while creating employment and generating incremental consumption. The insurer enables parents to plan for their family's financial future and prepare for important expenses such as children's education without having to worry about catastrophic loss of life or property upending their financial planning; in doing so, the insurer mobilizes savings and spreads risks across a large number of people.

   Since the 1990s, a dynamic area of research has demonstrated a positive linkage between financial development and growth, and between financial and economic development.[19] Financial development has also been shown to generate various other benefits for society. Some benefits, such as boosting entrepreneurship, are intuitive.[20] Others are less so – for instance, research shows a positive relationship between financial development and education, and a negative one with inequality.[21] The most recent iterations of research exploring the linkages between financial development and economic development suggest limits to that relationship: Beyond a certain level of financial development, there are negative returns to more finance. Separate IMF and BIS studies released in 2012 came to these conclusions.[22] An update of one of these studies shows that an increase in credit relative to GDP tends to raise economic growth but once it exceeds about 100%, that relationship appears to turn negative.[23] Too much finance can result in a credit boom. Excess credit is often channeled toward lower-productivity sectors, typically property development and construction, which can increase the risk of an asset bubble and a financial crisis.

The increase in the weight of finance in the economy does not inherently signal that finance is a social wealth-creating activity. Adair Turner makes the analogy with a world in which the frequency of divorces increases, leading to a surge in the demand for divorce lawyers and in their compensation. From an economic point of view, the outcome of the professional services rendered by divorce lawyers is close to being purely distributive – their increasing weight in the economy is not meaningful from a social wealth-creation perspective.[24]

When macro-economic research considers the impact of finance, it looks at it as a black box. It doesn't differentiate between different types of finance. It typically defines the level of financial development as the size of the banking sector or of private credit relative to GDP. It is difficult to say empirically from a top-down perspective whether some types of finance are more or less social wealth creating than others. But, as economist Luigi Zingales has argued, the lack of published evidence suggests that it is difficult to prove a positive correlation between economic growth and certain types of finance such as derivatives.[25] Moreover, we do have a sense, anecdotally. For instance, we know that securitization had an important role to play in the genesis of the Global Financial Crisis.

Because the finance industry appeared to be thriving prior to the Global Financial Crisis, there was little urgency to question its value to society. The industry's contribution to GDP kept rising while return on equities of financial institutions climbed. Unsurprisingly, rent extraction, or the act of obtaining economic gain by extracting value from society rather than creating new wealth, has come into focus since the financial crisis.[26] The traditional assumptions of finance, that markets are efficient and self-correcting, have been discredited, paving the way for a harsher critique of financial capitalism. A wave of academic research has documented widespread rent extraction across the industry. Pushing the argument further, rent extraction is increasingly understood to be a defining aspect of the system, and to have driven much of financial product innovation in recent years.[27] The increased sophistication of financial products has gone hand in hand with increased opacity, creating more opportunities for financial intermediaries to arrogate to themselves a greater proportion of profits.

A seminal empirical study by Thomas Philippon and Ariell Reshef documents a significant increase in financial innovation in the early 2000s and estimates that rents accounted for 30–50% of the compensation differential between the finance sector and the rest of the economy.[28] The presence of rent extraction of such magnitude suggests that economic power has become too concentrated in the financial industry. That is reflected in the influence of the lobbying bodies of various segments of the finance industry, which can press for outcomes that suit their particular subset of finance professionals and no one else. A striking example lies in the carried interest tax loophole which allows private equity professionals and some hedge fund managers to be taxed in the United States at a far lower rate than most workers (i.e. at capital gains rate rather than the income tax rate).

Value extraction in finance can take several forms. For instance, it exists when intermediation costs imposed on customers are too high (in which case, the provider's fiduciary responsibility to faithfully look out for the interests of its customers is also breached). Excessive intermediation costs can be facilitated by limited competition and the concentrated market power of several dominant players.[29] One of the most thoroughly documented examples of systematic rent extraction in the form of excessive fees relates to the asset management industry. As discussed in the previous chapter, for the past four decades, academics have consistently shown that active investment managers tend to underperform their index benchmark and thus to destroy value for retail investors.

Financial advisors and investment managers can provide services that add value to customers and are not captured by average return numbers. At their best, financial advisors provide bespoke advice based on one's life stage, financial situation, and personal goals and preferences. They are also shown to benefit financially illiterate individuals.[30] Still, the numbers speak for themselves. Consider US investment managers: Over a fifteen-year period ending in mid 2019, 90% of US large-cap funds underperformed the S&P 500, 95% of US mid-cap funds underperformed the S&P MidCap 400 benchmark, and 94% of all small-cap funds underperformed the S&P SmallCap 600 benchmark.[31] Only in recent years have decades of conclusive academic research and staggering numbers such as those cited above been reflected in a trend away from actively managed funds toward passive index funds and exchange-traded funds (ETF).

Value extraction often appears to be correlated with short-term approaches to profit generation. Andrew Haldane, the Chief Economist of the Bank of England, and co-authors Simon Brennan and Vasileios Madouros hypothesize that much of the excess returns to finance recorded since the 1970s can be attributed to increases in balance sheet risk in the form of increased leverage (both on- and off-balance sheet), increased assets held in proprietary books marked at prices reflecting a mispricing of risk in the economy, and the writing of deep out-of-the-money options.[32]

Value extraction in finance often involves generating a private gain via a risk premium while transferring the downside risks to the public. When mortgage providers signed up individuals with limited ability to repay their loans absent an increase in real estate values and then sold the mortgages down the chain to securitize them, they crystallized their gains at the point of sale, passing on the risks to others. At the end of the chain stood the government, which was forced to intervene once the real estate bubble was pricked. This also illustrates the pervasive importance of information asymmetry in the value extraction process.[33] Finance is an extreme example of an industry whose complexity, opacity, and dynamic innovation allow professionals to routinely take advantage of their insider knowledge to exploit outsiders, as we discussed in the previous chapter with the example of the egregiously complex products sold by Banque Postale in France to less sophisticated households.

One caveat to this discussion is that it is tempting but misguided to project a cynical approach on all finance professionals and to assume that by default, they extract value by pursuing narrow self-interests that are in conflict with those of their customers or the rest of society. Other factors can also contribute to bad outcomes for customers of financial services and to negative repercussions on the rest of society. For instance, a study found no evidence that during the run-up to the financial crisis, mid-level managers in securitized finance were more aware of a real estate bubble in the making and of a pending crash on the basis of their personal real estate transactions.[34] A cynical approach by these mid-level managers would have implied them using the asymmetric information they possessed about the boom and bust dynamics underway to their benefit, by buying before the surge in price and reducing their exposure prior to the crisis while they were actively promoting greater exposure to their clients. Compelling arguments have been made that they were just as ill-prepared for the crisis as anyone else because of contagious over-optimism, cognitive biases, or plain incompetence.[35] Financial ethicist Boudewijn de Bruin argued that incompetence was an important driver of the Global Financial Crisis, observing, for instance, that the fact that many of those involved with mortgage-backed securities in the run-up to the financial crisis did not understand the product is akin to a doctor prescribing a drug without knowing the side-effects.[36]

To be sure, anecdotal evidence of cynicism across various parts of the industry abounds – witness JP Morgan's endeavors to mask the Italian government's true level of indebtedness or the internal emails of Goldman Sachs' employees mocking clients (e.g. "I think I found a white elephant, a flying pig, and a unicorn all at once") who agreed to buy from them complex derivatives providing long exposure to mortgages, while Goldman Sachs was massively short the same market as a firm.[37] While self-serving approaches of this sort may characterize only a subset of professionals in the industry, their impact can be massive.

Rent extraction on a large scale inevitably leads to a widespread sense of inequity, and, ultimately, public outrage. The Occupy Wall Street movement of 2011 and the election of Donald Trump as US president in 2016 have been the clearest expressions of that sense of outrage, so far. The widely documented loss of trust in our financial institutions has been another negative consequence.

Identifying Social Value Creation

How can financial professionals position themselves to create rather than extract value from society? To begin with, models of value creation should promote the long-term, sustainable productive capacity of the real economy. Some financial activities clearly conflict with that goal. Going back to the JP Morgan Italian derivative example at the beginning of this chapter, complex structuring to achieve tax or regulatory arbitrage is unlikely to create any value at the collective level. On the other end of the spectrum, one would assume that anyone engaged in the basic functions of the financial industry – in other words, those who contribute directly to the functioning of the real economy that produces goods and services – help society to the extent that they uphold their fiduciary responsibility to their clients.

In practice, however, differentiating between value-adding and value-extracting financial activities can be challenging. It is difficult to separate activities which promote the sustainable functioning of the economy by, for instance, prudently extending credit to businesses or retail segments with limited funding access, from activities that create an overwhelming debt burden on borrowers and systematically contribute to inflating an asset bubble. Adair Turner pointed out that, on the surface, complex credit securitization, a critical enabler of the crisis, filled one of the financial system's basic functions: financial intermediation between savers and borrowers, albeit in a more sophisticated manner than prevailing products. It increased the extent to which assets on offer could be tailored to specific risk–return and liquidity preferences.[38] By doing so, it promoted "market completion," along the First Fundamental Theorem of Welfare Economics by Kenneth Arrow and Gerard Debreu, thereby contributing to greater market efficiency.[39] The clearest near-term impact was to increase the supply of credit and broaden its availability to socio-economic segments that had previously limited access to funding – a nominally positive effect.[40]

Yet the impact of these products turned out to be disastrous for both the recipients of the enhanced credit and for the economy as a whole. Turner points out that at the individual level, the life-cycle smoothing benefits were overwhelmed by the fact that the sustainability of this credit extension was entirely predicated on continued asset price increases. At the macro-economic level, it contributed to an asset price bubble. The industry failed at one of its fundamental roles as an intermediary between savers and users of capital by failing to adequately measure and price credit and liquidity.

How to say, then, whether a finance professional operates in a corner of the industry that delivers value to society? Of the four pillars of our model, this is by far the most challenging to define precisely. Perhaps simple low-brow questions might help guide us: First, is the activity promoting real-economy activities that are truly sustainable? The question emphasizes the importance of financial services supporting real-economy activities. By explicitly considering whether a financial service promotes an economic activity that is sustainable, it also explicitly takes into account the activity's potential impact on financial stability.

In practice, it may be only feasible to parse out extreme examples of activities that promote real-economy activities in a sustainable manner from those that don't. For instance, an investment in esoteric, complex derivatives, such as a multi-leg contingent option, will likely not support the production of goods and services in the real economy. At the margin, it may create risks in the system that are difficult to monitor and may even contribute to financial instability. Investing in synthetic collateralized debt obligations will likely not support sustainable economic activity since it will tend to promote asset bubbles. Extending a NINJA loan (i.e. a loan to an individual with no job, no income, and no assets) also exemplifies what can be seen as an unsustainable economic activity – absent a rise in real estate prices or a change in the beneficiary's economic status, he or she is likely to default. Direct investments in real estate present a dilemma. Piketty makes a plausible argument that they should be considered a productive use of capital as real estate provides "housing services" which are essential to the functioning of the economy.[41]

For retail products specifically, a simple question, akin to a litmus test, should be whether the finance professional would advise her children, assuming for the sake of the argument that she had children with a similar socio-economic profile and needs as her target customer, to purchase her product or service.

In assessing value to society, a final consideration should be whether the financial activity contributes to promoting or reducing inequality. For most activities, the impact on inequality will be inevitably difficult to ascertain, and many may ultimately qualify as indeterminate. Here too, the extreme examples are more enlightening. Extending loans to small businesses targeting low-income populations would likely register positively; advising high-net-worth individuals on the use of offshore structures to reduce their taxes would likely not.[42]

While this broad-brush approach may lack the certainty of precise categorization, it would weed out many, and perhaps the majority of, value-extracting financial activities, whether the peddling of dubiously underwritten mortgages, the financial engineering whose sole purpose is to mask a company's or country's true indebtedness, or the structuring and selling of exotic options that have no purpose connected to the real economy.

The Promise of Innovation

Even before the great spurt of innovation that led to the proliferation of derivatives and securitized products, the economist William Baumol argued in 1980 that historical evidence going back to ancient Rome and the Middle Ages suggests that contribution to society of entrepreneurial activities varies significantly, depending on the extent to which they lead to productive activities versus largely unproductive ones such as rent seeking.[43] A prime example of rent seeking he invoked was tax avoidance, a scenario that has been particularly widespread in recent years via innovative tax inversions by mergers, the process of relocating a corporation to a country with lower taxes following a local merger. With the financial crisis has come mounting suspicion that much of the financial innovation of the past three decades may not have been beneficial to society.

Nevertheless, innovation can create value by pushing the boundaries of how finance serves society. Examples abound of entrepreneurs and innovators who developed new social wealth-creating financial tools and activities. As will be discussed further below, Georges Doriot pioneered the institutionalization of venture capital investments, an asset class of investments that is broadly seen as beneficial to society. By cracking open the door to vast amounts of institutional capital backing the commercialization of new technology and products, Doriot helped stimulate technological development in the United States post-World War II and contributed in a small but tangible way to creating a more vibrant economy. Although Doriot stands out in his impact on the development of the venture capital field, many other early venture capitalists were instrumental, including contemporaries of Doriot such as Ralph Flanders and Karl Compton, who helped Doriot in the founding of the pioneer venture capital firm American Research and Development (ARD) in 1946, JH Whitney and Benno Schmidt Sr., who founded at about the same time JH Whitney & Company, and Arthur Rock, who helped finance some of the initial tech companies that came to define Silicon Valley.[44]

In recent decades, a wave of innovators has sought to harness the power of for-profit financial activities and markets to help address specific economic and social problems.[45] In the 1970s, Muhammad Yunus, founder of the Grameen Bank, and Fazel Abed, founder of the Bangladesh Rural Advancement Committee (BRAC), developed the concept of micro-lending, which seeks to fund the professional activities of poor people via small, uncollateralized loans in order to promote their financial independence.[46] Grameen was established as a for-profit bank under a cooperative model, meaning owned by its borrowers. Yunus demonstrated that micro-loans on reasonable financial terms extended to women with no access to bank funding could be the basis of a sustainable lending business. Under this model, 97% of loans are made to women, who as a group represented less than 1% of debt holders in Bangladesh when Yunus launched Grameen.[47] In the early years, Yunus found that women were more responsible debtors than men, focused on building for the future rather than spending the money on themselves.[48] Much of the early successes of the model lie in payback rates in excess of 97%.[49]

Yunus' micro-lending model has proliferated, earning him a Nobel Peace Prize in 2006. It eventually drew the attention of for-profit capital allocators who saw an opportunity to generate outsized returns from an under-served population while contributing to society. The scaling up of that model has had mixed results and has generated controversy – for instance, when two high-profile microfinance institutions, Compartamos Banco and SKS Microfinance (now called Bharat Financial Inclusion), publicly listed their shares, in 2007 and 2010 respectively, generating significant wealth for their founders and high returns for their investors.[50] The industry was a victim of its success, with anecdotal evidence of a surge in credit availability in many Indian villages, leading to the over-indebtment of women targeted by multiple lenders.[51]

In the wake of various repayment crises and scandals at several micro-lending institutions, more recent research, including randomized controlled trials, has questioned the micro-lending model itself, suggesting that access to credit is only one tool, necessary but insufficient, to lift large groups out of poverty.[52] Even if the effects are not as transformative as appeared at first, the industry that Yunus and Abed have pioneered is now estimated to provide access to microfinance to 200 million clients.[53] It has also allowed many organizations to learn from the micro-lending experience and develop more effective approaches to poverty alleviation using market mechanisms. In fact, Abed's BRAC broadened its efforts at an early stage to move toward "micro-franchising," which entails providing branding, inventory, and training to micro-entrepreneurs, in addition to credit.[54]

The reach of "innovative finance," which uses market mechanisms to tackle economic and social problems, is now broad.[55] Take London-based Wagestream, which enables employees to access their earnings before they receive their month-end paychecks, for a small fee. Addressing the challenge faced by employees who struggle to make ends meet as they await their payment, Wagestream provides a cash advance on money already earned.[56] Co-founder and CEO Peter Briffett has vowed to put out of business the payday loan industry, which typically targets low-income workers with usurious interest rates, by providing workers with a low-fee alternative that is not a loan, for a flat fee of £1.75.[57]

Financial innovations with a social bent are often brought about by market practitioners who apply their profit-maximizing skill set to a different arena. Christopher Egerton-Warburton headed the Sovereign Supranational and Agency Debt Capital Markets group at Goldman Sachs when he was asked by the Chancellor of the Exchequer to help the UK government reach its Millennium Development Goals (MDGs) to alleviate poverty.[58] Using the deep market expertise and experience he had accumulated at Goldman Sachs, he helped create the International Finance Facility for Immunization (IFFIm), which launched the world's first vaccine bonds. It converts long-term pledges from donor governments into immediately available capital for immunizations. It raised more than $5.7 billion between 2006 and 2016.[59]

The market for these types of social bonds has grown significantly in recent years. Climate bonds (also known as green bonds) have become its highest-profile expression, driven by the rising sense of global urgency around climate change. Climate bonds are issued by governments, multilateral development banks, and companies to fund projects that are deemed to contribute to climate change solutions or are simply environmentally friendly. Sean Kidney, a former marketing advisor to Australian pension funds who co-founded and heads the Climate Bonds Initiative, has been perhaps the highest-profile individual associated with climate bonds. But, as is often the case in the development of a new market, a large, loose, and fast-growing coalition of individuals can claim credit for it, including market-oriented professionals from not-for-profit groups such as the Climate and Development

Knowledge Network, supranational institutions such as the United Nations Environment Program, investment banks and rating agencies, and capital allocators such as the New York City Pension Funds. They have helped grow that market from less than $2 billion of issuance in 2007 to $162 billion in 2018.[60]

The market faces significant obstacles – including the thorny issue of developing widely accepted standards, the challenge posed by "greenwashing" or the risk that any bond tangentially linked to the environment gets promoted as "green," and the related question mark as to whether these bonds truly add capital to the climate cause and help mitigate it.[61] But anecdotal evidence of increasing numbers of thoughtful and experienced market-oriented professionals developing innovative finance applications suggests that momentum will persist.

The Case for Moderation

Do these examples imply that a finance professional should seek to both serve clients *and* positively impact social welfare in order to be virtuous? I would argue that this takes the concept of virtue, as defined in this book's framework, a step too far. Financial firms such as JP Morgan and Goldman Sachs have a fiduciary responsibility to serve their clients' interests, not to make the world a better place. However, impacting society in a negative way, even if it serves their clients' interests, can make their activity unethical. Is there such a thing as a financial activity whose social impact is neutral? Although it is hard to measure, many financial activities likely fall in that category – not clearly supporting or improving the real economy, but not clearly extracting value from it.

In fact, some finance professionals can positively contribute to the economy and society by simply refraining from pursuing financial activities that could extract value. Richard Davis, the CEO of Minneapolis-based US Bancorp between 2006 and 2017, stands out as a rarity among CEOs of large retail US banks in having shown caution and prudence in the run-up to the Global Financial Crisis. Going against the grain of the US banking sector at a time of exuberance and high growth, he chose to maintain relatively conservative leverage and to forgo pursuing opportunities in the subprime loan market. That restraint reflected true leadership given the pressure he likely felt from board members and shareholders envious of the growth achieved by the bank's more aggressive peers. It served his employees and clients well, as US Bancorp was able to survive the financial crisis not only unscathed, but stronger compared to its peers. By contrast, Washington Mutual, a bank of similar profile, aggressively sought under CEO Kerry Killinger to roll up regional banks and to pursue the subprime opportunity, leading to the bank's collapse in 2008.

Davis's discipline imbued the culture that he and his predecessor, Jerry Grundhofer, instilled at US Bancorp. His ability to avoid being distracted by whatever new shiny financial opportunity peers were pursuing is characteristic of the way he managed the bank. It is consistent with the bank's outstanding efficiency ratio (a ratio of costs over revenues), which stood in the low 50% range versus above 60% for most of the bank's peers at the end of Davis's tenure, and its low loan loss ratio.[62] Starting his career as a bank teller at 18, Davis was known for his detailed knowledge of the bank's operations, his proclivity as CEO to engage in casual conversation with low-level employees, and his reluctance to implement layoffs during difficult times.[63]

While the temptation is to focus on the highest-profile individuals such as Muhammad Yunus or Richard Davis, contribution to society as a finance professional doesn't necessarily entail being in a senior position, being an innovator, or performing any heroic feat. The most junior person engaged in real-economy-supporting functions, be it the junior teller at a retail bank, the loan officer at a mortgage company, the back-office specialist at a passive fund manager, or the analyst at an insurance company, is likely to play a useful role in our economic system. By operating in a corner of the finance industry that directly supports the real economy in a sustainable manner, and by fulfilling their fiduciary commitment to their clients, these finance professionals can contribute positively to society.

The Social Value of Investments

As a case study of the direct and indirect economic and social effects of finance, I will delve more deeply into one segment of finance with particularly broad reach, investment management. At a macroeconomic level, the fundamental purpose of investments is to channel capital to its most productive uses. The efficiency of markets – their ability to price financial assets correctly and to enable investors to acquire and divest financial assets in a liquid manner – is relevant to that economic function. As business ethicist John Boatright argues, that efficiency can be seen as an ethical value in and of itself since it enables a better allocation of capital, leading to more output for a given input and thus greater social wealth.[64] However, there are at least two limitations to that argument. First, while efficient markets can facilitate better allocation of resources, they do not necessarily lead to the most desirable outcomes, in part because they don't take into consideration any distributional aspect. Market efficiency should not be deemed the sole moral value to be pursued. A second limitation is that any individual investor, even one working for a large institutional fund, will have negligible impact given the diffuse nature of markets.

At a micro-economic level, the fundamental purpose of investments is to generate attractive financial returns on behalf of the owners of capital. In determining the economic and social impact of an investment, the first line of inquiry should be whether it benefits the investor, meaning the owner of capital and the fund manager, who benefits when the investment succeeds. This question merits attention, even from an economic and social point of view, because an investment that doesn't generate an adequate financial return over time reflects an unproductive and unsustainable allocation of capital. However, generating attractive returns doesn't in and of itself guarantee that the act of investing is helpful to society.

One conundrum is that the formal objective of many institutional investors is to generate alpha, or excess returns relative to the risk they take, by beating an appropriate market benchmark. The challenge with that aspiration is that alpha is technically a zero-sum concept – for any positive alpha generated by one manager, there must be negative alpha generated by other investors. Some have contested this argument by arguing that investors don't have homogeneous preferences and operate along different time horizons.[65] But William Sharpe's simple statement that "properly measured, the average actively managed dollar must underperform the average passively managed dollar, net of costs" is hard to refute.[66] As Eugene Fama and Kenneth French have argued, since the aggregate portfolio of all investors (active and passive) is the market portfolio, and passive investors hold the market portfolio, then the aggregate of active investors must be the market portfolio. Any gain relative to the market benchmark by an active investor must be reflected in a loss by another active investor.[67] As a result, generating alpha may help an investment professional fulfill her fiduciary duty but may have limited, if any, social impact on its own.

Assessing the economic and social value of investments can be a layered, complicated affair. It entails parsing out indirect effects and unintended consequences. It requires weighing positive effects against negative ones, an inherently subjective exercise given the breadth of their nature. Some effects are immediate, others take years to materialize.

The economic and social benefits of investments that, on the surface, should contribute to society can be limited in various practical ways. For instance, there can be a substitution effect at play, meaning that the impact might have happened regardless of the investment, via another mechanism. Meaningful economic and social benefits of an investment should only be evaluated based on changes that would not have happened absent the financial transaction.

With this in mind, I propose two channels by which investments can create economic and social value, consistent with a concept of value that reflects an increase in the long-term productive capacity of the economy. Again, the economic and social benefits of these investments are predicated on an assumption that they generate more private return on capital than their private cost of capital, absent which, an investment is unjustifiable and likely unsustainable, unless backed by philanthropic sources of capital.

The first channel in which an investment can benefit society is by simply fulfilling a role in supporting the sustainable functioning of the real economy. That can be reflected in positive contribution to certain economic indicators, such as growth, employment, productivity, R&D, and innovation, even if the transmission mechanism is indirect and the effect small. It can also be observed in a diminished environmental footprint, as, for instance, measured by emissions, water usage, and waste per unit of production. Another meaningful consideration, albeit difficult to ascertain, is the extent to which an investment either promotes or reduces inequality.

One caveat is that seemingly positive effects can be misleading, at times clouding the data's interpretation. For instance, some of these metrics might register positive boosts during periods of unsustainable growth, followed by busts, as was the case with the Global Financial Crisis. Decreases resulting from investments can also be misinterpreted as negative effects. They may stem from the greedy, short-term orientation of investors, but not systematically so. For instance, R&D is generally understood to generate positive social effects beyond the benefits accrued by the company which funds it because it adds to the general body of knowledge.[68] But cutting R&D at a mismanaged firm where the research function has poor prospects of productively developing innovation may redirect capital to better uses. By the same token, a cut to the headcount may boost a firm's short-term productivity and contribute to enhancing at a small scale the long-term productive capacity of the economy. Reduced employment at a bloated, unproductive factory can register as a net negative effect in the short term but may enhance productivity and have long-term positive economic effects. At its extreme, a state-owned enterprise in a country such as China may be incentivized to employ people for the sake of employing people, at great costs to taxpayers who subsidize unproductive jobs. Similarly, a steep increase in the headcount of financial firms that generate growth from value extraction should not be considered a positive development.

Still, with these caveats in mind, data points on the indirect impact of investments on growth, employment, productivity, and R&D can suggest a pattern of social impact, either positive or negative. Looking at the data over longer time periods, across economic cycles, can help mitigate the risk of misinterpretation.

The second channel by which investments can contribute to the economy and society is by actively improving the underlying business or asset. On one end of the spectrum, an investment that simply effectuates a passive change of ownership between investors will do little to change the recipient company (and will have only limited impact in sustainably supporting the functioning of the real economy). On the other end of the spectrum, certain investment strategies explicitly seek to influence and improve targeted companies in significant ways. In this chapter, we will devote particular attention to three prominent "activist" strategies: venture capital, private equity, and shareholder activism. Venture capital seeks to commercialize new technologies, products, and services that can generate consumer demand and create new jobs. Private equity and shareholder activism aspire to improve the productivity and governance of firms. At least theoretically, these investment strategies should have a positive impact on their targeted companies and, consequently, on the real economy, beyond allocating capital judiciously.

A closer look, as we will see, warrants a more nuanced perspective. Venture capital funds are as likely to bring to the world *Candy*

Crush, a mobile game application whose effects on economic productivity are questionable, as a new drug to treat a form of cancer. Private equity and shareholder activism necessarily abide by their own institutional imperatives and the need to show investment returns, the sooner the better. Their timeline – shorter for activist hedge funds than for private equity funds – can put them at odds with other stakeholders, such as employees, bond holders, and long-term equity holders, and conflict with sustainable value creation.

Our intuition that certain types of financial transactions or investments are inherently wealth creating is not always supported by the existing research. There is also a question mark as to whether the positive spillover effects are at a scale that can make a difference at the macro-economic level. Firm-level improvements stemming from activist investment strategies may not be significant enough to register at an industry, regional, or national level. Research finds evidence of firm-level benefits stemming from shareholder activism but almost no research documents its macro-economic effects. Still, the benefits are intuitive enough, at least in certain circumstances, that the Japanese government under prime minister Abe has implicitly supported shareholder activism as part of its efforts to revive the Japanese corporate sector and reform the economy.[69]

Outside of these activist strategies, the case for the social value of traditional (i.e. financial value-maximizing) investments is supported by fewer arguments. Liquid investments in equity and bond markets play a critical role in the good functioning of our financial system at an aggregate level. However, it is hard for an individual pursuing any of these liquid market strategies to claim that he or she is making a positive difference given how negligible a contribution any one investor, even a large institutional one, might make to market efficiency and to the cost of capital of portfolio companies.

A few investment strategies explicitly purport to make the world a better place. In the traditional investment world, venture capitalists and shareholder activists routinely invoke their social mission, and anecdotal evidence suggests that they deeply believe in it, even if they explicitly target only financial returns. By contrast, impact investments explicitly target both economic and social impact. In the rest of this chapter, we will explore the economic and social impact of several major investment strategies, starting with those within the financial value-maximizing universe that, I would argue, contribute the most to society.

Venture Capital

Venture capital (VC) may be the one traditional, returns-maximizing investment strategy that is mostly immune to the second-guessing of its social value. Venture capital is widely recognized as having played a critical role in the development of some of the last decades' most important technologies and in the commercialization of products and services that have become ubiquitous. The positive spillover effects of venture capital are highly visible. Whether googling some information on an iPhone, grabbing a coffee at Starbucks, FedExing a package, buying groceries at Whole Foods, or driving Tesla's latest electric car, we are benefiting from venture capital's broad reach. In fact, all but one of the five largest companies listed in the United States was initially backed by venture capital (Apple, Alphabet/Google, Facebook, and Amazon).[70] As of 2014, US-listed companies with venture capital backing employed four million people and accounted for one-fifth of total market capitalization and 44% of the R&D investment of listed companies.[71] This is remarkable for a funding channel that backs significantly less than 1% of new companies created.[72]

Venture capital funds invest in companies that are in their initial stages of development. They typically invest capital on behalf of large institutional investors and high-net-worth individuals. Once they back a new venture, VC professionals become deeply involved: They typically take a board seat, act as advisors, and, often, as mentors to the venture's management team. They take an active role in helping develop the company, whether by sharing industry analysis, providing strategic or operational advice, introducing potential partners, customers, or additional funders, or hiring employees. It is not uncommon for a VC professional to be involved with a portfolio company on a daily basis. The quality of a VC fund's advice and network plays a significant role in the success of its portfolio companies. The most promising start-ups strive to be backed by the top VC funds in the industry, which in turn bring to bear their differentiated support system. Over time, this cycle has contributed to highly skewed returns in the industry.

Pioneers in the industry were publicly minded. They responded to a specific need: Small businesses had a hard time raising capital, in large part because banks were reluctant to provide long-term loans to businesses that were considered high-risk.[73] They also saw venture capital as a means to improve society through the development and commercialization of new technologies that would enhance people's lives. Prominent among those who helped define the industry was Georges Doriot, a French-born management expert. He became a popular professor at a young age at Harvard Business School (HBS), where he developed and taught courses on manufacturing and business policy, starting in the 1920s.[74] Doriot believed that businesses had a social purpose that went beyond seeking profitability. In his closing statements to students at HBS in 1966, he argued that his students had a "particular and superior form of responsibilities as businessmen, as citizens."[75]

After managing the US Army's Military Planning Division during World War II, Doriot co-founded in 1946 the American Research and Development Corporation (ARD), which he headed until the early 1970s. ARD was the first institutional venture capital fund, in the sense that the fund took in capital outside of wealthy families, the traditional source of venture financing. During its close to three decades in existence, ARD backed 120 ventures. Its most prominent and successful investment was Digital Equipment Corporation (DEC), which introduced the first computer with a screen in 1960 and the first "minicomputer" (albeit as large as a refrigerator) in 1965.[76] ARD's initial $200,000 investment became worth hundreds of millions of dollars by the late 1960s, one of the first high-profile examples of venture capital's potential to generate multiples on an investment.[77] In the post-war years, dividing his time between running ARD and teaching at HBS, Doriot spawned not only many successful innovative companies but also multiple industry leaders through his teaching. Among the 7,000 students he taught over four decades figured some of the venture capital industry's future leaders, including William Elfers (HBS MBA'43 and founder of Greylock), William Draper (HBS MBA'54 and founder of Sutter Hill Ventures), and Walter Curley (HBS MBA'48 and long-time partner at JH Whitney & Company).[78]

The precursors to institutionalized venture investing were the wealthy New England families that financed new industrial ventures in the early nineteenth century. The Boston Associates, a group that included prominent individuals such as Francis Cabot Lowell and Nathan Appleton, backed in 1813 the Boston Manufacturing Company, which paved the way for the development of New England's textile industry.[79] In the same vein, a handful of firms, notably JH

Whitney & Company and Rockefeller Brothers Company, were established to channel wealthy families' capital into new ventures, at about the same time as ARD. Greylock, founded in 1965 by William Elfers, Doriot's former student and right-hand man at ARD, followed in ARD's footsteps and raised capital from a broad base of institutional investors.[80]

While the institutional fundraising of firms like ARD and Greylock marked a new stage, the industry did not truly take off in the United States until a regulatory change, the relaxation of the Prudent Man Rule in 1979, enabled pension funds to allocate capital to VC funds. From $2 billion in assets under management in 1980, the VC industry in the United States has grown to $400 billion as of year-end 2018.[81] Exuberance for VC deals peaked during the 1999–2000 "dotcom" bubble. In 2000, VC funds invested over $100 billion in new ventures, close to four times the average of recent years. As of the late 2010s, another bubble may be in the making, with the rise of the "unicorn" phenomenon, which refers to start-ups that are valued at more than $1 billion. A number of factors account for the high valuations of leading start-ups, including the large amount of capital at the disposition of VC funds, a widely adopted strategy to "get big fast" by targeting large and frequent funding rounds, and a propensity to stay private for longer periods of time given the availability of later-stage VC capital as an alternative to an initial public offering (IPO). The availability of capital has significantly increased from the surge in participation by public market institutional funds driven to seek illiquid risks due to the low interest rate environment and the difficulty in generating performance in public markets.

With the IPO market significantly less active than it was during the dotcom boom, many unicorns, which numbered 452 as of May 2019,[82] will either need to continue raising private equity capital or be acquired by a strategic buyer.

Interest in VC has risen steeply in Europe and Asia, although levels of investment remain much lower than in the United States. As a proportion of GDP, venture capital investments in 2007–2014 in the United States were eight times greater than in the EU.[83] China has experienced a surge of interest in recent years, accounting for one-third of global VC capital deployed in 2015, more than three times the capital deployed in Europe and sixty times the capital deployed in Japan.[84]

Has the Industry Served Its Investors Well?

At face value, the VC industry has delivered high returns. The Cambridge Associates' thirty-year industry internal rate of return (IRR) stands at 19.6% as of Q2 2018.[85] A seminal paper analyzing VC funds raised between 1980 and 2001 showed a median return IRR of 13% and an average return of 17%.[86] It also constructed a comparison of VC returns to public market equivalents (PMEs), an important benchmark given that investors should require a premium in returns relative to liquid equivalents since their capital can be locked up for ten years or more. The study found a PME of 1.21 for the average return (indicating outperformance of VC funds relative to the PME) and 0.92 for the median return. In the same vein, one study creating a NASDAQ-based public market equivalent over twenty-eight years, this one based on actual cash-flow data from limited partners, shows that the mean return from its representative sample of venture funds would have been 1.59 times that of the PME but exactly equal when using the median fund return.[87]

The significant difference between average and median returns reflects the fact that there is no such thing as an "average" return in VC because the industry's returns are extremely skewed, with the vast majority generated by a small group of funds at the top for which persistence of returns is very high.[88] Venture capital has become a "winner-take-all" industry. The highest-performing funds attract the most attractive ventures, creating a self-reinforcing cycle. The leading VC funds generally target returning more than three times their committed capital after ten years.[89] At the very top, the returns that have been achieved are extraordinary. As of year-end 2015, Sequoia Capital had generated 8× returns on both its 2003 and 2006 vintage funds and 5.5× returns on its third fund, driven by investments in LinkedIn and YouTube for the first fund, Airbnb and Dropbox for the second, and WhatsApp for the third.[90] The challenge for any investor seeking exposure to these funds is to be able to secure an allocation, as demand is greater than these funds' willingness to accept capital.

Does the Venture Capital Industry Create Social Value?

This is an implicit aspiration for many venture capitalists. Investors in other strategies typically emphasize solely their interest in generating high returns. The language used by venture capitalists often signals an ambition to impact the world in a way that extends beyond their fiduciary responsibility to their own investors, even if they don't adopt an explicit dual objective of returns and social impact, as impact investments do. Their philosophy draws parallels with the old saying that "what is good for GM is good for America," with a global twist. For instance, Benchmark Capital states that they "believe that great entrepreneurs change the world for the better."[91] In describing its activities in China, Kleiner Perkins presents itself as "focused on promoting economic development, employment growth, and industry innovation."[92]

By and large, the evidence suggests that VC funds benefit society. On the surface, the value of their role is easily apparent – they fund new ventures and help them grow. Decades ago, entrepreneurs would have had to rely on a very small group of wealthy individuals and banks to obtain funding. Few people would have had the right type of connections to even aspire to be considered. Today, connections still help but the industry has become institutionalized and decentralized. Resourceful entrepreneurs with compelling business ideas can plug into a vibrant ecosystem of potential funders motivated to find the next venture to back.

There are two broad ways in which venture capitalists create social value. One is by boosting and improving the businesses in which they invest. The other is by creating positive spillover effects into the economy. On the first point, the evidence suggests that VC-backed companies grow faster than non-VC-backed companies,[93] are faster to commercialize their product, and faster to professionalize their organization.[94] Venture capital also has a positive impact on the production of patents at the industry level, more clearly than on R&D investment.[95] Research generally points to a greater role for VC in the commercialization of venture products and services than in incremental innovation.[96]

One important question is whether VC-backed start-ups would have received funding from another source absent the availability of VC funding. The research points to a real gap in funding filled by venture capital funds.[97] The VC industry has a positive impact on the creation of new businesses.[98] A study of US metropolitan statistical areas (MSAs) shows that the availability of VC capital tends to stimulate the creation of new firms and is positive on economic growth.[99] The study implies that each incremental VC-backed firm stimulates the creation of between two and twelve firms. This positive spillover effect may stem from spin-offs created by former employees of VC-backed start-ups. It may also be driven by an emulation effect, as the desire to become an entrepreneur can be triggered by the example set by others starting new firms.[100]

Does venture capital generate any negative economic or social effects? The costs seem relatively limited compared to the industry's positive contributions. The herd mentality of VC funds may be one of the least productive aspects of the industry. At any given point, the industry typically channels capital to start-ups that all operate in the same narrow markets.[101] In recent years, a large proportion of the capital has gone to mobile applications, smart transportation, and clean energy ventures, to name a few. Even if the evolutionary battle taking place between competing technologies and products in the same space ultimately leads to better products, the over-abundance of capital in highly specific sectors implies over-investment – how many new image messaging mobile applications make sense from an economic and social point of view? It also renders these sectors prone to bubbles. For start-ups that fall outside of the sectors in vogue, it makes it much harder to raise capital from VC funds. Very few funds would consider investing in a hardware technology company at this point in time. Few VC funds would contemplate investing in a start-up unless it has a very steep growth trajectory. This means that the vast majority of start-up firms fall outside of the industry's de facto purview.

Another concern relates to the vast accumulation of unregulated power of leading technology companies such as Facebook, Alphabet/Google, and Twitter, which were initially backed by venture capital. Multiple scandals have surfaced, from the casual monetization of private data to the irresponsible spread of fake news and hate speech, all pointing to these companies' blind obsession with growth at all costs. It is difficult to tease out the role VC has played in these developments but at a minimum, VC's worship of viral growth must have influenced these technology companies' culture, suggesting some responsibility.

Is venture capital the answer to the challenges developed economies have faced in creating new jobs? Many countries have explicitly promoted VC as a form of economic policy. Areas that have become focal points of venture investments have clearly economically benefited, whether Silicon Valley in the United States or Cambridge in the United Kingdom. However, it is not clear to what extent the positive spillover effects of VC can be scaled up. The study reviewing the impact of venture capital on MSAs found that even in Silicon Valley, the VC industry funds less than 4% of all start-ups, at a level that is less than 1% of GDP.[102]

Private Equity

Despite all the negative publicity private equity has garnered in recent years, the fundamental underpinnings of that strategy should make it at least theoretically a force for good for society. In the strategy's most common form, the leveraged buyout (LBO), a private equity fund acquires a controlling stake in a firm that is mature and cash-flow generating. The general partner of the private equity fund typically seeks to create value by improving the operations of the firm, establishing better governance, and levering up the firm's balance sheet. At its best, private equity professionals can instill greater analytical rigor in the firm's capital allocation decisions and discipline in measuring and monitoring performance. They bring management consultants, industry experts, or experienced board members and connect the acquired firm to a new network of potential partners. They act as a sounding board to the CEO. New incentive mechanisms are often put in place to align the interests of senior managers with those of their new owners and ensure renewed motivation in improving and transforming the company.

LBOs gained prominence in the early 1980s. Since then, their popularity has surged, as large institutional allocators have followed the lead of David Swensen, the Yale Endowment CIO, who showcased the benefits of having significant allocations to illiquid alternative assets. Assets under management for private equity firms worldwide have doubled over a ten-year period, reaching $4.1 trillion as of the end of 2019.[103]

Compared with many other types of investments, private equity is hard work. To perform well, private equity investors need to demonstrate skill across a broader spectrum of the value chain than is typically the case for their public market peers who don't take control of their portfolio companies. They need to be able to source and identify attractive investment opportunities, negotiate a purchase, and help run the company once they have acquired it. In essence, senior private equity professionals need to combine the skills of an investor with those of a CEO.

With 4.4 million employees at over 7,500 companies controlled by private equity firms in the United States alone, the industry's public profile has necessarily grown since its days as a niche asset class.[104] It took the 2012 US presidential candidacy of Mitt Romney, co-founder of Bain Capital – one of the industry's most successful firms, to raise the industry's profile to front-page news in the United States. During that campaign, an acerbic controversy followed the release of Romney's tax returns and the public disclosure of his large earnings and low effective tax rates. Often referred to as the "carried interest loophole," a quirk of the US tax system allows private equity investors to have the bulk of their earnings taxed at the capital gains rate rather than the income tax rate, which is close to twice as high for high earners.

A more fundamental question was broached as well: Does private equity benefit society? This question can be addressed from two distinct and complementary angles: Are private equity professionals good fiduciaries? Does private equity create positive spillover effects on the economy?

Are Private Equity Fund Managers Good Fiduciaries?

In the previous chapter, I discussed the fiduciary concerns related to the private equity industry, including relatively high standard management and incentive fees, and additional fees charged to portfolio companies, albeit tempered by recent scrutiny from LPs. Nevertheless, any criticism that private equity investors are poor fiduciaries must be balanced by the fact that private equity has generated some of the highest returns among all asset classes.[105] A 2016 survey shows that 84% of investors have a positive perception of private equity, the highest among alternative asset classes.[106] As of 2017, 88% of institutional investors had an allocation to private equity.[107] The asset class is well established in Europe, which now accounts for almost one-third of global private equity assets under management, and has grown rapidly in Asia in recent years. There is no doubt that part of the asset class's success stems from low interest rates during the past decades given the fundamental role of leverage in the private equity model.

Do the returns justify private equity's popularity? On the surface, yes. The Cambridge Associates' US Private Equity Index returned 13.4% annually net of fees over twenty-five years up to Q3 2019.[108] This compares to the 8.9% annual return for the Russell 2000 Index over the same period. The volatility of private equity returns is lower than that of listed equities, although that comparison may be misleading given the discretion afforded to private equity general partners in determining valuations, leading to "return smoothing."

A deeper dive into private equity returns provides a more nuanced perspective. Companies acquired by private equity funds tend to be smaller on average than representative companies of the large equity indices, have significantly more leverage, and reflect a different industry composition. Risk-adjusting equity benchmarks for these factors leads the comparison to show either smaller outperformance of private equity or even underperformance, depending on the specific factors used to adjust performance and the methodology.[109] Private equity should theoretically show clear outperformance relative to synthetic replications in liquid markets since investors require an "illiquidity premium" for having their capital locked up for up to ten years. In addition, private equity needs to compensate investors for the risk of committing capital that may not be fully invested for long periods of time, until the general partner finds suitable investments.

To account for these investor requirements, private equity professionals typically structure their carried interest to be contingent on a minimum annual internal rate of return of 8%, creating a fiduciary safety net of sorts. These hurdle rates are generally aligned with the long-term target returns of pension funds. In this light, the private equity standard compares favorably to the hedge fund standard. Hedge funds offer more liquidity but typically have no hurdle rates and take incentive fees on an annual basis. However, while the typical private equity terms help align interests, they don't guarantee outperformance relative to public benchmarks.

It is surprising that the data does not show clearer private equity outperformance versus synthetic benchmarks in liquid markets given that private equity returns should be boosted by the resources deployed by private equity professionals in helping improve operating performance of portfolio companies. One reason may be that private equity funds often have to compete in bidding wars, which can erode their returns.[110] Perhaps one hidden advantage of private equity's long holding period is that its very illiquidity creates a potential safeguard against selling assets at the bottom of the market – a temptation that is often overwhelming when holding liquid assets. The popularity of secondary markets now mitigates that safeguard, allowing investors to sell their illiquid assets at any point. Harvard University's endowment famously sold between $1 billion and $1.5 billion of private equity assets in 2009, at discounts that were said to approach 40%.[111]

Private equity's very success creates challenges for the industry to fulfill its mandate of generating attractive risk-adjusted returns on behalf of its limited partners. Since so much capital is now chasing similar types of opportunities, acquisitions are bid up. Unsurprisingly, private equity returns have been negatively correlated to flows into private equity funds on a lagged basis. Companies that have been passed on from private equity fund to private equity fund are a symptom of how crowded that space has become. With the global private equity industry having raised more than $300 billion annually for a record five years and having more than doubled its assets under management between 2007 and 2017, private equity funds have to find new ways to generate returns and hit their benchmarks.[112]

The Social Value of Private Equity

The second angle into whether private equity helps society requires broadening the inquiry beyond private equity's fiduciary responsibility towards its investors. Put simply, do private equity funds help the economy? Two aspects are relevant here: Do they help improve their portfolio companies? Do they generate positive spillover effects beyond their portfolio companies?

The public perception on the first question has been mixed at best. Private equity funds have been criticized for making large sums of money at the expense of the long-term health of their portfolio companies. At their worst, private equity funds are seen as "gutting" their portfolio companies, by increasing leverage to extreme levels and cutting costs, including research and development costs, in order to boost their portfolio companies' short-term cash flows at the expense of their long-term competitiveness.

Case studies of abusive and self-serving behavior by private equity funds abound. They often revolve around dividend recapitalizations or the process by which private equity funds leverage their portfolio company up significantly and take a significant proportion of the proceeds to pay themselves back and significantly de-risk their investment. This leads to incongruous situations in which a private equity firm can generate returns shortly after the acquisition of a portfolio company, and declare the investment a success, while its portfolio company is burdened by high levels of debt, resulting at times in eventual default and bankruptcy. This stark contrast in outcomes illustrates the risk for private equity funds to become acclaimed fiduciaries by generating high returns for their investors and for themselves, while extracting value from other stakeholders, and society more broadly.

Dividend recapitalizations are widespread in the industry and growing. Steve Schwarzman, co-founder and CEO of Blackstone, one of the largest and most successful private equity funds in the world, stated in reference to portfolio companies during a public call to investors that "you just sell them if the sale market is good and if not you recap them and you make money that way. So we just sort of go with the flow if you will."[113] As is often the case in these situations across the financial industry, the initial impetus is not unreasonable, but excesses in the implementation can lead to indefensible outcomes. The pressure to deliver high internal rates of returns in an increasingly competitive environment has led private equity funds to devise new mechanisms along the lines of dividend recapitalizations to show returns over shorter time periods.

It is not in any private equity fund's interest to "gut" a portfolio company and push it to the brink of solvency. Any bankruptcy under a private equity fund's watch has negative reputational effects, which can impair the willingness of company owners to sell to that fund down the road. But the asymmetric risks in favor of private equity funds and the potential for quick outsized returns can too easily incite reckless behavior.

The poster child of dividend recapitalizations gone awry may be Simmons Bedding Company. Founded in 1870 in Wisconsin, Simmons filed for bankruptcy in 2009 after having been sold seven times in over twenty years by a slew of private equity funds to one another.[114] Simmons' debt load grew from $164 million in 1991 to $1.3 billion in 2009. Boston-based private equity fund Thomas H. Lee Partners (THLP) drew the brunt of the criticism for having made $77 million in profit after having bought the company in 2003 and seen it go bankrupt. Those profits came in the form of special dividends, transaction fees, and monitoring fees. THLP raised debt capital on behalf of the company twice after its purchase, paying itself $375 million as a dividend, thereby recouping more than the $327 million it paid for the acquisition. In addition, THLP received special fees of $28 million.

As noted in a *New York Times* case study, senior executives of THLP justified their payout by arguing that the company performed well, with 40% sales growth and 26% operating income growth between 2003 and 2007, but that it was hit by a difficult economic environment. Simmons was acquired out of bankruptcy by another private equity fund, a unit of Ares Management, and the Ontario Teachers' Pension Plan. A majority interest in its parent company was sold to yet another private equity fund, Advent International, in 2012.

This is not to say that dividend recapitalizations always end in tears. Twinkies, the beloved American cream-filled bakery products, was bought out of bankruptcy in 2013 by two private equity firms, Apollo and an entity owned by Dean Metropoulos. They downsized the company substantially, from 8,000 employees at the time of the bankruptcy to 1,200. The two firms led Hostess to raise $1.3 billion in debt, of which $900 million went to de-risk their investment via a dividend recapitalization. After investing $186 million in the equity of Hostess in 2013, their investment was valued at 13× their initial cost by 2016.[115] They sold most of their stake in 2017 via a public offering. In 2017, the company generated $776 million in revenues and $131 million in free cash-flow – a resounding turnaround.

However, the speed at which private equity funds are de-risking their investments raises concerns that interests between funds and their portfolio companies are increasingly diverging. A case in point is Platinum Equity's December 2013 acquisition of Volvo Construction Equipment Rents (renamed BlueLine Rental). Platinum managed to repay itself the $201 million it had deployed for the acquisition within two months of the deal's completion. In less than three months, Platinum secured financing for the LBO with a $760 million senior secured high-yield bond and added a $252 million bond to pay itself a dividend that covered 100% of its investment in BlueLine Rental.[116] It subsequently sold the company for about $2.1 billion in September 2018.

Private equity-backed retail companies have made headlines with increased frequency. The Payless shoe company, which was founded in 1956 and employed 22,000 people, went bankrupt in March 2017 after struggling to compete in the discount footwear segment while carrying an enormous debt burden of $665 million. The firm was acquired in 2012 by private equity firms Golden Gate Capital and Blum Capital, which generated a profit on the deal via a dividend recapitalization that enabled them to take out $350 million before the bankruptcy.[117] Excess leverage in an unforgiving retail environment also engulfed iconic toy store Toys "R" Us, which filed for bankruptcy in 2017 after failing to pay more than $250 million a year to service its $5 billion in long-term debt. To be fair, retail bankruptcies have sky-rocketed as changes in consumer behaviors have benefited online plat-forms. Still, the massive increase in leverage has to have played a critical role in these firms' demise.

The appetite for dividend recapitalizations shows no sign of abating. Historically low interest rates throughout the 2010s have supported demand for dividend recapitalizations. They reached $50 bil-lion in the United States in 2016, up from $38 billion in 2015. Highs of $70 billion were attained in 2013. Those numbers exceed the pre-Global Financial Crisis peak of $49 billion reached in 2007.[118] As of Q1 2017, private equity portfolio company multiple marginally exceeded the US Fed's guidelines published in 2013 that debt to EBITDA (earnings before interest, tax, depreciation and amortization) ratios should, for most industries, not exceed 6×.[119]

Another trend has been for private equity funds to first invest by using bank loans and then deploy equity capital, in order to shorten the effective investment period and boost reported IRRs. Since private equity funds compete with each other for capital allocation primarily based on performance, a ratcheting effect is pressuring them toward ever greater credit use. Of course, this can end in tears, as was the case for EnerVest, a Houston-based private equity fund which had aggres-sively used bank loans which it could no longer service as its energy portfolio companies slowed down.[120]

Criticism of the industry has not solely focused on financial engineering. 3G Capital, a high-profile Brazilian private equity fund, has earned a reputation as a ruthless cost cutter (in addition to being willing to highly leverage its companies). 3G and Warren Buffett's Berkshire Hathaway jointly acquired Heinz, the US packaged food company, in early 2013.[121] Consistent with the roll-up strategy favored by 3G, Heinz acquired Kraft Foods in early 2015. Deploying its "zero-based budgeting," which requires each department to justify every cost anew, 3G was able to boost the operating profit margin of the combined company from 15% to 21% in less than a year – a remarkable result. Yet it did so in large part by laying off 13,000 employees from the 55,000 the two companies had before the 3G acquisitions. Extreme cost cutting creates short-term profits but may not create value over the long term. In the drastic cost-cutting process, Heinz Kraft lost significant managerial talent. The uncompromising approach has also made 3G an unwelcome owner for many companies. When Kraft Heinz made an offer in February 2017 to acquire Unilever, a giant Anglo-Dutch consumer goods company, there was much concern that the 3G approach would clash with Unilever's focus on sustainable growth.[122] The bid was retrieved two days after it was made for reasons that were not made public.

Time will tell whether 3G will be more successful over time than other companies that in the past deployed sharp-elbowed strategies to shock companies into generating greater profits. The recent data suggests not – as of mid 2019, weak performance and a $15.4 billion writedown had led shares in Kraft Heinz to collapse more than 60% from their 2017 peak.[123]

While the negative anecdotal evidence is striking, research aggregating industry-wide statistics has generally shown the industry in a more positive light. Research on the impact of private equity, typically consisting of large sample studies in the United States or the United Kingdom, suggests that private equity firms tend to improve the companies they acquire. On average, operating margins, cash-flow margins,[124] and productivity improve.[125] Productivity improvement in industrial companies tends to be caused by reallocation of resources to more highly productive manufacturing plants. A study on French LBOs shows that in the three years following a buyout, acquired firms tend to grow faster than their competitors and increase capital expenditures.[126] Another study highlights that target plants in the UK experience significant improvement in productivity after a buyout, due to a decrease in the labor intensity of production.[127]

Following their acquisition by a private equity fund, companies also demonstrate more prominent innovation, as measured by patent citations, and show no evidence of decreased patenting activity, belying the widespread perception that private equity funds severely limit long-term investments.[128] A study also showed that private equity portfolio companies do not go bankrupt more often than their peers – with the caveat that this study was only conducted over the 2000–2008 period.[129]

The overall picture on employment is more mixed: Recent studies have shown that employment increases after a buyout, but more slowly than at other firms in the same industry[130] or that employment decreases slightly in the context of substantial gross job creation and destruction.[131] Studies of employment effects on target companies in the UK find either some employment growth[132] or no significant effect.[133]

Two caveats relative to private equity's impact on employment are worth mentioning. One is that private equity funds tend to invest in mature, and, at times, distressed companies. One challenge is to benchmark realized outcomes at a portfolio company against expected outcomes had the private equity fund not invested in that particular company. The other caveat relates to the risk of focusing on nominal changes in employment levels in isolation. In some situations, increased productivity via lower employment levels may be a preferable outcome at a societal level (obviously not for those who lose their jobs), even taking into account job losses.

The positive impact of private equity on portfolio companies makes theoretical sense. As Michael Jensen argued already in 1989, the private equity model can effectively address the principal–agent conflicts inherent in the diffuse ownership of public corporations.[134] These conflicts are particularly pronounced for companies in industries with weak long-term growth prospects and whose managers find limited opportunities to re-invest cash flows. Increased leverage creates a forcing mechanism to prevent hoarding of excess cash. Owners sit on boards to closely monitor managers. Interests between owners and managers are also better aligned with improved managerial incentives.

Academic research so far suggests that the externalities of private equity investments – beyond the impact on the specific companies acquired by private equity – are positive. Using a database of global private equity investments across various industries, a recent study found that labor productivity, employment, profitability, and capital expenditures increased for publicly listed companies in the same industry and country.[135] This suggests that even when private equity investments result in reduced employment or curbed capital expenditures at their acquired companies, their investment may have a broader positive effect on the industry as a whole that runs counter to that effect. Another study documents increases in R&D expenses and strategic alliances among competing firms within an industry when a leveraged buyout takes place.[136]

Anecdotal evidence also suggests that some of the operational improvements at private equity-backed companies can spread to competitors. The buyout of Hertz Corporation in 2005 has been cited as an example.[137] Following efficiency gains at Hertz, its two biggest competitors, Avis-Budget and Dollar-Thrifty, implemented various customer experience enhancements and cost-cutting initiatives, leading to increased profit margins and labor productivity gains.

The theoretical case for the benefits of private equity to society appears strong. Private equity funds help improve companies, with potentially positive spillover effects on their industries. Still, too few studies have delved into the broader impact of the private equity industry and the direction of causality cannot always be fully ascertained in existing studies, preventing us from drawing definitive conclusions.

Shareholder Activism

In theory, shareholder activism should also benefit society. Activist hedge funds seek to influence management teams of listed companies by pushing forward specific, highly reasoned, often well-researched agenda items. Those recommendations, or demands depending on the fund's level of assertiveness, can take the form of a more considered approach to capital allocation and greater focus on return on invested capital, greater transparency with shareholders, or a change in strategy. At times, they target a specific decision that management has to make – for instance, a divestiture, acquisition, or merger. They can also press for changes in the management team or the governance structure. More often than not, they simply ask for returns of cash to shareholders in the form of higher dividends or share buybacks. Ultimately, they always seek to boost shareholder returns since activist hedge funds live and die by their returns. Activist hedge funds typically build up a position owning 5% to 20% of the firm's equity in order to be taken seriously by management and, potentially, by other shareholders if at some point they need support. They often seek one or more board seats in order to have a more direct impact on company strategy.

As the frequency of activism has increased, power has shifted from boards toward shareholders, at least in the United States.[138] Yet the stakeholder-centric theory of governance has gained followers since the Global Financial Crisis, in both academic circles and managerial ranks. Jack Welch, the former CEO of General Electric, who is one of the pioneers of the shareholder value maximization approach, famously stated in 2009 that shareholder value is "the dumbest idea in the world," as "shareholder value is a result, not a strategy ... Your main constituencies are your employees, your customers and your products."[139] In a landmark decision announced in August 2019, the influential Business Roundtable redefined the purpose of a corporation to serve the interests of all stakeholders. The increasing appeal of a stakeholder-centric approach appears to be in large part due to the perception that the shareholder-centric view of the firm has led to the excesses that caused the crisis.

Shareholder activism's roots lie in value investing, an approach that seeks to buy securities and assets below their intrinsic value as determined by fundamental analysis. Benjamin Graham, often referred to as the father of value investing, was a pioneer shareholder activist. An investor and professor at Columbia Business School, his seminal texts on value investing – *Security Analysis*, written in 1934 with David Dodd, and *The Intelligent Investor*, written in 1949, laid the intellectual foundation for activist investing.[140] His campaign to get the management of Northern Pipeline to divest its excess investment securities between 1926 and 1928 is seen as a precursor to modern shareholder activism.[141] Graham determined that the company owned about $90 per share worth of investment securities while its stock traded at $65 and it generated over $6 per share in annual earnings. From his point of view, there was no reason for the company to hold on to these excess investment securities. The company should focus on its operations and return the capital to shareholders. After getting rebuffed by a management team incredulous that an outsider would tell them how to manage their company, Graham ran a proxy fight to get seats on the board. A successful grassroots campaign to elicit support from multiple shareholders yielded him and his lawyer two seats on the board. Despite being short a majority on the five-seat board, the pressure was enough for management to return cash to shareholders shortly thereafter.

Shareholder activism did not enter the public consciousness until the 1980s, when a more bare-knuckled approach, often referred to as corporate raid, took hold. Names like Carl Icahn, Nelson Peltz, Sir James Goldsmith, and Ronald Perelman made headlines with hostile take-overs of large publicly traded companies. While enormously profitable for these so-called corporate raiders, these activist interventions have generally been painted negatively from a social perspective due to their practice of "asset stripping" and ruthless tactics.

The typical playbook entailed taking control of a company, increasing its leverage dramatically, and selling off the assets, often to repay the debt. Their actions were not inherently antithetical to social value creation – in fact, the timing of these corporate raids coincided with a growing perspective in academic circles that corporate diversification tends to destroy value unless it is demonstrably synergistic. Opportunities to sell off assets and subsidiaries that could not be defined as core businesses abounded after the conglomerate-building trend of the 1960s. However, the indiscriminate selling, obsessive focus on short-term returns, and the seeming lack of interest in the long-term viability of the targeted firms often overwhelmed these investors' ability to generate positive spillovers. The spike in corporate raids diminished, following a slew of failed investments and the demise of Drexel Burnham Lambert, an aggressive investment bank that had raised investment pools on behalf of several of these high-profile investors, including Nelson Peltz and Ronald Perelman.

Over the last two decades, a new form of shareholder activism has gradually taken hold, focused on remedying breaches of corporate governance and improving performance. This strategy is less focused on breaking companies apart, emphasizing instead demands to return excess cash to shareholders and to reconfigure egregious CEO pay packages when shareholder returns are lagging. Spinning off non-core businesses and other corporate transactions remain a focal point, but demands tend to pay heed, at least publicly, to the medium-term positioning of the firm rather than the short-term proceeds of selling off various business units indiscriminately. Corporate raiders have morphed into governance proselytizers, and, in the process, have gained wider acceptance.

As opposed to European and Japanese markets, where discretion tends to be more effective, activists operating in the US market readily consider getting involved in proxy contests, whereby they propose a change and try to attract as many votes as they can during a company's annual meeting. Two proxy firms have great influence in the process, Institutional Shareholder Services (ISS) and Glass, Lewis & Co, which advise large institutional investors on how to vote in these contests. These firms are inclined to side with activists,[142] helping tip the balance in their favor. In 2018, the activists won at least one board seat in 50% of proxy votes.[143] This understates the influence of activists since deals between management and activists are often struck before the vote takes place.

The role of large asset allocators has also evolved drastically and become central to the development of activism. In the 1980s, only aggressive investment banks like Drexel Burnham Lambert dared support activists. Pension funds traditionally shied away from engaging with their portfolio companies. A 1988 Department of Labor directive to pension funds attempted to spur greater engagement by stating that they have a fiduciary duty to vote their shares. Still, many relented. John Biggs, the CEO and Chairman of the country's largest pension fund, TIAA-CREF, between 1993 and 2002 was the first head of a large pension fund to press for changes in the fund's portfolio companies.

The large asset managers have typically been reluctant to engage with their portfolio companies because of the inherent conflict they have in criticizing the management of a firm whose pension fund business they would likely be targeting simultaneously. Because every large listed company is a potential client, asset managers prefer to remain discreet.

Even more complicated is the position of passive asset managers such as Vanguard. Like active asset managers, every large public company is a potential client. Additionally, since they passively replicate the market, they can't threaten to sell or short a company's shares. They can, however, threaten to vote against management.

Of particular significance has been the stance of Blackrock, Vanguard, and State Street, since they manage more than $14 trillion combined as of early 2018 and continue to attract a disproportionate share of investor flows given investors' shift toward passive management. For years, John Bogle pressured his successors at Vanguard to become more active in sharing views with management. Frederick McNabb, CEO for a decade starting in 2008, decided in 2015 to shift to a more assertive stance. In June 2016, Vanguard adopted a new set of voting guidelines on annual proxies. This could lead to a shift from its historical support of management. Larry Fink, the CEO of Blackrock, has been another important voice in that debate. Illustrative of the shift was the decision by Vanguard, Blackrock, and State Street Global Advisors to vote against the management of Exxon Mobil in May 2017 to require that the company issue a report on climate change.[144] This points to a more assertive stance, with many of these large allocators having now set up their own internal proxy vote departments to determine how they should vote. As a mark of that greater assertiveness, they have expressed their frustration at the increasing frequency of settlements between corporates and activists without being consulted.[145]

In recent years, large asset managers have developed behind-the-scenes alliances with activist hedge funds. One solution to their conflict of interest in challenging management teams is to quietly invite activists to invest in portfolio companies that are ripe for intervention. They can facilitate activist interventions by signaling to the activist their likely support in a future proxy vote. In turn, this allows asset managers to create catalysts in their portfolios and help boost returns. Examples include support by the California State Teachers' Retirement System (CalSTRS), one of the United States' largest pension funds, of activist hedge fund Relational in pressuring The Timken Company, a traditional steel and bearing manufacturer, to break up.[146] One effect is that activist funds can now punch significantly above their weight. Even with a small stake, they can wield significant influence if they start with the implicit backing of large owners. A case in point was ValueAct's ability to get a board seat at Microsoft while owning less than 1% of its shares.

Confrontational activism continues to make headlines by the likes of Pershing Square and Third Point – hedge funds that often berate publicly the CEO of their target companies to garner support from other investors and shame the board into acting. While these activist funds tend to attract most of the attention, a fund like San Francisco-based ValueAct better exemplifies a new type of "constructive" activism, focused on governance, often acting in concert with, or at least with the blessing of, large allocators, and emphasizing discrete conversations over public letters and the front pages of newspapers. Importantly, they are also willing to be a long-term shareholder.

Since co-founding ValueAct in 2000, Jeffrey Ubben has shaped it to be a quiet giant in an industry dominated by large and loud personalities. ValueAct adopts a private equity approach to public investing, targeting ten to fifteen concentrated investments at any point in time. The fund typically seeks a board seat and gets deep in the trenches, advising the company on capital allocation and other CEO-level decisions, without seeking control. While ValueAct is known for its patient, fact-based approach, it doesn't shy away from applying pressure when performance doesn't improve. In one of the firm's most significant interventions, ValueAct helped instigate the ouster of Steve Ballmer at Microsoft, and did so without fireworks. Not all of its investments have been successes nor models of social wealth creation – most notably, ValueAct was a long-term investor in pharmaceutical company Valeant. It is credited for having picked the now disgraced CEO Michael Pearson and for having been the architect of Valeant's executive compensation plan, which is perceived to have spurred the unhinged value extraction that led to Valeant's collapse.[147]

Ubben developed his skill set as a value investor working under the famed Peter Lynch at Fidelity and later as a private equity investor at Blum Capital. His willingness to adopt a three- to five-year time frame for his investments stands out against peers that are typically pressed to show returns over a shorter period of time. The bulk of ValueAct's investors are locked up in the fund for several years, a key differentiator in the face of many activist hedge funds that either have shorter lock-ups or no lock-up.

In a move remarkable for its rarity in the industry but consistent with Ubben's persona, he decided to step down from the daily management of the $16 billion fund in May 2017, at the relatively young age of 55 and at a time when the fund appeared to be doing well, having produced annualized returns of 15% – in other words, without being pressured to do so.[148]

Do Shareholder Activists Fulfill Their Economic Mandate?

In the past decade, activist hedge funds have generated high returns in comparison with the rest of the hedge fund universe. Between 2010 and the summer of 2017, Hedge Fund Research's (HFR) activist hedge fund index shows an annualized return of 8.5% versus 4.7% for the composite hedge fund index and 13.3% for the S&P 500. Going back to the beginning of 2008, when data starts becoming available, annualized returns decline to 3.3%, in line with returns for the broader index and versus 7.7% for the S&P 500. As predominantly long-only strategies, activist strategies tend to be exposed to major market downturns. They showed an average 40% negative return in 2008, more than twice the average for the composite index.

As a result of their strong relative performance, assets flowing into activist hedge funds have dramatically increased. They have more than quintupled since 2008, from $32 billion to $176 billion at the end of 2016, according to HFR.

In a parallel development, the frequency of activist campaigns has surged in the United States in recent years. On average, 347 activist campaigns, defined by the filing of a 13D Schedule (an SEC filing that must be submitted within ten days of acquiring more than 5% of publicly traded securities in a company), were recorded annually between 2014 and 2016, more than twice the average recorded between 1994 and 2007.[149]

Those numbers understate the true influence of activism. The increasing frequency of activist interventions and their high rate of success has caught the attention of CEOs and boards of listed companies, notably in the United States. Good corporate hygiene now requires proactively addressing governance issues before they can be seized on by an activist fund, as well as keeping in closer touch with one's large institutional investors. Boards are now routinely focused on pre-empting the type of demands that activist funds might make. They hire consultants to better prepare them. Articles with titles like "Your Board Should Think Like Activists" are emblematic of that structured paranoia.[150] A case in point is Allergan's reaction to Valeant and Pershing Square's attempt to take it over: The firm decided to proactively cut its workforce by 13% (versus Valeant's 20% goal) and to cull R&D spend to 13% of revenues, from its historical average of 16% to 17%.[151]

Why has shareholder activism gained such prominence? One simple observation is that the ability of alternative asset managers, and particularly hedge funds, to generate alpha has eroded significantly over the years. A natural response to the frustration of undervalued securities remaining undervalued indefinitely, at least for value investors, is to create their own catalysts by attempting to influence management on specific decisions.

Other factors enabling more frequent activism in the United States include the increased sway with large allocators of proxy advisors, specifically ISS and Glass Lewis, which typically support activist interventions, and the steep decline in the prevalence of staggered boards, which constrain the election of directors to only one-third of the board at each election,[152] thereby insulating a majority of directors from removal in any given year. Another critical factor has been the "Wolf Pack" tactic, as defined by academics John Coffee and Darius Palia, or the ability for hedge fund activists to share views about a target company and invest in parallel without being considered a "group" from the perspective of the SEC, allowing them to file 13Ds individually rather than as a group and thus delay the point at which they have to publicly disclose their ownership.[153]

European markets have also experienced an increase in activist campaigns, although those have always been more discreet than they were in the United States because the culture has generally been less accepting of confrontational tactics and short-term gains.[154] The number of activist campaigns has just about doubled between 2012 and 2017.[155] One driver for that increase has been the inevitable crowding of the US market given the surge in assets under management allocated to activists operating there. Large American funds have increasingly targeted European companies – examples include Third Point going after Swiss conglomerate Nestlé and Elliott Management pursuing Akzo Nobel, a Dutch paint company, and BHP Billiton, a British–Australian mining firm.

Paradoxically, there tend to be fewer regulatory constraints in European markets. Shareholders generally have broader rights than in the United States and protections such as poison pills and staggered boards are less common.[156] In the UK, shareholders can call general meetings of the board and shareholders as long as they own 5% of the shares, putting the bar much lower than in the United States.[157]

In Continental Europe, other obstacles exist. German companies often have founding family members with a majority of the shares as well as a two-tier board structure that creates a buffer between activist funds and the management board.[158] France enacted in 2014 the controversial Florange Law which bestows twice the voting right to shares owned for more than two years. Protectionist measures can also come into play when the government is the dominant shareholder.

The most successful activist funds in Europe have favored a quiet approach to management and have tended to have a long-term outlook. Cevian, a Swedish activist fund managing $15 billion, and operating primarily in the Scandinavian, German, and UK markets, typically targets owning up to a third of a company's shares for four to five years. With a concentrated portfolio of about a dozen positions, its "active ownership" approach has significant overlap with private equity. Fund manager Christer Gardell has steered clear of public missives and proxy fights, preferring a collaborative approach that rests on trust built over time as the largest shareholder with a board seat.[159] In the countries Cevian operates in, a board seat often comes automatically or in a straightforward process for its level of ownership, allowing Gardell to eschew public fights.[160] While Gardell is known to be constructive and patient, he is comfortable applying pressure when changes are slow to materialize, resorting at times to releasing analysis to support his arguments.

Is Shareholder Activism Helpful to Society?

In theory, activist hedge funds should benefit society since a primary objective of their strategy is to improve the performance and governance of target companies. That promising potential drew me to "constructive" activism as an investor. My anecdotal experience has reinforced this notion that activism is a force for good for all stakeholders of targeted companies. However, evidence from academic studies is mixed. Multiple studies have sought to identify the impact of activism on long-term investment in R&D. Most of them show that activists tend to reduce it. One study conducted in 2015 showed that a representative sample of firms targeted by activism in 2009 reduced their R&D expenses as a percentage of sales from 17.3% in 2009 to 8.1% in 2013.[161] By contrast, a random control group slightly increased its spending from 6.5% to 7.6%. The fact that the targeted companies had significantly higher R&D expenses to begin with also suggests that they may have been targeted in part because of that high number.

Not all studies show a decline. A study by the *Economist* of the fifty largest activist positions between 2009 and 2014 shows an increase.[162] One study also shows that patent applications tend to increase at firms targeted by activism,[163] although it is not intuitively clear why that would be the case. Lucian Bebchuk, a prominent supporter of shareholder activism, has argued that while activism does negatively impact spending on R&D, in doing so it serves a pro-social function by swaying firms toward more optimal investment levels given that they tend to over-invest.[164]

Evidence of the impact of activists on the operating performance of targeted companies is also mixed, with most studies showing little tangible impact[165] and a subset showing negative or positive impact.[166] This is surprising as one would expect activists to have a clear positive impact on the operations of their targeted companies since they often explicitly seek to improve productivity.

On the whole, research findings generally support the possibility that activism pressures companies to focus on shorter-term outcomes. John Coffee, a prominent skeptic of the impact of hedge fund activism, has argued that the weight of the evidence lends credibility to the thesis that activism trades off short-term private gains against long-term social costs.[167] Some have even pushed the argument further, stating that the pressure from shareholder activists is directly responsible for the type of short-term emphasis that caused the Global Financial Crisis.[168] While that may push the argument too far, there is no question that the interests of activists can all too easily be at odds with longer-term stakeholders, whether management, employees, bondholders, or long-term shareholders, since even a temporary bounce in the share price may be enough to achieve the activists' ultimate goal of generating returns and exiting their position. The average holding of activist funds, under one year to one and a half years depending on the study, illustrates the inherent short-term bias of activists.[169] In fact, the shorter the period of ownership, the better for the activists since the higher their internal rate of return.

In the same vein, activism has contributed to the increasing appeal for listed companies to privatize, even if activism is far from being the only cause. The combination of constant pressure to focus on near-term results and higher compliance and reporting costs associated with being listed since the Sarbanes Oxley Act of 2002 has led many companies to forgo the liquidity of public markets. Michael Dell decided to delist his company in 2013 in order to move away from quarterly earnings pressure. The net effect has been a massive reduction in the number of listed companies in the United States, about 50% lower in 2016 compared to twenty years prior.

Similar to private equity, shareholder activism typically leads to increased leverage at targeted firms and increased cash returns to shareholders. This implies that the higher returns to shareholders may be driven in part by increased risk, with some studies suggesting that they simply represent a form of wealth transfer from bondholders to shareholders.[170] Another parallel observation to private equity is the possibility that the higher returns represent a wealth transfer from the employees to the shareholders, due to stagnant or reduced salaries, layoffs, or diminished future pension payouts.[171]

As with private equity, high-profile stories abound illustrating the strategy's negative aspects. The pioneering partnership between pharmaceutical company Valeant and activist hedge fund Pershing Square to acquire in a hostile take-over Allergan, another pharmaceutical company of similar size to Valeant, is a case study of the type of excesses that activism can lead to. Valeant was as pure an interpretation of focused activism as one could find. Its business model, under the helm of former McKinsey consultant Mike Pearson, was to make serial acquisitions of pharmaceutical companies with established drugs and boost their profitability by aggressively culling their R&D,[172] raising the price of selected drugs, while benefiting from economies of scale. Valeant was backed by Pershing Square and ValueAct, which were deeply impressed by Pearson's efficiency and aggressiveness. Pershing Square and Valeant filed a 13D schedule in April 2014, disclosing that their joint entity had acquired close to 10% of Allergan's shares. Valeant targeted reducing Allergan's R&D spending, once it was acquired, by 69%,[173] and planned to cut its workforce by 20%.[174] This was consistent with the fact that Valeant spent less than 3% of its revenues on R&D compared to as much as 20% for large pharmaceutical companies.[175] It also planned on reducing Allergan's tax rate from 26% to about 9% by moving its headquarters to Canada.

David Pyott, the mild-mannered CEO of Allergan, fought back, writing to Pearson that he had doubts about the long-term sustainability of Valeant's business model, that "Valeant's strategy runs counter to Allergan's customer-focused approach," and that he questioned how Valeant would achieve the level of cost cuts it was proposing "without harming the long-term viability and growth trajectory of our business."[176] In the end, Pyott found a white knight in Actavis, a large drug company, that was willing to acquire Allergan at a price that Valeant and Pershing Square could not match. Importantly, the deal limited the reduction in Allergan's R&D expenses to one-third, drastically less than what a Valeant deal would have entailed.[177]

Pyott's skepticism toward Valeant's business model turned out to be prescient. Valeant's excessive zeal in extracting value eventually drew political and media opprobrium. Its share price collapsed by 75% between the beginning of 2014 and April 2016, when Mike Pearson resigned. This also illustrates the downside risk taken on by activists. While Pershing Square ended up making a profit estimated to be close to $2.5 billion on its purchase of Allergan shares,[178] its overall losses on its investment in Valeant are estimated to be about $4.2 billion.[179]

Despite the risk of excess eagerness to improve short-term profits, on balance, the deterrent effect created by activists should support a stronger corporate sector. In this environment, CEOs and boards constantly need to demonstrate that they have a clear plan for value creation in order to pre-empt any external actor from filling a vacuum. It is also harder for CEOs to cajole boards into awarding them egregious pay packages. In addition to the risk of being called out by an activist, "Say on Pay," a non-binding shareholder vote for US-listed companies instigated by the Dodd-Frank reforms, has had a growing impact on CEO compensation. The very fact that shareholders now have a channel to engage with companies on executive compensation, even if it is non-binding, raises the bar for CEOs to justify their compensation. It has also contributed to curtailing CEO perks by creating greater transparency.[180] While the vast majority of investors continue to back executive compensation plans, investors have voted for increasing the frequency of Say on Pay votes to keep up the pressure on CEOs and boards.

One potential remedy to the risk that shareholder activism bolsters short-termism is to introduce regulations along the lines of the French law that grants double voting rights to any shareholder that has held shares in the company for two years or more. But this is no panacea. While the spirit behind it is commendable, in practice it creates a new set of distortions. On one hand, it would force most activists to extend their investment horizon, helping mitigate (albeit not resolve) inherent conflicts of interest with longer-term stakeholders. On the other hand, it might allow certain minority shareholders to lock in effective control, and potentially wield that power to insulate management companies from the influence of other shareholders.

In order to add real value, activism requires a willingness to share gains with other stakeholders, and particularly employees. The challenge is that incentives in the existing financial system are not conducive to self-imposed restraint. Investors are pressured to avoid leaving money on the table. As a result, what starts as a reasonable framework of engagement with management to create value for all stakeholders often ends up being pushed to its narrow limits as a mechanism to extract value on behalf of shareholders.

How can activists afford to show restraint and seek balanced rewards? There is no perfect solution, but when they can convince their own investors to entrust them with longer time horizons, as San Francisco-based ValueAct and Stockholm-based Cevian have done, their interests tend to be better aligned with those of other stakeholders. They no longer need to show quick returns and can feel less compelled to, for instance, force drastic cuts in R&D in order to boost margins.

Finally, one reason why the data on the social impact of activism in the United States may not be as conclusive as one might expect may lie in the fact that shareholders already exert significant sway in US markets. The social value of shareholder activism should be more pronounced in markets where there is a clear imbalance between stakeholders at the expense of shareholders. While shareholder activism is a quintessentially American form of investing – it embodies more closely than just about any other form of investing the credo that firms are run primarily for the benefit of shareholders, perhaps the best illustration of ways in which activism can deliver social value is to be seen in Japan, where the corporate sector tends to be structurally skewed in favor of employees. In most Japanese companies, any push toward delivering value to shareholders is a step toward more balanced governance that can benefit all stakeholders in a sustained manner. The current wave of constructive activism in Japan illustrates how investors can deliver real value.

The Japanese Experience

Since 2013, Prime Minister Abe has made corporate governance reforms a pillar of the third arrow of his Abenomics program, which comprises restructuring efforts and deregulation initiatives that are meant to have a long-term impact on the Japanese economy (the first two arrows target monetary and fiscal policies). This may be the first time that a government has made corporate governance reforms a central part of its policy platform. In doing so, the Abe administration has implicitly supported shareholder activism, in a bid to encourage the adoption of his Corporate Governance Code by Japanese listed companies. It has explicitly encouraged greater engagement between fund managers and portfolio companies by enacting a Stewardship Code. The investment by government-run GPIF, Japan's largest pension fund, in Taiyo Pacific, an American engagement (meaning friendly activist) fund targeting Japanese companies, illustrates the point. Abe has even met with one of the most prominent American activists, Dan Loeb, in a well-publicized encounter, implying he sees value in foreign involvement in Japanese markets.

A surge of flows in the first two years of Abe's second tenure as prime minister (his first stint in 2007 was short-lived) was driven primarily by the adoption of an aggressive quantitative easing program by the Bank of Japan. But Abe's corporate governance reforms have also been seen as an important driver of international capital flows, and a significant factor in the renewed interest in Japanese equities from global fundamental investors.

The corporate governance push in Japan comes out of necessity: At the onset of the Abe administration, Japan performed poorly in international corporate governance rankings, at levels consistent with emerging economies. This is incongruous, as one would expect an economy with a mature, sophisticated financial system to exhibit relatively good corporate governance because a capital markets-based funding system creates far more pressure points to redress bad corporate governance than a less developed bank-centric system. Companies that get most of their funding from bank loans have to satisfy the transparency requirements of a finite group of bank loan officers, some of whom may be part of long-standing relationships, whereas companies that rely on bond and equity issuance are constantly vulnerable to being exposed by hordes of analysts who are kicking the tires of their investment and opining on the prospects of the company.

The governance shortcomings of the Japanese corporate sector are core to the sclerosis the economy has experienced since the 1980s. Japan's corporate sector has been hampered by managers who don't act as owners. CEOs who are not founders or part of a founding family typically have only limited share ownership and are not compensated based on share price performance or operational metrics. This also points to a fundamentally different concept of the purpose of a firm. Despite recent challenges to it, the mantra that companies are run on behalf of their shareholders has held sway in the United States since Milton Friedman's seminal article came out in 1970. By contrast, firms in Japan have traditionally been viewed as vehicles to benefit their employees while serving their customers. This "community" concept of the firm, even pertaining to listed companies, has held firm since the end of World War II.[181]

Persistent deflation during much of the post-Bubble era provides context for a generation of managers who often perceived survival of the company and passing on the reins to the next non-owner CEO as an accomplishment in its own right.[182] But by valuing long-term stability and continuity over performance, many listed Japanese companies have plodded along and turned themselves into "value traps," i.e. companies that look very attractive on paper to value investors but fail to deliver returns to shareholders due to their fundamental lack of interest in their share price and the limited influence shareholders ultimately have on them.

Many small and mid-sized listed companies fit that profile: industrial companies with a proud engineering culture, at times led by descendants of the founder. While they don't typically show much growth given the maturity of the Japanese economy, they often generate stable cash flows, have fortress balance sheets with limited debt and significant amounts of excess cash. That cash is generally seen by management as a buffer against future economic crises and a retirement safety net for senior managers. In their mind, the cash was generated by years of employees' effort and craftsmanship, and belongs to employees, not shareholders. These companies tend to trade at valuation multiples that attract the attention of value investors – multiples that can be half of those for their international peer set. In this context, any push toward more balanced governance should spur firm performance and benefit all stakeholders, including employees.

Prime Minister Abe's corporate governance reforms attempt to remedy an endemic lack of dynamism and efficiency in Japan's corporate sector by applying a mosaic of pressure points that are uniquely suited to Japanese culture. They appeal to the shame factor and the visceral Japanese fear of sticking out. The Corporate Governance Code adopts a "comply or explain" approach rather than a legally binding one. Peer pressure has slowly built up and triggered virtuous behavior in some corners of Japan's corporate sector. It has led to increases in independent board directors and in returns of cash to shareholders, either in the form of increased dividends or share buybacks. In certain sectors with a clearly delineated group of competitors, an announcement by one of the companies of measures to implement a Corporate Governance Code recommendation has more often than not led to similar announcements by its peers.

Shareholder activists apply one additional pressure point. Japan has experienced an even more accentuated turnaround in the perception of the public utility of shareholder activists than the United States: from the bullies and, ultimately, pariahs of the 2000s to the corporate governance proselytizers of Abe's code since 2014. In the 2000s, a wave of activists hit Japanese listed companies under the premise that the Japanese corporate sector offered an abundance of "low-hanging fruit" that could be tackled via shareholder pressure. These activists generally adopted confrontational approaches similar to those prevalent in the

United States. By and large, they failed. Whether they were American funds, such as Steel Partners, British funds such as TCI, or Japanese managers, such as Yoshiaki Murakami, they found that the entire system conspired to support the embattled companies, no matter how impaired their corporate governance. Steel Partners famously lost a public battle with sauce-maker Bull-Dog, after the company issued a warrant that surgically diluted Steel Partners' stake. An egregious move by any standard, the Tokyo High Court nevertheless deliberated in favor of Bull-Dog.[183] The era of confrontational activism ended with its Japanese leader, Yoshiaki Murakami, in jail (after being accused of insider trading), and most Western activist funds in retreat.

Since the Global Financial Crisis, a new wave of "constructive" or friendly activists, often called engagement investors, has tackled the same corporate governance issues, but with an explicitly low-key, humble approach. Rather than berating management publicly, these funds have led quiet discussions behind closed doors. They have often presented themselves as advisors who can offer "free" consulting services to senior management. They earn management's trust by demonstrating their patience and refraining from asking for board seats or challenging them in proxy fights. Rather, they try to win them over by frequently sharing with them well-researched analysis that provides them with insights into their industry and comparisons with peers. Pioneer funds of this approach include Asuka, Taiyo Pacific, Simplex, and Governance for Owners.

Taiyo Pacific has developed the most involved form of engagement in Japan by offering a highly productized suite of services to its portfolio companies. In addition to sharing industry presentations, the fund invites the CEOs from funds in which they have publicly disclosed investments to attend offsite seminars on a regular basis. In those, senior executives from Taiyo often give presentations on simple concepts of value creation. They might, for instance, devote a session to discussing the concept of return on equity. This is basic knowledge that top Japanese executives at small and medium-sized listed companies often lack because they have never been formally trained in value-based management, having typically come from engineering backgrounds and risen through the ranks on the manufacturing side. These events can also promote the cross-pollination of ideas between CEOs and, at their most successful, even create a group identity that supports the image of Taiyo Pacific as a desirable shareholder that can help management.

Even confrontational activists have shifted their strategy in Japan to adopt a more constructive approach. Dan Loeb's Third Point illustrates the point. While he still telegraphs which company he targets, his discussions in Japan have played themselves out behind closed doors, rather than via the type of excoriating public missives he is known for in the United States. That may have yielded results. An example is Fanuc, the leading robotics company in Japan and one of Japan's most retrograde listed companies when it comes to investor relations. Third Point led a quiet campaign to create more transparency. After Third Point's stake was revealed, Fanuc announced that it would establish an investor relations department – a low bar to be sure. It is not clear whether Third Point's engagement was the determining factor or whether it merely coincided with a decision by Fanuc to abide by some of the demands of the Corporate Governance Code. At a minimum, the fact that Third Point's involvement did not backfire reflects a new stage in relations between Japanese corporations and shareholder activists.

Since the creation of the Corporate Governance and Stewardship codes, the number of constructive activists in Japan has proliferated. This is a rare occurrence where shareholder activists can justify pushing their agenda with management by invoking government policy. Whereas activists were historically seen as attempting to selfishly extract value from the system, their demands can now be framed as a form of civic engagement, contributing to the revival of the Japanese economy. There is less of a need to engage in philosophical debates about the primacy of shareholders.

Is it working? The jury is still out. Naysayers point to low adoption rates in broad swaths of the corporate sector, hollow participation by companies that are keen to follow the code in form rather than in spirit, and continued resistance to outside influence by large numbers of listed companies. Optimists point out encouraging metrics: The percentage of companies listed on the Tokyo Stock Exchange level 1 with at least two independent board directors has increased from 17% in 2012 to 91% in 2018.[184] Listed companies have returned record levels of cash to shareholders, via dividends and share buybacks. Divestitures of non-core businesses are on the rise. More importantly, companies are significantly tuned into the Corporate Governance Code. Many companies have gone from being completely oblivious to being solicitous of investors' perspective on the Corporate Governance Code. Optimists see the emergence of a snowball effect.

The most critical metric remains cross- or strategic shareholdings (share ownership by business partners to signal their long-term commitment to the business partnership). They provide the ultimate buffer against outside influence. The Abe administration is merely attempting to accelerate their elimination. From an estimated 34% of total market capitalization in 1990, they are currently estimated at 10.3%, according to Nomura Securities. The mega-banks have announced plans to reduce their own cross-shareholdings by 20–30% in the next few years. Absent these cross-shareholdings, many CEOs will need to completely reassess how their firm will be perceived in the marketplace and either take action or run the risk of encountering more aggressive types of activism, unfettered by obstacles to majority ownership.

Public Equity Investing

In public markets, the scope for social value creation is more limited than in private markets. By investing in the stock of a listed company without trying to influence management, equity investors can only aspire to have an impact by affecting that company's cost of capital. Theoretically, that impact should be meaningful given the centrality of the cost of capital in a well-functioning capital market-centric financial system. Yet the practical impact of investing in listed equities is severely limited for several reasons.

Counterintuitively, stock markets have had a limited role in raising capital for productive uses in developed economies. Since the mid 1980s, net equity issuance by non-financial corporations – meaning new stock issuance minus the retirement of outstanding stock via repurchases and mergers and acquisitions – has turned negative in US markets.[185] A similar pattern is observed in UK markets.[186] A contributing factor has been the shift in the function of IPOs, which historically raised funds that were predominantly targeted at financing productive investments and that are now more often than not meant to provide liquidity for early investors. The financing of productive activities has been increasingly covered by the private equity and corporate debt markets. As the Kay Review of UK Equity Markets noted, "equity markets today should primarily be seen as a means of getting money out of companies rather than a means of putting it in."[187] Another important driver of this trend has been the increasing sway of the shareholder-centric model and the view that returning cash to shareholders creates a safeguard against unproductive capital allocation by managers.[188] Because the primary function of IPOs in developed markets has increasingly been to provide an exit mechanism for early investors rather than to raise additional capital for future growth, investing capital in newly issued shares has less direct economic impact than one might expect, at least in these markets.

In emerging markets, stock issuance still fulfills an important funding role in the corporate sector. The surge in Chinese IPOs since the early 2000s has channeled much-needed capital into many high-growth companies. Pointing out the trend in developed markets is not to say that stock markets don't serve an important role there. While US markets may not serve the same function they used to in financing productive uses, they form the core of our financial system, creating virtuous incentives for early-stage investors to support new companies. But they are no longer a significant direct funding channel into productive uses.

Even if you assume that equity issuance can play a significant economic role, as it does in many markets, can investors have a discernible impact on listed companies' cost of capital by investing in their equity?

The demand for a company's traded stock theoretically affects the company's ability to raise additional equity and to borrow capital in order to fund new projects. An active investor, meaning one that picks stocks rather than invests across the market, thereby contributes in an infinitesimal way to a healthy liquid market. Each stock-specific investment decision should help refine price discovery, providing instant and constant feedback on the prospects of individual firms. In practice, however, being a market participant, even a discriminating one, cannot in and of itself provide much basis to claim impact on cost of capital. The effect of secondary market transactions, which represent the bulk of trading activity in any given day, is indirect at best since each investment simply signifies a change of ownership in the shares of a company without that company's direct involvement. The impact of any individual or institutional investor in public equity markets is further limited by the wide diffusion of ownership, whether investing in a new stock issue or in the secondary market.

The lack of direct, discernible impact is compounded by the fact that an increasing proportion of investments in listed equities is done passively. Passive asset management entails indiscriminate buying across equities, precluding any presumption that the capital is allocated to its most productive uses, that the investment decision helps markets become more efficient, or that it might help address a particular market failure. There are also rising concerns that the massive shift from actively to passively managed funds may impair the market's price discovery mechanism.[189] Passive management's neutral, and perhaps even negative, impact on market efficiency doesn't refute, at this stage at least, the argument that the surge of flows into passive management is a force for good, given the simplicity of its model and the efficiency with which it allows savers to invest their capital at a low cost. It simply limits any potential claim that passive investors can have an economic or social impact.

If any investment inherently falls short of influencing companies because of the lack of a direct transmission mechanism, could collective action make a difference? That is the contention of a growing movement that argues that investors should embed environmental, social, and governance (ESG) factors in their investment decisions. But the reasoning of ESG proponents increasingly goes beyond social value creation. There are at least three separate reasons why investors might choose to consider ESG factors in their investment process. It can be seen by socially minded investors as a way for their capital to have a positive impact on the world, despite the limitations noted above. For others, it may be a way to exhibit their values – they may not believe that their capital allocation can have a significant economic and social impact, but they care enough about being true to their values that they would not want to contribute to the financing of a business they perceive to be detrimental to the world, no matter how remote their impact in that process; nor would they want to generate returns from it.[190] The third, and rapidly growing, reasoning holds that investors must incorporate ESG factors in their investment decision in order to fulfill their fiduciary duty, because risks associated with these factors are sooner or later going to be priced in securities, and doing so today represents an important risk-management exercise and could generate alpha.

Climate change has become a focal point in the development of an ESG framework. To proponents of ESG factors as a catalyst for social change, finance has a role to play in the transition from a fossil-fuel-dependent economy to a low-carbon economy fueled by cleaner forms of energy. But the majority of institutional investors cannot alter their investment strategy in order to accommodate social goals. They have a fiduciary duty to maximize their clients' returns. For them, a critical question is whether incorporating ESG factors can be justified solely under the premise of value maximization.

The evidence increasingly suggests that it makes sense to do so. One reason is simple risk management – as the world moves toward limiting greenhouse gas emissions, adapting portfolios in that manner appears prudent. Increasing awareness of the contribution of untethered emissions to climate change has spurred global mobilization, epitomized by the Paris Agreement concluded in 2016. Signed by the vast majority of countries, the agreement seeks to limit global warming to less than two degrees Celsius above pre-industrial levels. Environmental regulatory risk is expected to rise as countries plan to deliver on their pledges. Historically, companies that pollute have often passed on the cost of that pollution to taxpayers. Going forward, new regulations will likely require companies to internalize at least part of these costs.

A related reason why incorporating ESG factors in financial analysis is consistent with the fiduciary responsibility of traditional, value-maximizing institutional investors is that environmental risks appear to be getting increasingly priced in markets. Research by Blackrock shows that global companies that improved their carbon efficiency the most between 2012 and 2016 outperformed significantly those that improved the least.[191] During that period, the top quintile of MSCI World companies outperformed by over 4%, while the bottom quintile underperformed by more than 4%.

Among traditional value-maximizing institutional investors, the argument to "climate-proof" portfolios particularly resonates with the most long-term investors, such as sovereign wealth funds and pension funds, since they are the most likely to be invested long enough to experience the pricing of environmental risks in markets. However, new financial products now allow all investors to environmentally de-risk their equity portfolios with limited trade-offs. MSCI, the most prominent benchmark index provider, initiated a low-carbon index (MSCI ACWI Low Carbon Target Index) in 2014, opening the door to a new generation of low-carbon passive funds and ETFs. Asset managers such as Blackrock can optimize the MSCI World Index by diminishing the index's carbon footprint by 70% with a similar tracking error of only 0.3%.[192] In other words, the MSCI World Index can be substantially "decarbonized" by having its exposure to carbon risk significantly reduced without significantly affecting its performance. That kind of positive screening with low impact on volatility and low cost can be appealing to investors across the spectrum, with or without an ethical mandate.

There is also evidence that sustainable equity mutual funds have outperformed traditional funds on average, based on a Morgan Stanley study covering performance between 2007 and 2014.[193] The highest-profile sustainability-focused investment manager, Generation Investment Management, co-founded by former Vice President Al Gore in 2004, has outperformed its benchmark sharply. As of early 2019, its Lombard Odier Generation Global Fund generated total returns since its launch in November 2007 of 150% compared to below 6% for the MSCI World Index.[194] An acceleration in the trend, partly due to increasing concern by executives to be called out for not engaging, led Gillian Tett, the Chair of the *Financial Times*' US editorial board, to hypothesize that 2019 would turn out to be the year when ESG considerations entered the mainstream.[195]

Momentum toward the incorporation of ESG factors in standard financial analysis has increased significantly in recent years. Swiss Re, one of Europe's largest insurers, decided in 2017 to benchmark its entire $130 billion portfolio to ESG indices.[196] Perhaps even more telling, GPIF, Japan's largest pension fund – an allocator not known for its propensity to jump on fads – announced in 2017 that it had allocated 3% of its equity portfolio to track ESG indices, and that it planned to raise that allocation to 10%.[197]

Several people and institutions can claim to have been pioneers, although few have had as much impact as Frédéric Samama, Patrick Bolton, and Mats Andersson. In the late 2000s, Samama, a manager at Amundi, a large French asset manager, took the personal initiative to convene financiers and academics to consider how long-term capital holders could address market failures such as climate change.[198] Samama organized conferences at Columbia University and at the Bellagio in Italy in partnership with Bolton, an economist at Columbia Business School, to discuss market solutions to climate change. During the course of these discussions, Andersson, the then head of Swedish national pension fund AP4 and a long-time skeptic of ESG approaches, experienced an epiphany of sorts and announced that he would commit to pricing in climate risk in his equity portfolios.

Bolstered by the prospect of a first client, Samama and his team developed the first mainstream low-carbon equity index, in partnership with MSCI, contributing to the development of a new market in low-carbon or "decarbonized" ETFs and funds. Samama framed the use of a decarbonized index by investors as a "free option on carbon."[199] The low tracking error of a low-carbon index ensured that the investor would not be penalized in a status-quo scenario under which polluting companies continued not to be penalized, but would outperform the standard market index if the costs of pollution were to be borne by these companies, due to the low-carbon index's reduced exposure to them.

AP4 swiftly shifted all of its US equity exposure to a low-carbon index.[200] Along with AP4, FRR, the largest French pension fund, and the United Nations Joint Staff Pension Fund were the first large pension funds to incorporate these indices into their portfolios. They were soon followed in the United States by the New York State Common Retirement Fund and CalSTRS, and in Japan by the GPIF.

Can incorporating ESG factors in financial analysis help investors collectively put pressure to effect real change in corporate behavior? To assess the potential for real social impact, it is worth considering the historical impact of divestment campaigns, the precursor to the adjusted index approach. On their own, divestment campaigns have had little impact in influencing corporate or governmental behavior. A study has shown that the high-profile divestment campaign targeting the Apartheid regime in South Africa in the 1980s had little tangible impact on its own on South African financial markets or on banks and firms with South African operations.[201]

For every ethically motivated seller in the secondary market, there is a buyer who may not have the same moral lens or may be completely oblivious to any moral dimension related to the stock transaction. On any controversial issue linked to a subset of corporations, from gun control to animal testing, purchasing stock from a seller primarily motivated by ethical considerations could represent an opportunity for a traditional value-maximizing investor to generate alpha, or excess returns relative to the stock's market risk exposure.[202] As discussed, that is not necessarily true for many issues associated with sustainability. Since there is a high probability that new regulations will require companies to internalize the public cost of their greenhouse emissions, the alpha opportunity is skewed toward those who are diminishing their exposure to companies with high carbon footprints, to the extent that environmental regulatory risk is not yet fully priced into markets. This is consistent with the argument that the Yale endowment CIO David Swensen made in a letter in April 2016 announcing that the endowment was starting to divest from fossil fuel producers.[203]

Could the incorporation of ESG factors in financial analysis have greater social impact than divestment campaigns have had? Possibly, despite the severe limitations of non-activist investing as a catalyst for social change – for the simple reason that a much greater scale of capital could be involved given the fiduciary argument in favor of ESG factors. But the real impact of ESG factor inclusion is yet to be tested given the early stages of this approach.

The most successful social campaigns targeting stocks have generally been those that bolstered the call to divest with shareholder activism, typically in the form of submitting a shareholder resolution (or proxy proposal). As opposed to the anonymity of the daily sweep of buying and selling in the secondary market, shareholder activist campaigns can force management to engage. At a minimum, it brings the issue to the company's attention. In US markets, the bar for submitting a shareholder resolution is low. An investor needs to have held a minimum of $2,000 in the company's stock for at least one year prior to submitting a proposal – although companies have leeway in excluding certain proposals from the firm's annual proxy. The number of shareholder resolutions related to sustainability issues has increased significantly over the years, with the proportion of votes in favor of ESG proposals rising from 8% in 1999 to 25% in 2018.[204]

Successful social campaigns led via shareholder activism have not necessarily hinged on a resolution being adopted. In fact, a review of the proxy proposals related to sustainability issues submitted to Fortune 250 companies in the United States between 2006 and 2014 shows that only four won a majority vote.[205] Additionally, shareholder proposals are typically non-binding. Yet, over time, they tend to be associated with improved performance on the sustainability issue targeted by the activists.[206] Examples of successful consumer campaigns involving shareholder activism abound. They can be highly targeted. In 2011, a resolution by a shareholder activist group pressed McDonald's to replace its Styrofoam cups with a more environmentally friendly alternative. The resolution failed but management decided two years later to make the switch.[207] A clue as to the effectiveness of shareholder activism for social movements is that many issue-driven organizations have set up shareholder activism groups to buy shares in targeted companies and submit proposals.[208] PETA, or People for the Ethical Treatment of Animals, was a pioneer shareholder activist among social organizations, launching its first campaign in 1987. As of 2016, it held stock in fifty-six targeted companies.[209]

In the past, activist campaigns on sustainability issues have also often led to the establishment of committees on social responsibility and a commitment to publish an annual report on social responsibility. The mere fact that corporations now need to document their activities tends to have a positive effect on their adherence to sustainability goals.[210]

Engagement is not always a viable path. In some cases, divestment may represent the only moral alternative, even if it is clear that on its own, it will not have any tangible impact in addressing the issue at stake. If an investor believes that cluster bombs are an unacceptable weapon and all a company does is manufacture cluster bombs, then there is limited scope for engagement with the company's management.

One of the most intriguing initiatives using equity markets to advance economic or social goals has been the launch in 2014 of JPX-Nikkei Index 400, a Japanese equity index which weeds out underperforming large companies by weighting operating profits and return on equity in addition to market capitalization, the traditional way in which equity indices are constructed. Illustrating how mid-level managers in large financial organizations can at times have vast impact, the index was created by Daisuke Tanaka, a product developer at Japan Exchange Group, who had only been introduced to equity indices four years prior.[211]

The index, which has been enthusiastically backed by the Abe government, has become an unlikely policy mechanism by nudging large underperforming Japanese companies to focus on improving their operations, and, in particular, to make productive use of their dormant cash, or else risk being excluded from the index, a shameful outcome. This is one of the first attempts, if not the first, to use a broad country equity index as a tool of public policy. It was not initially clear that leading Japanese companies would care whether they were included in this index of national champions, particularly if they already qualified as one the 225 constituents of the Nikkei index, the best-known national equity index in Japan. However, anecdotal evidence suggests otherwise. The CEO of Amada, a $4 billion industrial company, famously mentioned in his first results meeting after the establishment of the JPX-400 that he was disappointed that his company was not in the index, despite being in the Nikkei index, and announced that he would return 100% of the firm's net income over the next two years in the form of increased dividends and share buybacks in order to ensure his firm would qualify for the index in the future. Trevor Hill, the global head of equity for SMBC Nikko Securities, one of the major Japanese investment banks, commented in June 2019 that he is frequently asked by CEOs and CFOs of non-index constituent companies for advice on corporate measures to increase the probability that their company be included in the next iteration of the index.[212]

Global Macro Strategies

Global macro strategies can play a useful role in the setting of economic and monetary policies. Global macro funds express top-down views on economic and political trends by investing in instruments across equity, fixed income, currency, commodity, and futures markets. Central banks pay particular attention to forward indicators of inflation and other economic metrics in the setting of their rates. Those are highly influenced by global macro funds and bond funds. In some circumstances, large macro hedge funds have played a critical, and at times controversial, role in bringing about economic policy changes, putting them at odds with national governments and central banks. Two of the highest-profile episodes of global macro interventions include the "breaking of the Pound," which forced the British Pound out of the European Exchange Rate Mechanism (ERM) in 1992, and the forced de-pegging of South East and East Asian currencies during the Asian Financial Crisis of 1997–1998.

"Black Wednesday" refers to the day (September 16, 1992) that Great Britain was forced out of the ERM. Great Britain had joined the ERM in 1990 as part of an effort to integrate further with the rest of the European Community. In order to maintain its currency within the ERM band, the Bank of England had to maintain interest rates that were consistent with those of Germany, the dominant European economy, whose currency, the Deutschmark, acted as a benchmark. Prime Minister John Major perceived the ERM as a beneficial mechanism that would inject anti-inflationary discipline on British policy. But German and British economic conditions diverged sharply as Germany was grappling with the effects of its reunification and decided to raise its interest rates following a spurt of growth and inflation. By contrast, Great Britain had experienced a recession in 1991 and needed to stimulate its economy.[213] Market forces were putting pressure on the British Pound to depreciate and on the Bank of England to raise rates in order to stay within the ERM band of plus or minus 6% of the Pound's peg to the Deutschmark.

Several hedge funds, including most prominently George Soros's Quantum Fund, took a view that Britain's inclusion in the ERM was detrimental to its economy by forcing it to adopt economic policies that were inconsistent with its domestic priorities. Believing that the Pound's position within the ERM was unsustainable, they shorted the currency, exacerbating downward pressure on it. The British government and the Bank of England fought back by supporting the Pound, spending billions worth of foreign currency from its foreign exchange reserves and raising interest rates. After a show of fiery resistance, the British government abdicated, realizing that market forces were overwhelming its ability to defend the Pound. It decided to let the Pound devalue beyond the lower limit of the ERM's band and float. The Pound fell by about 15% over the next few weeks, helping British exports rebound and the country's trade deficit to be eliminated by 1995. Interest rates were cut, gradually reaching 6% by early 1993. This paved the way to a period of expansion that lasted sixteen years.[214] Inflation followed a largely downward trajectory over the next decade. In hindsight, economists consider the move out of the ERM to have been beneficial to the British economy. Many have concluded that joining the ERM in 1990 was a policy mistake, or at least that the timing was off and the pegged exchange rate with Germany too high.[215]

Soros's hedge fund reportedly made a profit of about $1 billion by shorting the Pound and another $1 billion from various parallel positions in interest rate futures and other instruments.[216] On the other side of the equation, the British government lost $27 billion in foreign exchange reserves as it fruitlessly tried to defend the currency.[217] Of that, Soros is deemed to have accounted for $10 billion.[218] The shocking magnitude of private gains and public losses – all generated in the course of days – might make us uncomfortable. However, the evidence points to the fact that the Pound's abrupt exit from the ERM was a force for good over time, even taking into account the drain in foreign exchange reserves incurred by the government's futile attempt at maintaining the status quo. Soros and a handful of other hedge funds contributed to the British government adopting a wiser economic policy.

To what extent were they instrumental in that turn of events? On the surface, they seem to have provoked the crisis. Soros is routinely described as the man who "broke" the Bank of England. Yet, Soros claimed that the Pound's exit would "have unfolded more or less the same way even if I had never been born."[219] That seems inconsistent with his own theory of reflexivity, which holds that a feedback mechanism in markets can allow participants' perspective to shape reality.[220] On balance, Soros's involvement probably accelerated an event path that would have occurred regardless. The size of the assets he managed, his willingness to make big, aggressive bets, and the fact that other funds made the same bet, allowed the shorters to swiftly overwhelm the government's defenses. Over time, it is likely that an increasing number of market participants would have come to the same conclusion, even absent Soros's participation.

The British Pound's ERM exit example illustrates how macro hedge funds can serve a useful social function: as an early warning system for misguided economic policy, regardless of whether the policy lapse is driven by a government's bad analysis, incompetence, or political calculations.[221] By doing so, they can sway government actors to rectify the course earlier than they might have done otherwise and benefit taxpayers, corporations, and investors.

This is not to say that macro hedge funds always deliver a social service, even when they have foresight. Often, the signal they provide does not affect policy in any way or ends up being muddled in a swamp of contradictory signals. These signals can also be overwhelmed by the prevailing psychology of the market at any given point, which can swing from over-confidence to over-pessimism. Lynn Stout posited that a fundamentally correct signal may be socially useless. The traditional example of the wheat futures trader that drives up wheat prices in correct anticipation of a drought, leading farmers to plant more wheat and mitigate the future drought is, in practice, unsupported by evidence.[222] Invoking an analysis made by Jack Hirshleifer as far back as 1971, she argues that whether the proverbial trade in anticipation of the drought benefits society all depends on its timing and whether it is too late for anyone to do anything about it.[223]

What if Soros's views were wrong and he acted on faulty assumptions or a misunderstanding of macro-economic fundamentals?

There is a risk that he could have led the British government astray, being large enough to move markets on his own. However, few fund managers are large enough to be able to influence large, liquid markets such as the foreign exchange market. The rest of the market participants also provide a de facto safety net against erratic flows by having the ability to think on their own as to the wisest economic policy and take an opposing view. In a much less publicized trade, Soros's fund and a few other macro hedge funds lost money in betting that the French Franc would also be forced out of the ERM.[224] The French economy's fundamentals enabled the government to withstand the pressure from short sellers, forcing them to cover their positions at a loss. In practice, few situations are as clear-cut in hindsight as that of the British Pound's exit of the ERM. In fact, sophisticated economists constantly disagree with each other on the best course of action at any given point.

What about the risk that a powerful market participant seeks to manipulate a commodity market for its own private gains? By hoarding a physical commodity, a substantial trader can have disproportionate impact on prices once liquidity dries out. To be clear, attempting to corner markets is illegal. The negative effects on the real economy can be significant, much greater than insider trading, for instance, where the ill-gotten gains of a trader typically don't have a clearly identifiable victim. Well-known past attempts at market cornering are sporadically invoked as cautionary tales – from the cornering of the New York gold market by Jay Gould and James Fisk in the 1860s, to the Hunt brothers' cornering of the silver market in 1980, to the cornering of the copper market in the mid 1990s by the head of a Japanese metal trading company.[225] Evidence suggests, however, that attempts at cornering markets typically falter in part because the manipulator eventually has to sell, and in part because governments and regulatory authorities can intervene when the commodity market appears erratic and threatens to disrupt productive economic activities that rely on the commodity.[226]

Trading and Derivative Strategies

Investment strategies that are trading-oriented and short term in nature are harder to justify from a social perspective. Since they largely take place in the secondary market and rely on short-term, often technical signals, their contribution tends to be confined to providing incremental liquidity to their markets and enabling greater price discovery. It is not clear that ever greater liquidity and price discovery provide commensurate social benefits. If anything, they tend to benefit short-term traders.[227]

Options and other derivatives present an interesting case as these financial instruments serve an important risk-sharing and risk-management role in the economy. The classic case is that of airlines, whose largest cost is oil. Airlines typically want to hedge their oil costs because oil prices can fluctuate dramatically. They generally do so by purchasing call options, futures, or swap contracts, or by implementing more complex option strategies. The financial industry has thus created much value over the last decades by creating tailored financial instruments that can satisfy the specific needs of their clients.

However, what started as a smart, thoughtful mechanism to share risk has sprouted into an ever greater set of complex products that are often completely disassociated from any real-economy role. Exotic options are particularly challenging to justify. The size of the exotic derivative industry appears to exceed any economic rationale justifying its existence. The traditional justification relies on the efficient market hypothesis. Complex derivatives theoretically enable a more efficient risk allocation, allowing participants to hedge specific risks. In practice, however, information asymmetries may be a more accurate description of the underlying driver for these transactions, as John Kay has argued.[228]

The absence of a robust, transparent exchange – the hallmark of fair and well-functioning capital markets – makes these products attractive for banks to sell on the basis of their high friction costs.[229] We discussed in the second chapter how European banks have marketed complex derivative products to the least sophisticated retail customers, in transactions that clearly benefited the banks at the expense of their customers.

For institutional investors, the information asymmetries are less pronounced. Typically, there is no one seller on the other side of the transaction, as there is when buying or selling equities for instance, since the broker pieces together different autonomous parts in order to structure the option. It is plausible for both the buyer and the structurer to make a profit – the buyer from exercising the option and the structurer by earning a commission. But even when there is no clearly defined "loser" on the other side of an exotic option that performs well, the impact on the rest of the industry and society is mixed at best.

More often than not, there is no underlying economic rationale for exotic options. A common example might be a two- or three-"legged" option that will only be exercised if two or three specific conditions are met. Structuring and transacting the option may marginally enhance market efficiency by contributing to price discovery, but that argument is stretched in the context of a security that is more often than not completely disassociated from any real-economy need. The most significant downside comes from the opacity of these products, which muddle the picture of where market risks lie. A combination of potentially high private returns and negative social returns can occur when the accumulation of risk that is not well understood leads to increased systemic risk.

For all their limitations, trades in derivative instruments between banks and institutional investors tend to be pursued in good faith (a case that's harder to make when these types of products are sold to retail customers). They enable institutional investors to express an alternative perspective on the pricing of specific securities and add a risk exposure to their portfolio that fulfills a specific role in the context of their other exposures. That spirit of good faith can't be said of many sophisticated trading strategies that intend to manipulate the market.[230] "Spoofing" comprises a broad range of trading tactics that seek to deceive the market, and specifically trading algorithms which buy and sell along pre-determined criteria, by making bids and cancelling them before execution. For instance, a "quote dangling" algorithm seeks to artificially raise the price of a security by sending multiple bid orders to buy a security and immediately cancelling them, leading other algorithms to readjust their bids based on artificially inflated price indications.[231] As financial economist Maureen O'Hara argues, these trading strategies are designed to manipulate others and are unethical. They also impair the integrity of markets. Many of these tactics are illegal but can often be difficult to prosecute because of the challenge of proving intent.

Impact Investments

The investment industry has experienced a surge of interest in investments generating socially beneficial outcomes. Historically, that interest had been confined to "socially responsible investments" (SRI), which initially screened out "sin" investments from investment portfolios. One of the movement's leading thinkers, Brian Trelstad writes of a "spectrum of capital," which is bounded by traditional financial value-maximizing investments that are part of a fiduciary mandate on one end (where SRI resides) and philanthropy on the other.[232] Sustainable investing evolved from SRI in the late 1990s and early 2000s out of the belief that allocating capital could generate social or environmental benefits, and not simply avoid creating harm.[233] A subset of socially minded investors believed that excess financial returns could be generated from incorporating ESG factors by enhancing the quality of due diligence on investments. As discussed earlier in this chapter, embedding ESG factors allows investors to identify risks that might be overlooked and could increasingly affect company value.

Over the past decade, much attention has been devoted to impact investments. In contrast to traditional financial value-maximizing investment strategies, impact investments explicitly pursue dual objectives, seeking both financial returns and measurable social impact. They typically target private ventures at an early stage of development. This approach is seen as distinct from traditional investment approaches, even when those lead to positive social outcomes as a by-product of their financial objective, although some industry leaders have argued against imposing intent as a litmus test.[234]

An important debate addresses whether financial returns are inevitably hurt by impact investments' dual objectives. Traditional financial theory would say so: Adding a social impact criterion to a financial returns objective inherently reduces the universe of investible assets, thereby acting as a constraint and pushing the efficient frontier of risk–return to a less attractive place. Yet "finance-first" funds, which seek to maximize financial returns while creating positive social impact, would argue otherwise. They contend that seeking social impact leads investors to investment opportunities that are often uncrowded, contrarian, and can generate alpha – for instance, by catering to under-served populations.[235]

One of the most successful private equity investors in Europe and a pioneer in the industry, London-based Bridges set the stage for finance-first funds, seeking positive spillover effects while targeting attractive returns. Its founder, Sir Ronald Cohen, was instrumental in turning the United Kingdom into a vibrant hub for impact investments, by establishing Bridges as a successful model for other finance-first funds and by helping found in 2012 the government-funded Big Society

Capital to seed new impact investment funds and centralize know-ledge.[236] Many of Bridges' investments could theoretically fit in the portfolios of traditional venture capital funds, except for the fact that VC funds tend to pursue at any given point narrow investment themes that focus on innovation – blockchain, smart transportation, and aug-mented reality are three in vogue – that often precludes the type of traditional "brick-and-mortar" businesses that Bridges might pursue. A case in point is the Gym Group, which operates low-cost fitness clubs in under-served areas in the United Kingdom. Over the span of five years, the firm opened thirty-five locations and returned more than twenty times its initial investment.[237] This type of investment, targeting the bottom 25% of the UK population on the basis of income, has enabled several of Bridges' funds since the firm's founding in 2002 to deliver returns that are consistent with or in excess of traditional private equity funds.[238]

San Francisco-based DBL Partners, another successful pioneer finance-first impact investment fund, was established by Nancy Pfund to target top-tier venture capital returns while delivering social, economic, and environmental impact in the regions in which their companies operate.[239] DBL invested at an early stage in companies such as Tesla Motors, SolarCity, an energy storage company that merged with Tesla in 2016, and Revolution Foods, a healthy-food company that delivered as of year-end 2016 two million school meals every week in fourteen states.[240] DBL's high returns in its first fund – Pitchbook ranked it second out of twenty-five funds under $250 million through 2019 – have enabled it to gain in scale, raising $400 million in its third fund in 2015.[241]

The prospects for generating market returns, or even excess returns relative to the market, while doing good have increasingly drawn mainstream financial institutions into impact investments. While still very small in absolute size, the industry has generated enough pull, particularly from a younger generation of individuals with savings to invest or purview over assets, to make it difficult for large financial institutions to dismiss it, at least conceptually. 2015 marked the begin-ning of a new stage when Bain Capital and Blackrock announced forays into the industry while Goldman Sachs acquired Imprint Capital, a leading impact investment consulting firm. Private equity firm TPG completed in October 2017 the largest fundraise to date in the industry, closing on $2 billion for its Rise Fund from large traditional allocators such as the Washington State Investment Board, Bank of America Corp., and the Regents of the University of California.[242]

An important limitation of the debate on the potential of impact investments is the lack of returns data given the relative novelty of the strategy and the small number of funds that have been operating for more than a few years. The early data is far too sparse to draw conclusions.[243] The Cambridge Associates Impact Investing Benchmark, a quarterly index of industry-wide pooled returns, shows as of September 2019 an average annual return over fifteen years of 7.2%.[244] However, its impact investing index only captures data from 77 funds versus over 1,800 funds for its venture capital index.

Another challenge has been measurability. Adopting a standardized approach to defining and measuring social impact has been a vexing challenge for the industry due to the multifaceted and intangible nature of many social outcomes. By contrast, financial returns rely on well accepted, highly standardized GAAP or IFRS accounting and financial metrics. At this stage, many impact investors focus on one or several of the seventeen UN Sustainable Development goals that were set in 2015.[245] A massive effort has led to the development of IRIS (Impact Reporting and Investment Standards) and GIIRS (Global Impact Investing Rating System) investment ratings, but the resulting 400+ IRIS indicators have done little to move the industry toward a consensus approach.[246] The International Finance Corporation has also developed nine principles of impact investing, with the verification of achievements one of the areas of emphasis. The result has been a proliferation of approaches, all focused on achieving measurability and rigor.

Acumen Fund, a pioneer "impact-first" fund founded in 2001 by Jacqueline Novogratz, has adopted a "lean data" approach which seeks to gather insightful data directly from end customers of social enterprises through surveys conducted by mobile phone interviews or text messages. More sophisticated approaches to data collection can help refine impact investors' understanding of the investments' social benefits, which can be difficult to predict. A case in point is SolarNow, one of Acumen's portfolio companies, an energy company that seeks to light rural parts of Uganda where less than 5% of households are connected to a national grid.[247] Acumen trained call center staff to survey a random sample of SolarNow customers. The data showed an average of two hours of additional light per day. Beyond the basic data, the survey highlighted how the social value expected to be created via the investment was different than the intended one. The initial thesis focused on health effects of switching away from traditional fuels, but the survey found that users valued more the positive impacts related to security and brightness of the light. The surveys allow Acumen and SolarNow to better measure the social impact of the investment and, over time, to refine how the company serves its customers' needs.

Impact investments show promise as a social impact tool but the question remains whether trying to achieve two separate goals at once can be more effective than pursuing them independently. That question won't be properly addressed until more data becomes available. The data will also help test the model, and to teach and adapt it over the next few years. So far, the level of attention devoted to the asset class, in particular from foundations and academic institutions as well as students and young professionals, far exceeds the scale of adoption among allocators. However, the emergence of impact investments as a new asset class has generated a tremendous amount of energy in developing new ways for finance to benefit society while drawing a younger generation into the debate – all positive developments.

Faithfully serving your customer is often, but not always, consistent with contributing to society. In this chapter, we attempted to define positive contribution to society, delving into the investment management industry as a case study. The existing empirical research suggests that not all investment strategies, even when they generate excess returns, serve society. That awareness can be helpful in and of itself. It may be unrealistic to expect an investment professional to abandon their specific investment strategy on the basis of these findings, but that consideration may inform which area of investment management, or finance more broadly, well-intentioned individuals may choose when entering the industry. Over time, it may also inform the investment allocation of capital providers, many of which have already shown a propensity to incorporate social impact into their decisions.

3 HUMANISTIC LEADERSHIP WITHIN THE ORGANIZATION

Treating Colleagues with Dignity, Empowering Them, and Fostering a Responsible Culture

Colleagues Matter

Virtue for finance professionals is not only defined by how they serve customers and whether they act responsibly toward other stakeholders. It is also defined by how they treat colleagues and the extent to which they influence them to act virtuously. A finance professional could perform admirably with respect to the first two pillars of this book's framework – be a great fiduciary to her clients and manage to generate social value in the process – and yet be a tyrant at work, manipulate and abuse colleagues, prevent them from developing professionally, discriminate against any subset, and generally create a miserable work environment.

Do these considerations rise to the level of the other three pillars of the framework? Typically not, for the simple reason that the community affected by these actions is much smaller than those affected by the customer mandate, social wealth, and citizenship pillars. Yet one can imagine extreme situations in which bad behavior that impairs human dignity – harassment, humiliation, or vilification of colleagues, for instance, could overwhelm any virtue exhibited otherwise.

This chapter looks inside the organization and examines dynamics with colleagues. It discusses the process, not the outcomes, and makes the point that process matters and that internal dynamics should not be systematically subservient to corporate goals. The manner in which a finance professional acts with colleagues should reflect a basic measure of humanity. As management scholar Michael Pirson has argued, a humanistic approach to management, which protects dignity and seeks to promote collective interests, can be contrasted with a traditional "economistic" approach, which values foremost efficiency, performance, and the pursuit of narrow self-interest.[1]

Of the four pillars of the framework, this one is the least specific to the finance industry. The dollar amounts at stake in finance may often be larger than those in other sectors and the resulting pressure may be at times greater, although certainly not systematically so (think of surgeons, police officers, or firefighters). However, negative organizational dynamics can be observed across professions as they ultimately pertain to the foibles of men and women working in groups, balancing their self-interests with the collective interest. As a result, useful examples of virtuous behavior and positive organizational dynamics can be gleaned outside of finance, as illustrated in this chapter.

While this chapter concentrates on the relationship with colleagues, its underlying message is relevant to relationships outside of work, including with family, friends, and other individuals with whom one would interact. Virtuous behavior should be considered holistically, not in a compartmentalized manner.

Consistent with the rest of the book's framework, this chapter does not address how financial professionals can be most effective in their daily activities or most successful in their career. The virtuous behaviors portrayed do not offer a fast track to power and, in fact, may detract from it. Rather, the chapter explores ways in which finance professionals can interact with colleagues without slipping into self-serving behaviors for the sole purpose of accumulating money or power. Most practically, it offers a conceptual lens through which the culture of a firm can be assessed and suggests that the most effective path to virtuous behavior within a firm is to choose to work at a firm that promotes standards consistent with that behavior.

What are the attributes of virtuous collaboration with colleagues? For employees across the organization, the Golden Rule may be as good a start as any: Treat others the way you would like to be treated.[2] It appears in one form or another across most religions and ethical traditions. Its appeal stems in part from the simplicity of its message. Yet its application can be complicated by differences in status within an organization.

For those in positions of authority, servant leadership, a long-standing behavioral model, offers a compelling set of guidelines that emphasize collective outcomes and empowerment over personal goals when those come at the detriment of the group. Influencing others to act along these lines is a meaningful marker of good organizational citizenship. At its best, an individual can help foster a corporate culture that values employees, emphasizes service to customers, and recognizes a responsibility toward other stakeholders. Promoting inclusion and diversity also counts as an important attribute. At a minimum, it works against discrimination and might even contribute to building a stronger-performing organization.

Developing and Empowering Colleagues

The manner in which colleagues are treated, developed, and empowered is meaningful, in and of itself. Servant leadership impels us to ask how much we should value financial leaders that rise through the ranks and succeed financially but do so by making their colleagues miserable, defensively failing to develop subordinates into leaders in their own right, hogging all of the credit, and awarding themselves disproportionate compensation. Resisting such behavior, servant leaders strive to develop and empower their colleagues to achieve the firm's goals rather than narrowly seek to have the firm serve their own personal interests.[3] They tend to put collective interests ahead of their own and do so in a quiet way, without systematically drawing attention to their contribution. Investment consultant and writer Charles Ellis invokes an analogy to good parenting.[4] Servant leaders show the traits of parents who quietly endeavor over the years to nurture and foster the development of their children to enable them to make their own decisions and flourish.

To skeptics, the concept, developed by Robert Greenleaf in 1970, points toward motivations that go against the instincts of many professionals. For instance, a cognitive bias leads most people to perceive their input to a group as having greater value-added than it does in reality.[5] This tendency to "over-claim" may be especially true in the finance industry, which draws much of its talent due to the perception that individuals can distinguish themselves by dint of their own performance and resourcefulness.

Jeffrey Pfeffer, a Stanford behavioral academic, points out that servant leadership is the exception, not the norm among corporate leaders. A self-proclaimed realist, he argues that in the real world, "assholes" tend to win, as much as we would like to observe the opposite.[6] Accordingly, leaders can get away with harmful or immoral behavior as long as they are perceived to be successful. Why? Because we too often live in a world in which money trumps all other considerations. While we espouse humanistic values, an objective assessment of our actions shows that we are systematically guided by considerations related to personal financial outcomes and upward mobility. How we get to individual or corporate goals matters less than whether we achieve these goals. The mistreatment of colleagues is all too often perceived by its perpetrators as collateral damage, an unintended consequence of ensuring that objectives are reached. This is illustrated by the ever growing list of celebrated leaders that are known to have made their colleagues miserable – Steve Jobs being a notably well-documented case outside of finance.

Certain areas of the finance industry, such as Wall Street trading desks where alpha-male culture predominates, are particularly vulnerable to these dynamics. Consider for instance the CIO of a multi-billion-dollar high-yield bond investment firm based in California. An investigative report paints the picture of a bully who intimidated colleagues for years.[7] Court documents describe him as someone who "punched walls, broke phones, threw pens, and slammed doors in employees' faces" (he denied punching walls). A physically imposing presence, he is reported to have yelled in a tense meeting at a much smaller colleague and to have threatened to fight him in the conference room. How can such behavior ever be justified? Certainly not by a lack of awareness across the organization – court filings invoke complaints to HR about an environment rife with "yelling, screaming, hitting or throwing objects." Indications of such extreme behavior started surfacing in 2014, in a litigation between ex-employees and the firm, leading to the involvement of HR consultants. The bond fund's parent clearly knew about the toxic internal culture and volatile temper of its star trader but stuck by him over the years (he stepped down in 2019 for health reasons, staying on as a senior advisor). In all likelihood, his lasting tenure can be explained by the fact that the bond fund outperformed its benchmark over his eight years at the helm, while he expanded the firm's global presence and grew its asset base.

Several psychological theories explain why people rationalize and accept bad behavior, including motivated blindness, the cognitive bias that leads people to be oblivious to transgressions of others if acknowledging the transgression and taking action would likely have a negative impact on the observer.[8] The common example for such behavior is auditing firms, which are hired and paid by the firms they are auditing. An inherent bias tends to seep in, hindering these firms from acting objectively when signs of irregularities surface. At times, this leads to disastrous outcomes – for instance, the well-documented failure by Arthur Andersen, at the time one of the oldest, most reputable auditing firms, to detect fraud at Enron prior to its blow-up (resulting in Andersen's demise), or PwC's failure to take action on the accounting fraud at Satyam Computer Services, one of India's global corporate champions at the time. PwC signed off on Satyam's financial results for five years during which Satyam had inflated its revenues with thousands of fake inventories. India's securities regulator found that PwC had failed to follow up on "glaring anomalies" in Satyam's financials and to independently check monthly bank statements.[9]

Embedded in these psychological dynamics is also the tendency for people to want to believe that their workplace is just and fair and to rationalize the success of fast-rising colleagues by assuming positive attributes to justify their success. In investment management, that justification is exposed to the fact that investment success can be driven by an element of luck, perhaps even more so than in other fields.

Pfeffer may well have a point that servant leadership has limited sway among corporate leaders and that, in reality, most CEOs are narcissistic, over-confident, self-important, and self-promoting. Moreover, "hagiographies" of servant leaders tend to rely heavily on stories woven by those being celebrated, influenced by people's propensity to embellish their own narratives and by their failure to reliably recollect things as they happened.[10]

Of course, this is a risk I am exposed to in this book, as an enthusiastic promoter of role models to illustrate desirable behaviors. Still, in my view, examples of finance professionals exhibiting virtuous behavior within their organization are worth exploring and emulating. Social commentator David Brooks calls them "heroes of renunciation," leaders such as George Marshall and Dwight Eisenhower, who are more likely to have reached their positions of power despite their reticence and humility.[11] He acknowledges that these traits tend not to offer the quickest path to power. Yet research shows that professionals who care about others' welfare can succeed. Adam Grant, a professor at the Wharton School, found in his research across a wide swath of professions that an individual's style of reciprocity has an impact on success and that givers, who help others without expecting reciprocity, tend to be both at the top and the bottom of the ladder, with takers, who try to extract from personal relationships more than they give, and matchers, who look for reciprocity, in the middle.[12] The givers at the top were self-interested and just as ambitious as takers and matchers, but they were also "other-interested." The ones at the bottom helped others without consideration to their own needs and ended up being taken advantage of.

As an example of a successful giver, Grant highlights David Hornik, a venture capitalist who helps others almost indiscriminately. In contrast to most of his peers, Hornik sees his role as one that is primarily about serving entrepreneurs. He responds to emails from strangers and reviews unsolicited business plans.[13] At times his instinct to be helpful goes against the advice of his partners. He was a trailblazing blogger in the venture capital industry, sharing in detail online how venture capitalists think in order to help entrepreneurs refine their outreach to potential funders. He contributed to lifting the veil on the industry, creating transparency at the risk of over-sharing and losing some competitive advantage. He created an annual conference, The Lobby, that convenes not only entrepreneurs but also competing venture capitalists. A more competitive character would have kept peers away in order to develop a proprietary source of new investment ideas. Grant argues that Hornik's generosity gives him an edge.[14] He has refused to be corrupted by standard practices and, in the process of expressing his values, has developed a vast network of entrepreneurs and peers that respect and trust him.

Hornik's giver mentality informs the design of the venture capital firm he joined in 2000, August Capital. The firm has a flat structure, with a small group of active partners who each hold equal equity and have an equal say in investment decisions.[15] The effect on the firm's culture is that each partner feels some level of responsibility to support each of the firm's portfolio companies, not solely the ones he or she sourced or is leading. Few of the prominent Silicon Valley firms have such a structure.

Consistent with the concept of moral muteness, servant leaders tend to underplay the extent to which their actions are driven by a desire to help others. John Bogle cringes whenever he is asked whether setting up Vanguard as a mutual company (i.e. owned by its customers) was meant as a public service. He typically retorts that it was a tactical decision made purely as a way to appease his former employers and gain market share. Yet Bogle's pattern of decisions throughout his career and his lifelong crusade on behalf of individual investors point to a more complex motivation that belies his simple explanation.

Certain firms have developed a culture that embeds servant leadership. The management consulting firm McKinsey & Company, where I spent several years at the beginning of my career, obsesses over the development of its professionals. Although not a finance firm, aspects of its thoughtful organizational design could be usefully applied at financial firms. An enormous amount of resources is spent training its professionals. Marvin Bower, McKinsey's legendary leader, invoked the servant leadership model in explaining the critical role of continuous on-the-job training and mentoring at the firm.[16] Structured feedback is frequently provided informally to younger members of the team during projects, and more formally at the end of projects. I remember routinely receiving highly considered feedback even on tasks as pedestrian as the manner in which I left voicemails. In a marked departure from year-end reviews in the finance industry, these meetings were, in my experience, almost entirely focused on a detailed parsing out of feedback from all of my managers and several of my peers, with my year-end bonus only mentioned at the end, almost as an afterthought. The ultimate objective is to enable consultants to develop over time the full array of skills that is expected of a partner. The flip side of that highly engaged approach to developing and empowering professionals is that the recipients of all of that attention have to continuously exhibit progress toward partnership or else be asked to leave the firm.

McKinsey is organized so that little credit goes to individuals as opposed to teams. All of the work is developed in teams that are assembled at the beginning of a project and disbanded at its end, with individual contributions difficult to tease out, by design. Consultants who survive and become senior partners are those who have not only developed the full array of skills but have also generated significant followership within the firm, a sign that they are givers and are perceived to care about the development of members of their teams. Emblematic of that disposition to value each member of the team as an important contributor and a potential future partner is the fact that each professional, no matter how low on the totem pole, is encouraged to exercise their "obligation to dissent." At its core, the concept implies that a first-year analyst straight out of college, with no experience in business, should feel empowered (and have the poise) to raise counter-points or objections to arguments made by senior members of the team.

Another core tenet of the firm's values consistent with the servant leadership model is the aspiration to find a balance between listening and asserting, implying that junior members of the team have a say and that senior members of the firm should take it into consideration. It was not entirely surprising to me that one of my mentors at the firm, Bernie Ferrari, wrote a book about the power of listening. His training as a physician drew him to ask "pesky" questions to his consulting clients in a direct and open manner.[17] A man of great versatility, who has been a surgeon, medical clinic manager, lawyer, consultant, and now business school dean, he embodies to me the ideal of a professional with deep humanistic values and a rich life experience. When working on one of his teams (many layers below him), I found him to be so interested in people, routinely probing into their views and passions, that it was often hard to keep the discussion focused on the task at hand.

Even if financial firms can tease out useful aspects from McKinsey's organizational culture, a challenge is that the finance industry may be a less natural fit with the servant leadership model than the management consulting industry. In her research project "Inside the Banker's Brain," Susan Ochs identified five mental models that are prevalent in the financial industry based on interviews of 700 financial service professionals.[18] Those include a bias toward complexity, a desire for financial success, a prioritization of self-interests, a need to have one's intelligence recognized, and a short-term outlook driven by a desire to maximize financial outcomes with every transaction. Such models are hardly consistent with any of the principles of servant leadership.

The potential for outsized compensation in finance tends to attract competitive individuals, a subset of whom may be particularly driven by the prospect of accelerated financial returns. Trading activities, which have become increasingly prominent within the industry, are associated with an "eat what you kill" mentality, meaning that compensation is largely determined by individual contribution rather than collective outcomes.

Still, true team spirit can be found in firms across the industry, with aspects of a servant leadership culture even appearing in unlikely corners. Take hedge funds, for instance. On one end of the spectrum, many hedge funds are organized so that analysts are siloed into narrow parts of the fund's value chain, acting as an extension of the portfolio manager's research efforts, but largely shielded from the idea-generation process, the decision to pursue an investment opportunity, and the execution of the trade. These dynamics make it difficult for analysts to grow into decision-makers or to claim credit for any successes in the portfolio. By contrast, some portfolio managers create a work environment where every young analyst is treated as a junior portfolio manager. Junior members of the team shadow the portfolio manager across the range of investment activities and learn from day one not only how to become a high-performing analyst but also how to grow into a portfolio manager. In an industry where junior analysts can be quickly promoted to portfolio manager, that apprenticeship model tends to be valued by portfolio managers who have enough confidence to enable subordinates to shine and get credit for successes. In my experience, managers who deliberately give their junior analysts opportunities to mimic their own responsibilities tend to perceive that empowering apprenticeship model as a core part of their edge in delivering value for their clients.

In a more staid corner of the institutional investment industry, Capital Group, a Los Angeles-based firm founded in 1931, illustrates how asset management firms can embed several aspects of servant leadership into their organizational structure. This privately held firm houses the American Funds, a group of over forty mutual funds. Despite managing $1.9 trillion as of mid 2019, the firm has remained relatively discreet, certainly compared to competitors such as Fidelity. Its emphasis on integrity goes back to the founder, Jonathan Bell Lovelace. Upon succeeding his father at the helm of the firm in 1963, Jon Lovelace syndicated the adoption of a three-way commitment that would come to define Capital's culture: The firm's objective would be to balance the interests of investors, owners, and the firm's professionals, while putting first the interests of investors.[19] An example of that commitment to investors' interests is the firm's reluctance to offer new "flavor of the month" funds that tap into popular investment themes that may not survive the test of time. As of 2019, Capital Group managed 36 funds, compared with 504 funds for Fidelity. In concentrating its offerings, Capital has positioned itself as a firm that is more focused on investing than marketing for the sake of asset gathering.

Describing the Capital Group, James Rothenberg, the former Chairman of the firm, stated that it "is clearly a culture of strong individuals in an industry notoriously afflicted with egotism, yet we accept and quietly seek anonymity as individuals in the work we do."[20] Each portfolio is managed using a "multiple counselor" structure.[21] Rather than having a single portfolio manager, multiple portfolio managers each manage their assigned parts across several portfolios. They can focus on their specialty without being overwhelmed by the size of the assets they are managing. As many as a dozen portfolio managers may be responsible for the returns of any given fund, leading to its performance being the result of a collective effort and preventing any fund from becoming too dependent on a star portfolio manager. An investment committee oversees the various parts, ensuring proper diversification. The fact that Capital Group's logo doesn't appear on its headquarter building reflects the firm's self-effacing culture.[22]

Other examples of servant leadership in the finance industry include founders and senior managers who "left money on the table" in order to make their firms more attractive for younger generations or to help instill a culture of moderation to strengthen the long-term health of the firm. Warren Hellman, a co-founder of San Francisco-based private equity firm Hellman & Friedman, illustrates the point. He came from a lineage of distinguished bankers, going back to Isaias W. Hellman, who bought Wells Fargo Bank in 1905 and turned it into a major funding source supporting growth in the American West.[23] At age 26, Hellman became the youngest partner in Lehman Brothers' history and eventually its president before co-founding his private equity firm in 1984.

Hellman characterized Lehman in the 1970s as a tormented organization whose professionals competed against one another, banded in factions, and hoarded information. At Hellman & Friedman, his guideline was to do the opposite of what he thought Lehman Brothers' "old guard" would do.[24] He gave every investment professional a vote in investment committee meetings until the group became too large to manage. In sharp contrast to the way the old guard at Lehman hogged the firm's equity, he gave out equity to younger colleagues relatively quickly in the early days of the firm, sometimes after only two or three years at the firm. He also required every investment professional to invest in each of the firm's deals to ensure consistent alignment of interest with the firm's investors.[25]

Upon retirement, he decided to sell his shares back to the firm at their book value, giving away much of their value to those who would carry on the firm's activities, with an eye to his legacy.[26] That is unusual. Most founders of investment funds who have reached this level of success seek to monetize their ownership, by selling part or all of their firm at a high valuation or by going public. Philip Hammarskjold, Hellman & Friedman's co-CEO, described it as a "Marvin Bower moment" for the firm,[27] referring to the McKinsey leader's decision to sell most of his shares to his partners at book value when he turned 60.

Hellman's inclination to support others extended into a deep engagement in philanthropic activities. His sustained giving to causes he cared about, centered on San Francisco-area organizations, kept him from appearing on the various Forbes lists of richest Americans.[28] While Hellman exemplifies many of the servant leader attributes, he also proves that no human being is perfect, particularly when subjected to close scrutiny. At Lehman, he was nicknamed "Hurricane Hellman" for the volatility of his temper.[29]

Another marker of servant leadership is the gap between the highest compensation and the average in an organization. The finance industry exhibits extreme differences, with the ratio of CEO pay to the median employee an average of 150 to 1 based on a 2018 survey of publicly listed financial firms.[30] Some firms make it a point to manage that gap. Bridgeway Capital Partners, a Houston-based asset management firm, is a rare financial firm that does so explicitly. It caps its highest-paid partner compensation at seven times that of the lowest-paid individual at the firm.

The moderation reflected in the partner compensation cap also informs other key tenets of the firm.[31] When John Montgomery set up the firm in 1993, he embedded in the foundational documents that 50% of the firm's profits would be donated to charitable causes.[32] Over time, he has found it to be an effective recruiting tool, attracting young professionals who share these values, are willing to forgo higher salaries they might get elsewhere, and are attracted by the long-term value-creation potential of the firm's stock option plan.[33] As of end 2019, the firm managed $7.5 billion and had donated tens of millions of dollars to more than 500 non-profits since inception.[34]

Fostering a Responsible Corporate Culture

Corporate culture encompasses the assumptions, values, and practices that shape how employees behave. It is worth considering on its own because it goes to the heart of whether employees are valued, treated with dignity, and empowered. It also informs how decisions are made, and inevitably seeps into how customers are treated and whether any consideration is given to impact on other stakeholders and the broader community.

Culture is defined at the top. Formal policies, codes of conduct, mission statements, and training programs tend to be superseded by the unofficial, core values of the firm which flow down from the head of the organization and senior managers, who signal what they care about to the rest of the organization. Gaps between official messaging and actual behavior abound. In a 2014 PwC survey, 30% of banking professionals believed that management decisions were inconsistent with communications regarding risk.[35] In fact, listed companies that use ethics-related terms such as "ethics" or "corporate responsibility" in their annual reports are more likely to score weakly on corporate governance metrics and be subject to class-action lawsuits.[36] Proclaimed values also appear to be irrelevant to a firm's performance, while employees' perception of senior managers as trustworthy and ethical is associated with stronger firm performance.[37]

By the same token, internally designated safeguards such as risk managers and compliance officers are not systematically perceived as having a binding authority since they ultimately report to the business leaders. In the same survey, PwC found that only 16% of banking professionals strongly agreed that the risk control function could take precedence over a business decision at their firm. The design of incentives reflects firm values and, more often than not, they reward employees solely based on performance relative to financial goals rather than behavior consistent with espoused values.

Financial institutions' emphasis on a fiduciary culture has waned over the years as competition has increased and financial activities have veered toward transactional activities, away from relationship-driven services. Financial institutions that have tarnished records of breaches of client trust tend to have a culture that implicitly supports, or at least condones, achieving financial results at the expense of values. Even at main-street retail banks such as Wells Fargo, we saw in the chapter on customer mandate how the incessant pressure on financial performance can sway the culture toward achieving performance at all costs.

Some institutions have managed to maintain their values despite the pressure to change. Nationwide Building Society, one of the last remaining British mutual financial institutions, stands out in this respect. Founded in the nineteenth century to provide working people the means to save and borrow money to afford the land and materials to build their own house, it has remained committed to its broad mission of building a better society. As a mutual, it is owned by its customers, who are referred to as members. While most of its peers demutualized in the 1980s and 1990s, it has kept its status, surviving calls over the years to convert to a bank status.

Nationwide often tops surveys as the most trusted lender in the United Kingdom. Its culture promotes an ethic of care, which endeavors to push beyond concepts of fairness by aspiring to treat the customer with respect, empathy, and compassion.[38] In order to effectively fulfill that mission, Nationwide has committed to maintaining its 680 branches and 200 agencies throughout the United Kingdom, at a time when the large for-profit banks are retrenching their brick-and-mortar presence. Occasionally, the mutual has used its credibility to sway the industry toward greater fiduciary conduct. In 1999, it went on a campaign to shame banks that charged issuer fees for using another operator's ATM machines, leading to the elimination of these fees throughout the United Kingdom.

A Servant Leader Who Influenced Generations of Bankers: John Whitehead

Senior managers have a particular responsibility in defining and carrying their firm's culture, not least because the default culture in contemporary financial institutions is one of obsession over performance and financial outcomes. John Whitehead, co-Senior Partner of Goldman Sachs between 1975 and 1984, stands out for his dedication to maintaining a responsible culture at the investment bank. Long before Goldman Sachs was hyperbolically described (to much acclaim) in *RollingStone* as a "great vampire squid wrapped around the face of humanity, relentlessly jamming its blood funnel into anything that smells like money," the firm could earnestly ascribe its success to its culture of stewardship, prudence, and long-term bias. These values are generally seen as having been cemented by chairmen Sidney Weinberg (1930–1969) and Gus Levy (1969–1976), who coined the phrase "long-term greedy" to describe the firm.[39] During his years as co-Chairman between 1976 and 1984, John Whitehead carried those values, becoming known for his long-term strategic vision as well as for being the proponent of significant initiatives to promote ethical standards.[40]

While Whitehead operated at a time when the pressure to generate short-term profit was less and many investment banks were still private partnerships, he remains a timeless exemplar because of the multiple decisions he made against boosting performance at the cost of eroding the firm's values. The pressure on the chief executive of a financial firm to follow competitors into the latest profit-making activity even if it entails lowering the firm's standards (wherever those happen to be at the time) is perennial, making Whitehead's example just as relevant in an age of more pronounced greed and looser standards.

The codification of Goldman Sachs' twelve business principles (eventually expanded to fourteen by Goldman Sachs' lawyers) is the legacy he was most proud of. They state first and foremost that "our clients' interests always come first." While codes of ethics and corporate mission statements have become pervasive today – with varying degrees of influence on the actual conduct of business – Whitehead's version was trailblazing.

Yet he refrained from presenting himself as an ethical vigilante and preferred framing his ethics initiatives as purely business driven. Goldman Sachs grew very quickly in the 1960s and 1970s, making the assimilation of new employees a challenging task for a firm with such a strong culture. Whitehead perceived a critical need to disseminate what the firm stood for, and presented his business principles as an important tool to do so.[41]

A small-town D-Day veteran, John Whitehead rose to the cochairmanship of Goldman Sachs after having been mentored for years by Sidney Weinberg, the legendary Goldman Sachs Chairman who is often referred to as the soul of the firm. One of the most significant decisions Whitehead made during his tenure as co-Chairman was to create bright lines regarding which businesses Goldman Sachs would and wouldn't take part of, based on ethical and reputational considerations. As Charles Ellis argued in his analysis of pre-eminent professional service firms, the strongest test of a firm's principles lies in its decisions to avoid activities that are profitable to its peers. In the 1970s, many potential client firms knocked on Goldman Sachs' door to support them on unfriendly raids. Morgan Stanley had broken the taboo on hostile take-overs by advising International Nickel in its bid for Electronic Storage Battery in 1974. While most investment banks joined the fray, Whitehead was steadfast in his refusal to take up that emerging line of business. He saw it primarily as a matter of integrity – it was important for Goldman Sachs to act in a "statesman-like" manner. While the decision led Goldman Sachs to lose some assignments, it helped position the firm in the long run as the advisor of choice on take-over defense. More significantly, by refusing to "go hostile," the firm's reputation for integrity grew. This helped propel the firm to its status as the benchmark investment bank.[42]

Whitehead showed strong conviction that he was doing the right thing. In his mind, upholding the firm's long-term interests often implied going against its short-term financial interests. He ascribed his success as a leader to his ability to see past his own short-term interests: "I could see that my interests *were* the firm's interests, and vice versa. The firm and I would succeed or fail together. I think that is the difference: My sense of my own interests is wider than usual, and includes those of the entire group. That is an essential element of my definition of a leader."[43]

His management style was heavily consensus-oriented. His guiding principle as chairman of an organization (of which there were many beyond his tenure at Goldman Sachs) was to eschew votes in favor of building broad-based agreement. He ascribed that proclivity to his time as an undergraduate at Haverford College in Pennsylvania.[44] Steeped in Quaker culture, Haverford instilled in him a preference for collective decision-making and civility. An Episcopalian, Whitehead eventually became the first non-Quaker chairman of Haverford's board.

This personality trait likely helped make his co-chairmanship of Goldman Sachs with John Weinberg a success. Rare are the co-leadership arrangements that have worked at the head of large companies. The two executives would talk on the phone in the evenings if they had not been able to get together during the day. They would speak on Sunday night every week to prepare the agenda for the Monday management committee meeting.[45] When the co-leadership structure was first announced, McKinsey's Marvin Bower quickly followed his congratulations with a prediction that it would not work, because it never does.[46] Smiling, he added that when they realize it doesn't work, McKinsey will be there to help fix it. Bower eventually had to admit he had been wrong as the partnership proved effective.

Whitehead stands out not only for having eschewed the easy path to incremental profits at the expense of values but also for having fought against the tide pushing Wall Street firms to change their legal structure from partnerships to publicly listed companies. In doing so, his motivation was primarily to maintain the firm's culture and values. This showed foresight given both the erosion of the firm's culture after Goldman Sachs listed in 1998 and the generalized evolution of incentives on Wall Street as most of the leading banks went public.

Proposals for an IPO had been discussed six times prior to being accepted by Goldman's 188 partners in August 1998. Many partners supported the IPO for justifiable reasons – most importantly, the need to compete against other listed investment banks such as Morgan Stanley and Merrill Lynch.[47] But it's hard to parse out strategic reasons from personal self-interest given the massive windfall expected by all partners in the event of an IPO. The public listing enabled Goldman Sachs professionals to sell shares at five times book value, whereas Whitehead sold most of his shares at book value upon retirement.[48] He is not the only prominent Goldman Sachs partner to have pushed back against an IPO over the years – many have, including his co-Chairman and co-Senior Partner John Weinberg. Several prominent senior partners from Goldman Sachs and from other leading Wall Street firms that debated the same issue could have also been portrayed to illustrate the point. John Whitehead stands out as a compelling example within that group given his lifelong emphasis on values and issues of ethics.

Whitehead and Weinberg were the last leaders of the firm who unambiguously emphasized fostering long-term relationships as the firm's primary business purpose. The shift toward trading gradually took hold with each subsequent leader, contributing to the erosion of the firm's professional values. Greater focus on short-term results and growing complexity, as new activities proliferated, led to greater conflicts of interest.[49] Whitehead made no secret of the fact that he was disappointed, and at times mortified, by the change in culture at Goldman Sachs over time, particularly in light of its involvement in selling toxic subprime securities to its clients in the run-up to the subprime crisis. Much like John Bogle, Whitehead did not shy away from criticizing the firm whose values he was widely perceived to embody. Long after he left Goldman Sachs, consistent with the integrity of his leadership at the bank, Whitehead continued to crusade in favor of ethical standards on Wall Street. For many, he has come to represent the lost culture of stewardship on Wall Street.

Promoting Diversity

Absent an active promotion of diversity in the workplace, passive discrimination becomes the default mode of operation. Research on behavioral psychology has long established that even well-meaning individuals have cognitive biases that lead them to unwittingly discriminate. Chief amongst them is the natural tendency to trust, hire, and promote people that have a similar profile to ours, a bias often referred to as in-group favoritism. Despite our best efforts, we carry implicit stereotypes that influence our decisions.[50]

Biases play an important role in the dismal representation of women and people of color in the finance industry. A global survey of financial service firms found that while women make up 46% of all professionals, they only account for 26% of senior managers and 15% of executive-level positions.[51] The skewed representation is more extreme for racial and ethnic diversity, which has been less of a priority than gender diversity in recent years. In the United States, African Americans represent 3% of senior positions in finance companies compared to their 14% share of the overall population.[52]

The challenges faced by women and people of color seem greater in the financial industry than most other industries. According to a PwC survey, only 35% of female millennials employed in financial services believe they can rise to senior levels versus 49% among female professionals across industries.[53] More than 70% of female millennials surveyed think that there is a discrepancy between the talk around initiatives to promote diversity and actual equality of opportunity.[54]

In practice, a firm cannot simply decide to increase its diversity and successfully hire a more diverse group of professionals. The barriers are deeply ingrained and systemic in nature. To be overcome, they require a concerted, multi-year effort driven by top management and supported throughout the organization. Years ago, I contributed to a management consulting study for one of the most prominent global investment banks. The bank was struggling to gain traction in recruiting, retaining, and promoting women. We found that one of its greatest challenges was to overcome institutional barriers. To begin with, the bank's pool of applicants for its Associate program was highly skewed toward male students. Once new recruits started, we found that the deck was stacked against female recruits.

Based on multiple interviews across the firm, success in the early stages of a career was determined by internal demand for a recruit to be staffed on the most desirable, high-profile mandates. What determined demand for staffing? The answer was always internal reputation, which was formed over the first sixty days or so on the job, based on the quality of a recruit's experience in that short window – meaning the desirability of the mandates he or she worked on, and their track record on these projects, evidenced by whether senior members of the team requested to staff them again on subsequent projects. The catch was that those who managed to get staffed early on desirable projects were often those who had natural mentors at the firm, typically Senior Associates, Vice Presidents, and Managing Directors who took an interest in guiding them through the system. More often than not, this meant that the men in the new Associate class had a leg up because they were much more likely to have natural mentors above them – perhaps a college varsity team mate or a fraternity brother, than new female recruits, who had few senior female mentors to turn to. Of course, women could and might develop male mentors but there were fewer natural ties. While some aspects of these dynamics may have been idiosyncratic to this particular bank, it is not hard to imagine that these types of institutional barriers bolster the perpetuation of existing hierarchies across the industry.

One angle into the disparity is the gender pay gap, whose disclosure is now mandated in the United Kingdom for companies with more than 250 domestic staff. In its 2019 release, the median pay gap across the financial industry was 22% in favor of men, finance being only edged out by construction as the most unequal industry in terms of pay.[55]

At the forefront of the movement toward gender pay equality in the United States has stood Natasha Lamb, co-founder of Arjuna Capital, a North Carolina-based wealth management firm. Since pursuing an MBA focused on sustainability, she has been motivated by the potential for business to act as a force for social good.[56] She co-founded Arjuna as an investment platform for like-minded clients. Its design also meant to address the practical constraints imposed by the financial industry's conservative culture, which make it more difficult for women to thrive – for instance, the unspoken rule that an employee's request for greater flexibility in hours or work location inherently reflects a lower commitment to succeed professionally.

With Arjuna, Lamb has taken the gender equity fight to the shareholders of large listed companies. Since 2014, she has filed shareholder proposals at twenty-five companies, requesting the disclosure of the percentage pay gap between male and female employees (which is not mandated in the United States) and firm targets to bridge the gap.[57] After initial difficulties, Lamb's initiative gained significant momentum in 2017–2018. It succeeded in getting twenty-two companies to publish gender pay gaps, including nine large financial institutions. Peer pressure is an important motivator: Once Citigroup became the first US bank to agree to the proposal, its main competitors quickly followed suit.

Will greater transparency make a difference? Early returns suggest it will. Research on wages at Danish companies, which have been mandated since 2006 to disclose gender pay data, indicates that the gender pay gap has shrunk compared to control firms.[58] Lamb also makes the point that firms don't simply decide to publish their numbers – they go through their internal data and will typically try to "clean house" before sharing them, by adjusting the pay of a subset of employees.

Publishing the data can also mark the beginning of a process to reach new targets and a new stage of discussion with the likes of Arjuna. When the targeted US firms first published their data, they generally shared "equal pay for equal work" data, or the gender pay gap comparing men and women in the same functions, geographies, and seniority levels. Lamb is now focused on getting them to publish their unadjusted median gender pay gaps, which tend to reveal the skew toward men in higher level roles.[59]

Citigroup disclosed in January 2019 that its "like for like" gender pay gap was just 1% in favor of men but that its median gender pay gap was a striking 29% in favor of men and 7% in favor of non-minorities. Citigroup was the first US-listed company to publish that data.[60] The very fact that it has shared these numbers makes a difference: The bank likely took action to mitigate the gap prior to publication and has now created expectations that it will both continue to publish these numbers and show progress over time. In conjunction with the disclosure, it announced that it has set a goal to increase representation at the Assistant Vice President through Managing Director levels to at least 40% for women globally and 8% for Black employees in the US by the end of 2021, as a starting point.

With such pressure coming from different corners of the industry, many more internal initiatives seek to address diversity than used to do so. In the same PwC survey cited above, financial firms with a strategy in place to promote diversity grew from 40% in 2010 to 59% in 2015. A significant driver is likely the fact that the business case in favor of diversity has grown clearer over time. In a study of large companies in the United Kingdom, Canada, Latin America, and the United States, McKinsey & Company found that companies in the top quartile of gender diversity on their executive teams were 21% more likely to generate financial returns above their national industry median.[61] Companies in the top quartile of ethnic and cultural diversity were 33% more likely to outperform their national industry median.

While these findings demonstrate correlation rather than a causal relationship, there are strong hypotheses regarding how diversity might improve performance. Greater diversity provides an edge in recruiting by broadening the potential sources of candidates. Research has also shown that it helps generate better decisions by injecting fresh perspectives and reducing the risk of group think.[62] Diversity on a sales team can also enable a financial service firm to connect with a broader group of customers.

Taking gender diversity as an example, women account for 85% of consumer purchases, make 89% of decisions on bank accounts, and own 40% of stocks, and yet 84% believe that they are not well understood by sales people.[63] These research findings are well enough established that in a survey of financial service firm CEOs, 85% believed that a strategy to promote diversity would enhance business performance, while 80% thought that it would strengthen brand and reputation.[64]

The weak representation of women is consistent across the industry, and notably pronounced in investment roles. In the fund management industry, a vexing paradox has grown increasingly untenable: The data consistently suggests that women have attributes that tend to make them better risk managers, but they represent only 3% of hedge fund managers and 9% of mutual fund managers. There are far fewer women who are money managers than doctors (37%) or lawyers (33%).[65] In private equity, real estate, and venture capital, women account for only a single-digit percentage of senior investment professionals.[66]

A recent study by Morningstar on mutual fund managers found that there was no statistically significant difference in performance between male and female mutual fund managers, denying the possibility that the industry's nine to one ratio between men and women managers could be explained by men's outperformance.[67] A simple (non-risk-adjusted) comparison of hedge fund managers shows that the HFRI Women index, which tracks single manager funds managed or owned by women, has outperformed the HFRI Fund Weighted Composite Index by almost 1% annually, between the inception of the HFRI Women index in 2007 and the middle of 2018.

In the United States, only two of the largest fifty hedge funds are managed by women – Nancy Zimmerman who leads Bracebridge Capital, a relative value fixed-income fund, and Qi Wang, who is the lead portfolio manager of PIMCO's global macro hedge fund strategies – while Dawn Fitzpatrick manages the family office of George Soros. In Europe, Leda Braga manages $8 billion in assets for her hedge fund Systematica Investments. But by and large, women are rarely in the highest-profile, highest-paying roles. They tend to be channeled toward "back-office" positions or marketing and investor relations departments, where they account for half of the lead positions in the largest fifty US hedge funds.[68]

Few senior women in finance are well known outside of their organizations. An exception in the United Kingdom may be Helena Morrissey. At a time of increased attention to the dismal representation of women in senior roles, she has become a celebrated case. She is, famously, the mother of nine children, who are looked after by her stay-at-home husband. At 54, she has risen to the very top echelon of the industry, as the head of personal investing at Legal and General Investment Management (LGIM), overseeing close to $1 trillion in assets. Like most women in the industry, her path hasn't been seamless. In her book *A Good Time to Be a Girl*, she asserts that she was passed over for a promotion at Schroders, one of the oldest and largest asset managers in the United Kingdom, because of a maternity leave early in her career. She was told at the time that her commitment was in question because she had a baby. She recalls how the atmosphere at Schroders was "clubby" in nature and constantly reinforced the existing hierarchy. Every afternoon a butler would serve tea and biscuits from a trolley only to those that were Associate Directors and above.[69] In reaction to the negative publicity, Schroders stated that the firm is very different today than it was twenty-five years ago (in fact, its CEO Peter Harrison was named one of the *Financial Times*' 2018 HERoes: champions of women in business).[70]

Morrissey (now Dame Helena) co-founded in 2010 the 30% Club, a not-for-profit dedicated to pressuring boards to reach at least 30% female representation. Its advocacy has emphasized the business case rather than simply the moral imperative. She believes that the most effective advocates are senior men rather than women.[71] The message, whether coming from the 30% Club or stemming from a broader trend, has gained traction. From 12% of directors for the top 100 UK-listed companies, the proportion has now risen to close to 30%. Her firm, LGIM, voted against more than 100 UK chairmen in 2018, up from 37 in 2017 and 13 in 2016, for failing to have a minimum threshold of gender diversity on their board.[72] Morrissey has been recognized within her industry. She was named chair of the Investment Association, the United Kingdom's trade association for fund managers, in 2014.

There are further reasons to promote gender diversity in finance. A dynamic area of behavioral research tackles the biology of risk-taking. This body of research argues that women have the potential to be better risk managers in part because they typically are more risk averse and show greater discipline, less over-confidence, and a greater long-term orientation. One study tested the premise, drawn from psychological research, that men are more over-confident than women, implying that men will trade more excessively than women. Based on household data from a discount brokerage, the study found that men traded 45% more than women and that trading reduced men's net returns by 2.65% versus 1.72% for women.[73] Research by neuroscientists also shows that higher levels of testosterone lead to greater potential for irrational exuberance on the trading floor.[74] This is particularly relevant since the financial crisis is widely perceived to have been exacerbated by a culture of aggressive risk-taking, over-confidence, and siloed thinking – all issues that can be mitigated by more diverse teams.

Few places have suffered as much from financial exuberance than Iceland. The role of gender in the build-up to the crisis is intriguing. A small island populated by 330,000 residents, Iceland reinvented itself in the run-up to the Global Financial Crisis as a European financial center, offering high interest rate accounts to foreigners and dabbling in derivatives. The size of the country's three largest banks grew from about 100% of GDP in 1998 to 900% of GDP in 2008.[75] As Icelandic banks flooded the economy with cheap liquidity, the net worth of the average family in Iceland grew three-fold between 2003 and 2006. An alarming number of Icelanders, whose male population historically had found employment in fishing or the aluminum smelting industry, turned to financial speculation, borrowing in foreign currencies at relatively low interest rates to benefit from the mid-teen rates offered by Icelandic banks and the rising Krona.[76] In Icelandic banks, equity that was meant to act as a safeguard against economic volatility turned out to be substantially financed by loans from each bank to itself or from one of the other Icelandic banks.[77] Once access to foreign funding dried up, the three dominant banks became unable to repay their maturing loans. They were nationalized in October 2008, causing the stock market to spiral down in excess of 90% from its pre-Lehman collapse levels and the Krona to devalue. The meltdown of Iceland's financial system overwhelmed the economy, leading to a $2.1 billion bailout from the IMF. As an IMF official related to writer Michael Lewis in 2009, "Iceland is no longer a country. It is a hedge fund."[78]

Iceland's Independence Party had governed the country for years preceding the crisis. Historically supported by fishermen, its philosophy skews toward free markets and individualism. It is also notable for being completely dominated by men. In the years preceding the crisis, the banks and many other state-owned enterprises had been privatized, sold to a small group of men who had attended the same exclusive Latin School. They became a prominent driver of Iceland's crazed expansion into speculative finance during the 2000s.[79] Of course, the example is too anecdotal to draw conclusions. But it suggests a relationship between financial exuberance and gender that has been empirically highlighted in different contexts.

Exasperated by the extent to which an aggressive male culture of risk-taking and speculation led to irresponsible management of financial assets, Halla Tomasdottir and Kristin Petursdottir, two Icelandic businesswomen, founded Audur Capital in 2007 as an investment fund explicitly managed along feminine values, which they interpreted as less testosterone-driven decisions, greater focus on risk management, and greater awareness of social impact.[80]

Petursdottir had risen to become the deputy CEO of an Icelandic bank in London but had quit in 2006, despairing over the male-dominated banking culture.[81] Audur would be run differently. It wouldn't invest in anything they did not understand. Profit with principle meant that capital would be deployed with an eye to its social and environmental impact. They would conduct an "emotional due diligence," which meant delving into people and corporate culture.

It emphasized straight talking, so that concepts would be understandable. Tomasdottir made the point that "women are willing to ask stupid questions. We want to understand. We won't take risks we don't understand, so we ask: 'what is sub-prime? Who'll pay these loans back?'"[82] Ultimately, the goal was to promote the financial independence of women.[83] As a result of these guidelines, Audur Capital navigated the crisis with aplomb, protecting its capital at risk, and growing at a time when almost all other financial institutions were going bankrupt or fighting for survival. Audur merged with another Icelandic financial service firm in 2014 and Tomasdottir went on to run for president in 2016, finishing runner-up.

The Canadian banking industry offers a striking counter-example to Iceland. Whereas most developed large-economy banks necessitated a government bailout during the Global Financial Crisis, Canadian banks remained profitable.[84] John Taft, former CEO of the wealth management unit of RBC, a Canadian bank, and author of a book on stewardship in finance, points to several reasons explaining the resilience of Canadian banks during the crisis: a mortgage market with an originate-to-hold rather than an originate-to-sell model, a single regulator with a principle- rather than rules-based approach, conservative capital ratio requirements, and a large proportion of bank funding coming from stable customer deposits.[85] But at the root of these various factors lies Canadian culture, which, Taft argues, is more community-oriented. He also invokes an argument that Canadian culture may be considered feminine – marked by a desire to plan ahead, concentrate on preserving what one has, and rely on cautious incrementalism to implement changes – in contrast to the masculine culture of the United States, which is more comfortable with risk-taking and innovation.[86]

These anecdotal stories prompt a question: Are there gender differences in attitudes toward ethical issues? In a seminal book, titled *In a Different Voice*, published in 1982, psychologist Carol Gilligan made the argument that men tend to approach moral questions through the prism of rules and rights while women are more readily guided by relationships and responsibilities. Along the same lines, financial ethics scholar John Dobson argues that the theory of the firm as a nexus of contracts creating incentives to pursue self-interest and maximize wealth can be considered to be a masculine concept, in contrast to the more feminine concept of the firm as a nexus of relationships, which calls for more emphasis on cooperation and collective objectives.[87]

A recent study, testing gender differences in tactical approaches to negotiations, suggested that women were less likely to act deceptively in order to secure financial gains.[88] Consistent with Dobson's analogy, empirical research has, on balance, albeit not consistently, supported the claim that women tend to have higher ethical standards than men – yet more reason to promote greater diversity in finance.

Implicitly underpinning all of the examples discussed in this chapter is the primacy of an organization's established culture. An individual can positively impact existing norms within a firm, but it is significantly more straightforward to behave virtuously within the organization by working for a firm whose norms are consistent with the standards discussed in this chapter and espoused by like-minded colleagues. John Whitehead was able to turn his business principles into a quasi-constitutional document at Goldman Sachs because the firm's culture was already anchored in a set of values that supported the thrust of his message. This pillar of the framework – to treat colleagues with dignity, empower them, and foster a culture of service to customers and responsibility toward other stakeholders – can both provide guidance on virtuous behavior inside the organization and function as a screen to assess the culture of a potential employer.

4 ENGAGED CITIZENSHIP
Contributing Expertise, Time, and Wealth to the Common Good

The Versatile Finance Professional

We discussed in the chapter on social wealth how finance can contribute to the common good. Finance fulfills a critical role in our economy, whether by facilitating savings for retirement, enabling seamless payments for the purchase of goods and services, or offering insurance against the financial risk of an early death, to name a few of its basic services. By and large, the primary purpose of finance is to help customers achieve their goals.

Serving customers with their interest in mind is a noble enterprise. But it is hard to argue that a successful finance professional should command the same respect for being a responsible, caring citizen as the low-paid nurse who has toiled her entire life in a selfless manner to care for others, the public school teacher who tirelessly instructs generations of students in overcrowded classrooms, or the military who puts his life on the line to protect his country. Even if finance professionals deliver critical services to their customers, their contribution to society is indirect since they act as intermediaries. Finance enables individual, corporate, or social goals but doesn't achieve them on its own in the way medicine or engineering might.

Moreover, few go into finance for the explicit purpose of serving others or helping humanity. A growing subset of finance explicitly targets social impact on a wider scale, via, for instance, impact investments, green bonds, or micro-insurance, but that sector remains small.

A career in finance has many appeals. It can often be intellectually stimulating, of broad relevance, global in nature, and potentially lucrative. But benefiting society simply isn't the driver of motivation for most entering the field, even if it is a welcome by-product. While the financier might have pursued her career with great integrity and moral commitment, and shown genuine care for her clients, she will likely have been motivated at least in part by the incentive of attractive compensation and the social status that tends to go with it.

She might have also pursued her career in a corner of the industry that extracts more value from society than it creates – in the asset management firm that overcharges fees on a retiree's savings, the credit card company that peddles complex, usurious terms on customers ill-equipped to understand them, or the mergers and acquisitions advisory firm which pushes its corporate client toward a deal that lacks synergies but will generate high fees. There is also strong evidence that too much finance can have a negative effect on an economy.

Moreover, finance's contribution to society is clouded by the extreme compensation garnered by professionals in significant parts of the industry and by the burgeoning sense that the narrow, selfish pursuit of personal interests by a subset of these professionals paved the way toward the Global Financial Crisis. As a result, finance professionals may be particularly motivated to contribute to society outside of the confines of their professional responsibilities.

Not everyone agrees that a career as a nurse is inherently more ethical or more beneficial to society than a career as an investment banker. Oxford philosopher William MacAskill has argued the opposite in a seminal paper, using a consequentialist argument, focusing purely on outcomes rather than intentions. In his framework, those who are primarily interested in having social impact should pursue the highest-paid job, even if it's in a field that is "morally innocuous" or even "morally controversial," to the extent that they donate a large portion of their earnings on an ongoing basis.[1] The net result is that by eschewing the traditional path toward social impact via, for instance, the not-for-profit sector, the highly paid investment banker can fund many other not-for-profit workers. Had she pursued a career in that sector, she would have done the work of one person, rather than funded the work of two or more people as a philanthropist. Since money is fungible, an objective reflection would lead even the most motivated altruist to opt for the highest compensated career, as long as it is not morally reprehensible.

MacAskill's argument is enticing, but it relies on tenuous assumptions. While money is a fungible resource, people are not. It is hard to imagine a highly motivated altruist, to take an extreme example, having the enthusiasm and commitment to successfully pursue a career as an investment banker absent an innate desire to do so. The investment banking field is extremely competitive and requires an enormous amount of dedication to succeed. Along the same "people-are-not-widgets" vein, the deeply motivated altruist would likely be more effective in her career in the not-for-profit sector. Had Wendy Kopp opted to work in investment banking like many of her Princeton University classmates who graduated in 1989, she would not have founded Teach For America, an organization that has had a tangible impact on US public education by having enrolled over 50,000 college graduates of top universities to teach K-12 grades for at least two years.

Another challenge to the thesis is that its implementation requires an extreme level of discipline to purposefully opt out of the lifestyle of one's socio-economic group. In his original paper, MacAskill implies that the investment banker should live a quasi-ascetic life in order to give away most of her earnings. That commitment may be manageable as an overworked single professional but becomes much harder if and when that worker starts a family. It would then likely entail numerous trade-offs that would be at odds with the choices made by other members of one's community of colleagues and friends, such as opting for a sizeable commute, since high-paying jobs tend to be in high-priced real estate areas, or forgoing private school for the children.

MacAskill's paper makes necessary simplifying assumptions. The effective altruist movement that it has spawned and the various organizations MacAskill has helped create to spur its implementation have become more practical since their conceptual origins in MacAskill's paper, moving away from an emphasis on personal sacrifice and on taking on jobs primarily to maximize compensation (and thus donations) at the expense of personal interest.[2] In his subsequent book, *Doing Good Better*, MacAskill advocates for an analytical, fact-based approach to improving other people's lives, without necessarily relinquishing a comfortable life.[3] He broadens the channels through which one can have impact – "earning to give," or maximizing one's earnings in order to donate more, is one of several tools, in addition to the labor one provides (to the extent that the organization is effective in doing good), and the influence one has on other people.[4]

This more nuanced approach to the argument takes into greater consideration the fact that people are not uni-dimensional. In practice, people are more productive when they pursue activities that they truly enjoy. They are not solely defined by their professional role at a point in time. They might pursue several distinct professional or semi-professional paths at once. The hedge fund manager may devote a substantial portion of his time overseeing a foundation, launching an economic development venture, or mentoring underprivileged children. The high-fee litigator may take on half of his cases pro bono. Finance professionals may switch careers, rotating between jobs that are primarily driven by self-interest and jobs that are primarily targeting social impact.

This chapter advocates in favor of that versatility. Finance professionals have much to offer to society beyond the services they render. In the next few pages, we will explore ways in which finance professionals can draw on their experience, expertise, network, and financial resources to benefit others outside of their professional interest in finance.

Donating Thoughtfully and Generously

Even if one finds MacAskill's original argument unconvincing, it is undeniable that for those who do choose a career in finance and generate a comfortable income, donating thoughtfully and generously can be a critical component of responsible citizenship. It may be the most common way in which finance professionals voluntarily contribute to society outside of their primary professional mandate. Fund managers that I host in my classes routinely invoke their philanthropy as one of the main channels through which they perceive themselves as being good citizens. In the United States, whose political economic foundations have supported a narrower role for government than in other parts of the world, there is significant social pressure on wealthy individuals to be philanthropic. For the wealthiest, Andrew Carnegie, a nineteenth-century industrialist-turned-philanthropist, set the tone by arguing that members of his class should thoughtfully and diligently manage their excess wealth in order to reduce inequality. In recent years, the pressure on those with large fortunes has been exacerbated by the public campaigning of Warren Buffett and Bill Gates, whose Giving Pledge challenges (some might say shames) billionaires into pledging at least half of their wealth to philanthropic uses. The media attention devoted to take-up of that pledge among the wealthiest financiers has made it increasingly difficult for any of them to evade the question.

Finance professionals engage in philanthropy for different reasons. For some, the appeal is to be recognized and celebrated. At the extreme end of the wealth spectrum, a finance professional putting his name on a building in an elite university highlights his material success for all to see and admire while creating an aura of benevolence. It associates the donor's personal brand with that of a highly pedigreed, socially beneficial institution. In some cases, it might even divert attention from the more controversial manner in which his wealth was created.

Consider Denny Sanford, a pioneer in subprime credit cards. After purchasing a Sioux Falls, South Dakota-based bank in 1986 and experimenting with various money-making initiatives, he found a golden opportunity: marketing to people with the worst credit profile credit cards whose terms take advantage of the state's unusually weak anti-usury laws. We discussed in the chapter on social wealth how some credit card companies have shown a propensity to target the least financially literate customer segments with the most complex, unattractive products. Sanford's First Premier Bank credit card routinely ranks amongst the worst offenders.[5] Its First Premier Mastercard has in the past been named the nation's worst credit card by Consumers Union, a non-profit watchdog. In 2018, a card offering a $300 credit limit would cost a combined $170 in processing fee and annual fee in the first year, and $120 in the second year, with a convoluted fee structure clearly designed to circumvent the Credit Card Act of 2009, which limits fees on a credit card in the first year to 25% of its credit limit.[6] Its Annual Percentage Rate exceeds that of competitors, at 36% for purchases and cash advances as of 2018. The bank can increase the credit limit after the account is open for thirteen months and charge a fee of 25% of the increase upon approval. The card's terms and their implications are not always clear to its customers: The firm agreed to pay a $4.5 million settlement on charges brought by the New York State Attorney General's office for deceptively marketing high-fee credit cards.

Sanford and his colleagues argue that their credit cards "provide a lifeline for credit-impaired people." A website devoted to Sanford's philanthropy also boasts about his companies having created

3,000 jobs in its communities.[7] But it is hard to justify the card's usurious terms, potentially exacerbating a cycle of debt dependency for many of its more than three million customers. Considering the first two pillars of our framework, it would be a challenge to portray Sanford as putting his clients' interests first and his bank as creating value for society rather than extracting value. The public data available is too limited to opine on how he would do with regard to the third pillar of our framework and whether he treats his colleagues and employees with dignity and empowers them. He would shine, however, when it comes to the fourth pillar of our framework: Outside of his professional activities, Sanford is a stellar citizen. He has given away close to an estimated $1 billion to various causes, a large portion of his overall wealth, with a particular focus on children's health.[8] Donations include $400 million to the Sioux City Health System, which has been renamed Sanford Health, and substantial gifts to the (now renamed) T. Denny Sanford Mayo Clinic Pediatric Center, T. Denny Sanford Pediatric Center at Florida Hospital for Children, and Children's Hospital of Los Angeles. He is also an advocate for "sunset philanthropy," having been vocal about wanting to "die broke."[9]

How should we evaluate Sanford through the prism of our overall framework? The framework is not meant to be a scorecard that naturally lends itself to summation of positive and negative behavior across its pillars or to a cost–benefit approach which might condone, for instance, exploiting and potentially trapping vulnerable customers to the extent that a certain threshold of philanthropy was achieved. This is all the more the case because those who benefit from the philanthropy are typically distinct from those who may have been abused by the core activity which generated the wealth at the source of the philanthropy. Customers may freely choose to enter into an agreement with First Premier to obtain a card, but in practice, they have few if any other choices, leaving them little bargaining power, and exposing them to deeply unfavorable terms. Additionally, First Premier cards' complex terms tend to obscure their potential toxicity. In our framework, the ends don't justify the means. Sanford can be simultaneously celebrated for his engaged and impactful involvement in philanthropic causes while being excoriated for the manner in which First Premier's credit cards may abuse customers in difficult circumstances. Sanford's complex profile makes him a thorny case, but he does illustrate the many finance professionals who primarily seek to have a positive impact on society via their philanthropy rather than their primary financial activity.

George Soros, perhaps the most well-known contemporary philanthropic financier, has had an undeniably large impact in his core causes. Born in Budapest to a Jewish family, he survived the period of Nazi control and immigrated to the United Kingdom in 1947 after the inception of Soviet occupation. After studying philosophy, he became a trader and developed into a legendary macro investor, his international reputation cemented by his bold short on the British pound sterling in 1992, which reportedly generated his fund a $1 billion payday and another $1 billion on parallel positions.[10] His outsized returns over multiple decades have been matched by a profound commitment to philanthropy, which started in the late 1970s to support the fight against communism in Eastern Europe and aid Black South African students under apartheid. In 1984, he famously donated photocopy machines to Hungarian universities and libraries in order to breach the government's monopoly on information.[11] Over the years, he has given away over $30 billion to promote human rights and democratic values, primarily via his Open Society foundations around the world.

Soros's giving reflects his deeply held values. He has not shied away from tackling controversial issues, becoming a lightning rod for conservatives in the United States, who fret at his support of liberal causes such as gun control and criminal-justice system reform, and for nationalists in Europe, who despise his promotion of immigrant rights and open-border societies.[12] He has increasingly become the object of vilification and scapegoating, much of it a thinly veiled appeal to anti-Semitic prejudice.

Soros stands out for the depth of his engagement in the causes he cares about. He has donated a greater proportion of his wealth than any other member of the current Forbes 400 list of the richest Americans – close to 80% at the latest count. The Open Society became the second largest philanthropic organization in the United States following an $18 billion donation he made in 2017. He plans on donating most of the rest of his fortune during his lifetime or at his death.[13]

Of course, the vast majority of finance professionals are not grappling with the public perception of their giving or the dilemma of whether to name a building or not. At the opposite end of the wealth spectrum, a growing movement has encouraged professionals to give early in one's career, regardless of one's income. Giving What We Can, an organization created by William MacAskill and Toby Ord, also an Oxford philosopher, challenges young people to make a pledge to donate 10% of their income on an ongoing basis. Those who take the pledge become members, with their names added to a public list on the organization's website.[14]

Whether a finance professional donates on a modest scale or in vast amounts, the choice of what organizations to support tends to reveal the donor's fundamental values and beliefs. Based on the observation that even good intentions can lead to bad outcomes, the effective altruism movement advocates focusing on the most effective organizations that can affect the most lives the most significantly and practically, in the most neglected areas, on the basis of empirical evidence.[15] The approach has roots in the consequentialist philosophy of academics such as Peter Singer and MacAskill. It has found particular resonance with professionals trained in math or philosophy, including many finance and tech workers, because of its analytical approach and emphasis on optimization.

For those who can give at a scale that commands attention, donations can be used as public statements, shining a light on a cause to attract greater support. Michael Bloomberg, the founder of financial services and media company Bloomberg L.P., has channeled his advocacy and giving toward issues related to climate change, public health, government innovation, education, and the arts. Hedge fund manager Paul Tudor Jones founded the Robin Hood Foundation to alleviate poverty in New York City; mathematician and quantitative investor Jim Simons has backed the Flatiron Institute to advance basic computational science; Blackstone co-founder Pete Peterson channeled much of his fortune during his lifetime into a foundation focused on fiscal issues; David Rubenstein gives to "patriotic" causes such as the National Archives, the Kennedy Center, the Lincoln Center, Mt. Vernon, the White House Historical Association, and the National Gallery of Art; Bill Janeway, a true "theorist-practitioner" who completed his Ph.D. in economics at the University of Cambridge and went on to build the information technology investment practice of Warburg Pincus, has funded institutions that are pushing the frontier of economic thinking, such as the Institute for New Economic Thinking, the University of Cambridge Faculty of Economics, and the Bendheim Center for Finance at Princeton (with which I am affiliated).

Curiously, a few wealthy finance professionals have gone to great lengths to donate anonymously. Andrew Schechtel, David Gelbaum, and

C. Frederick Taylor launched in 1989 TGS, one of the early quantitative funds. Their venture has been extraordinarily successful and yet largely unpublicized, perhaps because much of the capital was their own. Over the years, the three have reportedly donated more than $13 billion to a vast array of philanthropic causes, including medical research, human rights advocacy, and environmental protection. What is unusual about their giving, outside of its sheer size, is the near secrecy with which they have implemented their philanthropic activities. Several layers of overlapping company subsidiaries using the addresses of local law firms were meant to create a veil of secrecy. It took a highly resourceful investigative effort by Bloomberg reporter Zachary Mider to reveal a network of enormous charitable trusts donating funds to various causes on an anonymous basis.[16] For instance, Mider found that $700 million were donated between 2000 and 2014 to medical research targeting Huntington's disease, a rare form of fatal congenital disease – a sum larger than the National Institute of Health's own allocation to the disease.

It is unclear why they sought to donate anonymously – particularly since many of the organizations they have supported appear to be relatively uncontroversial (although some revealed political leanings). It is possible that they wanted to obscure the manner in which they generated their wealth, perhaps because they were sensitive about would-be competitors seeking to emulate their trading techniques, or perhaps because there was a whiff of controversy in their previous fund, where several employees were indicted (although not the three TGS founders, and charges on their colleagues were eventually dropped). There are few similar known instances of anonymous giving at such large scale – Chuck Feeney, the duty-free shopping magnate who gave away almost the entirety of his $8 billion fortune during his lifetime, is the lone stand-out. Perhaps the key to their mind-set could be found in an interview Gelbaum gave to the *Los Angeles Times* in 2004, stating that "I don't think that if you have a lot of money and you give away a lot of money, you should get a lot recognition. You shouldn't be able to buy that," adding that his investment success was "all a matter of chance. It certainly wasn't because I worked 5,000 times as hard as the average person, or was 5,000 times smarter than the average person."[17]

While many of the donors discussed above take an active role in the causes they support, some have gone further by explicitly switching careers, working primarily on advancing philanthropic causes rather than pursuing private interests. An increasing number of successful finance professionals have retired early from their financial activities to do so, perhaps emulating the example of Bill Gates, whose complete transition to the full-time pursuit of philanthropic causes at age 50 must count as one of the most socially beneficial pivots by any individual in recent history. In the same vein, Bloomberg left his eponymous firm to serve for three terms as mayor of New York. An engaged public servant, he instilled private sector management discipline into city hall. Since then, he has endeavored to improve the quality of city leaders by funding training programs and tools to facilitate the development of high-performing, innovative cities.[18] This leads us to a discussion about how financial professionals can apply their professional skill set and experience toward social purposes.

Contributing Expertise and Time

In the course of a career in finance, a practitioner is well positioned to acquire an adaptable skill set that can be put to use for the public good. It may comprise broad-based analytical, communication, and managerial skills, as well as more specialized skills, such as developing financial projections, identifying the most effective financing structure for a project, or assessing the impact of changes in macro-economic variables.

There is a long tradition of financiers who have put these skills to use by serving government. In the US government, they have converged in departments linked to foreign affairs or the financial system and the economy. Some of these positions require a skill set that few would possess outside of certain types of finance professionals. Richard Berner, the former co-head of Global Economics and chief US Economist at Morgan Stanley, illustrates the potential for a seamless shift when the content of private and public roles overlaps. From 2013 to 2017, he managed the Office of Financial Research (OFR), which was established by the Dodd-Frank Act to promote financial stability. The chief mission of the office is to develop more robust data standards and to conduct analysis to identify threats to financial stability, a close cousin to the type of activity he pursued for twelve years at Morgan Stanley, where he directed forecasting and analysis of the US economy and financial markets. Cynics might argue that the very fact that most banks were caught like the proverbial deer in the headlights during the

Global Financial Crisis would make someone like Berner ill-suited to identify financial threats on behalf of the government. But the very experience of having been in the trenches during the crisis may be an asset in itself, in addition to the eminently transferable skill set a seasoned financial analyst like Berner would bring to his role in government (and it turns out that Berner was the first leading Wall Street economist to call the recession in 2007, a fact that likely facilitated his appointment to the role).[19]

Most public-good-oriented positions taken up by former finance professionals require greater adaptation than was the case in Berner's example. They often draw as much, if not more, on managerial skills than specialized content.

The Public Servant Investment Banker: Robert Lovett

Robert Lovett stands out as an exemplar in the first half of the twentieth century. Born into privilege as the son of the general counsel of the Union Pacific Railroad, Lovett embodied the discreet, purposeful generation of American public servants who considered government service the noblest of callings.

He was one of the "Wise Men," a term popularized by writers Walter Isaacson and Evan Thomas to describe a group of US policy makers who helped build the post-World War II order.[20] Their pragmatic, non-partisan agenda was internationalist in nature, seeking to project American power across the globe in order to shape an international liberal framework. They were mostly members of the East Coast establishment, imbued with the sense of *noblesse oblige* which compelled members of the elite class to devote a substantial portion of their time and resources to the public good. They were educated at British-inspired boarding schools in New England and Ivy League colleges, developing lifelong friendships that often blossomed into close partnerships in later life.

Several established their credentials on Wall Street before entering government. This was a well-worn path. Members of Lovett's generation looked up to men like Henry Stimson, a Wall Street lawyer who served twice as Secretary of War and once as Secretary of State between 1911 and 1945. In turn, Stimson looked up to Elihu Root, the leading light among the original internationalists, who alternated between his Wall Street law practice and policy making, most notably as William McKinley's Secretary of War and Theodore Roosevelt's Secretary of State.[21]

A strong sense of service permeated Robert Lovett's life. As a college student in 1915, Lovett formed the Yale Flying Unit with a dozen of his undergraduate friends to join the fight in Europe. As one member of the group quipped, they did it "for God, for country, and for Yale," as the ending phrase of Yale's alma mater goes.[22] A quick study with a charming, patrician demeanor, Lovett became the group's de facto leader. The unit entered active duty in 1917 as part of Britain's Royal Naval Air Service. Distinguishing himself in service, Lovett became the acting wing commander of the Northern Bombing Group and earned a Navy Cross.

At the end of the war, after a short stint at Harvard Law School, he joined his many Yale classmates on Wall Street, pursuing a successful financial career for almost two decades before entering government. He joined his wife's family's bank, Brown Brothers, in 1921, working his way up from running messages. A stint in London and New York at Brown Shipley & Company, a Liverpool-based merchant bank, opened his eyes to international trade finance, an important theme throughout his professional life in finance. Once he became a partner of Brown Brothers, Lovett and Averell Harriman, a close childhood and Yale friend who was also a prominent member of the mythologized group of "Wise Men," decided to merge the century-old Brown family banking house with the more aggressive Harriman family's banking firms, forming Brown Brothers Harriman.[23] Over the next ten years, Lovett, Harriman, and their partners turned their firm into a banking powerhouse, dominating trade finance.

On the last of his European tours on behalf of the bank in May 1940, Lovett came to the conclusion that the United States was completely ill-prepared for the cataclysm that was about to unfold in Europe. Having stayed in touch with Yale Flying Unit colleagues who had gone on to senior positions in the United States War Department in the 1920s, it became clear to him that US military capability would be dwarfed by Germany's re-armament effort.[24] He resolved to do what he could to help prepare his country, joining the government as Assistant Secretary of War for Air in December 1940 at age 45. He deeply impressed General George C. Marshall, who took him on as his Under Secretary, first at the State Department and then at the Department of Defense.

A skilled administrator with a strong vision, he is credited for having overseen the massive expansion of the air force during World War II and, later, as Secretary of Defense, for having managed the country's partial remobilization and re-armament during the Korean War.[25] True to his investment banking background, he managed with great attention to detail, constantly requesting facts and numbers to form his opinions.[26] His experience in banking had also instilled in him a resourcefulness and can-do attitude that was in short supply in Washington.[27] While he was intellectually sharp and demanding, his warmth and humor endeared him to others. His facility with developing relationships proved to be an asset, both on Wall Street and in government. He was also highly pragmatic, as attested by the fact that he was a Republican who served under two Democratic presidents.

Such was his aura after he rejoined Wall Street that the young President-elect John F. Kennedy offered him his choice of position as Secretary of State, Secretary of Defense, or Secretary of Treasury. Ever self-effacing, he declined, invoking his health, while steering Kennedy toward alternatives.[28]

Although these men's ability to seamlessly shuttle between Wall Street and government brought great talent to policy making, their ongoing business affiliations and ownership could create what a modern eye would clearly consider to be conflicts of interests. Harriman, who became a central figure in US government policy toward the Soviet Union, kept his business interests, including Soviet securities, throughout his government service.[29] Lovett took a more disciplined approach. He resigned from his Brown Brothers Harriman partnership as he entered government in 1940. When he was called in 1947 by President Truman to return to Washington after he had been back as a partner at Brown Brothers Harriman for little more than one year, he accepted on the spot, despite the complexities of disentangling himself once again from his business interest at the firm – not a straightforward process in an unlimited liability bank owned by a co-partnership.[30] He quickly sold his interests in the thousands of companies that had any dealings with the US military.

"Government Sachs"

While most prestigious banks are reliable sources of policy-making talent, Brown Brothers Harriman stood out in the middle of the twentieth century for producing high-profile public servants, including Robert Lovett, Averell Harriman, and Prescott Bush, who went on from the partnership to represent Connecticut in the US Senate. In recent years, Goldman Sachs appears to have become the leading private sector source of talent for high-level positions in the US government. This is not an entirely new development for the bank. Sidney Weinberg, Goldman Sachs' long-standing senior partner starting in the 1930s, became President Roosevelt's Assistant Director of the War Production Board during World War II. He had been one of the few on Wall Street to support FDR in the 1932 election.

High-profile appointments have been common since then. Robert Rubin's tenure as Secretary of Treasury under President Clinton contributed to the perspective that Goldman Sachs was a reliable source of able, technocratic public servants, even if he was criticized in hindsight for his pushback on the regulation of derivatives. But it is during the George W. Bush administration that the number of senior positions filled by Goldman bankers became so large as to elicit the "government Sachs" moniker.[31] President Bush appointed former senior partner Stephen Friedman as a top economic advisor, former London employee Joshua Bolten as his Chief of Staff, and former senior partner Hank Paulson as his Treasury Secretary. In turn, Paulson brought into Treasury Vice Chairman Robert Steel as Undersecretary of Treasury and investment banker Neel Kashkari as Assistant Secretary.

The reach of the bank has been broad, going beyond the White House and the Treasury Department. Under the Obama administration, former partner William Dudley became the President of the Federal Reserve Bank of New York, while former partner Gary Gensler chaired the Commodity Futures Trading Commission. This isn't solely a US phenomenon, as reflected by Mario Draghi's tenure as President of the European Central Bank. Even Donald Trump, who had railed against Goldman Sachs during his presidential campaign, took on a noticeably large group of former Goldman bankers to fill top positions in his administration: former partner Steve Mnuchin to head Treasury, former COO Gary Cohn as Director of the National Economic Council, and former investment banker Steve Bannon as White House Chief Strategist.

"Government Sachs" triggers the concern that the government becomes captured by the special interests of financial professionals, materializing in the form of deregulation of the financial industry and lighter overall scrutiny. A related concern is the revolving door: the pattern of a professional moving from an industry to a government agency overseeing that industry and then back again into that industry, cashing in on the ability to sway government policy by representing the industry's interests. It has proven extremely difficult to stamp out, as the lure of monetizing insights and networks developed in government can prove too strong. President Obama had vowed in his presidential campaign to get rid of the revolving door, but gained only limited traction.[32]

Another personal incentive to move into government may lie in the tax break offered to US executive branch appointees who are required by ethics laws to sell certain assets. For some, this can represent a once-in-a-lifetime opportunity to sell assets either tax-free or with a tax deferral. Upon being nominated as George W. Bush's Treasury Secretary, Hank Paulson sold about half a billion dollars' worth of Goldman Sachs stock, avoiding an estimated $200 million in taxes.[33] The issue gained prominence again when several billionaires and mega-millionaires were appointed by Donald Trump.

Still, it is reasonable to assume that most finance professionals shift to public service out of genuine desire to help society. While there may be a natural interest in burnishing one's legacy and, for a few, some financial incentives, the trade-offs are stark. Those include an often steep drop in compensation, the opportunity cost of not pursuing new business opportunities, and, for high-profile roles, a loss of privacy that can have a harrowing effect on one's entire family in this age of hyper-partisanship.

Goldman Sachs has always put some emphasis on its employees contributing to society outside of the narrow definition of their professional responsibility, typically by being generous givers to philanthropic causes and by volunteering.[34] Among the many Goldman Sachs alumni who have contributed their time and resources to government or not-for-profit organizations, John Whitehead stands out. Even in the rarefied world of former leaders of prestigious investment banks, the sum total of leadership positions he accumulated over his lifetime is startling – US Deputy of State under President Reagan, Chairman of the Board of the Federal Reserve Bank of New York, Chairman of the Board of the UN Association, Chairman of the Andrew W. Mellon Foundation, the Harvard Board of Overseers, and the Brookings Institutions, and finally, Chairman of the Lower Manhattan Development Corporation in charge of rebuilding the site destroyed during 9/11.

Yet, he remained humble about his contributions. When he discussed issues of ethics and lessons learned from his life with my Princeton first-year undergraduates, he did not mention his most inspiring act of leadership, having landed a Higgins boat at Omaha Beach twice in the first wave on D-Day as a 22-year-old US Navy ensign. This was consistent with his preference for quiet leadership.

The Trailblazer Enablers: Michaela Walsh and Erin Godard

Michaela Walsh has never shied away from challenging norms. Working for Merrill Lynch in New York in the late 1950s, she sought a transfer to Beirut after hearing that some colleagues were planning to open an office there. The personnel department demurred, invoking the risk of sending a woman. Walsh proceeded to resign from Merrill Lynch USA, pay her way to Lebanon, and get hired by Merrill Lynch's Beirut office – all of this at age 26.[35] Her four years in the office were some of the most exciting of her professional career and personal life. It opened her world to new ways of thinking and sparked her propensity to question accepted ways of doing things. More than a decade later, her drive and take-charge attitude were critical in enabling the establishment of Women's World Banking (WWB), an innovative banking network mandated to provide credit services to entrepreneurial women for local businesses.

A self-described "trouble-maker" raised in Kansas City, Walsh was imbued at a young age with a strong yearning for social justice and a desire to travel that was at odds with the typical role of women in post-war Midwest America. She was particularly influenced by the work of her grandfather, Frank Walsh, who co-wrote a congressional proposal for the child-labor law and advocated all of his life in favor of living wages.[36] She admits to having always felt like the black sheep in her family and believes in hindsight that she had a learning disability, perhaps dyslexia.[37] She decided to join Wall Street because "women had to go where the money is, to get the power," starting as a sales assistant in her local Merrill Lynch branch office while attending night school.[38] Her drive and willingness to speak up made her valuable to the bank. During her tenure in Merrill Lynch's New York, Beirut, and London offices, she took on managerial roles, at a time when women working in investment banks were typically channeled toward executive assistant roles. She eventually became the first woman partner at

Boettcher & Company, a Wall Street sales and trading firm. Many of the existing partners were furious at her promotion, likely because of her gender.[39]

But her years as a private sector finance professional didn't fully satisfy her, despite her rise through the ranks. She became increasingly uncomfortable with the chasm between her day job on Wall Street and her strong convictions regarding social justice. Walsh developed a fascination for how finance could help improve people's lives. In 1972, she joined the Rockefeller Brothers Fund, a leading philanthropic foundation, where she was tasked to identify technology projects that could contribute to economic development.

A turning point in her life took place when she was sent to attend the First United Nations Conference on the Status of Women in Mexico City in 1975. Reflecting a rising global interest in understanding the magnitude and impact of gender discrimination, the conference laid out how women around the world were routinely excluded from the formal economy. Analysis by a Danish economist named Ester Boserup showed that women performed over 65% of the world's work but earned only 10% of the income and owned less than 1% of global property.[40] Women were often denied the ability to open bank accounts and rarely could gain access to working capital on their own. At the conference, she met social activists at the forefront of the emerging movement to address these issues – among them, Ela Bhatt, the founder of the Self-Employed Women's Association (SEWA), and Margaret Snyder, who later became the founding director of the United Nations Development Fund for Women.[41] For Walsh, the conference was "a game-changer for my life, a complete paradigm shift."[42] Among the women attending the conference, she had a distinctive perspective, being one of the few who had a background in finance.[43] The solution, in her mind, was to provide women access to credit. An internationally diverse group of attendees committed to collaborate on the creation of a movement for the financial inclusion of women in the global economy. From 1975 to 1980, Walsh chaired the committee to organize WWB and eventually led the organization during its first decade (she has since remained active on its board).

In addition to being a pioneer of micro-credit, WWB innovated in its emphasis on women-owned credit institutions, at a time when women were typically not allowed to have a bank account without a man's signature. Ultimately, its goal was to help low-income women set

up their own business by providing them credit and business development services – and perhaps more simply, to help embed women in the
formal economy. Early on, Walsh and her colleagues decided that it
would be most effective to work within the system – for example, by
acting as a guarantor to banks that considered their women entrepreneurs too risky.[44] WWB was structured to operate via local affiliates,
ranging from banks and for-profit lenders to not-for-profit organizations. The decentralized nature of the network reflects Walsh's deeply
ingrained belief from having worked overseas that it was critical to
avoid the pitfalls of imposing New York-based decisions across countries and cultures.

In order to link up to the WWB network, women founders of
local affiliates had to set up their own legal structures in their country
and seed them with at least $20,000, to ensure that they had full
agency.[45] To this day, the affiliates have to take ownership of their
activities and secure WWB's backing. As of 2018, WWB had 30 million
clients around the world, via a global network of fifty-three financial
institutions from thirty-two countries, committed to providing low-
income women access to financial tools and resources. Its mission
remains as critical as ever, with an estimated one billion women – more
than 40% of women around the world, without access to financial
services.[46]

In contrast to Walsh, whose decades of service have left an
enduring institutional legacy with Women's World Banking, Erin
Godard is at the very beginning of her career. While the social enterprise
she helped create in Rwanda is still at an early development stage,
Godard illustrates how a young, enterprising finance professional can
utilize her skills very concretely toward social impact.

We noted earlier in the book that the development of financial
institutions and associated skills in developing economies tends to have
a positive impact in various ways, such as boosting entrepreneurship
and spurring growth. Godard, a young accountant from Toronto,
experienced first-hand how the lack of financial skills can act as an
obstacle to development. In the summer of 2016, she took advantage of
her employer Ernst & Young's sabbatical program, volunteering for
two months in Rwanda to provide consulting services to a not-for-profit
in need of financial management guidance.[47] After five years working as
a public accountant in Canada, she was eager to apply her professional
skills toward social impact. Ever since she was young, her aspiration

had been to leave a positive mark on the world and she had thus far expressed that drive by being involved in multiple not-for-profit organizations in Toronto.[48]

During that summer in Rwanda, she found that her accounting skill set could translate into significant and lasting improvements in local organizations. An organization without proper financial controls and management can quickly founder. In a developing economy such as Rwanda, many firms and not-for-profits find themselves mismanaged because of the pervasive lack of financial training and experience. Godard spent two months volunteering at Gardens for Health International, which teaches families how to use agriculture to combat malnutrition, a widespread issue among Rwandan children. It provides guidance to caregivers, typically mothers, on creating gardens that can feed families nutritiously. After conducting an expense audit and analyzing its control systems, Godard revamped the organization's internal processes and systems while building its team's capacity to manage its finance and accounting function. The country head for the organization gushed about Godard's impact:

> [She] saved us time, and created better feedback systems within the
> organization . . . If you don't have good accounting systems in
> place, nothing really works that well. If you don't have the ability
> to account for your funds, it affects everyone from the person
> implementing up to [the] donor, who isn't able to understand how
> funds are being used.[49]

Godard found that the gap in Rwanda between the need for Certified Public Accountants (CPAs) and their availability is overwhelming. There are only about 400 CPAs in the country, for a population of twelve million. This compares to 185,000 CPAs in Canada for a population that is approximately two-thirds larger.[50] By the end of her summer, Godard was inundated by requests for support from various organizations which had heard of her services. She decided to go all-in: In the spring of 2017, she left her position at Ernst & Young to move to Kigali, Rwanda. After another Ernst & Young alumnus, Pascal Ambrosino, joined her, the two founded FinanceYOU, an organization dedicated to addressing the country's massive accounting and finance skills gap. As accountants, they wanted to differentiate themselves from the mass of struggling not-for-profits by structuring FinanceYOU as a for-profit social enterprise whose aspiration was to be self-sustaining.[51]

After a few months on the ground, it became clear that their greatest potential impact would come from training new university graduates, having observed that the pervasive lack of basic business and finance skills was preventing young graduates from getting employed, as most organizations lacked the ability to train them. This led to the creation of the African Accounting Academy, which they piloted in July 2018. The classroom module was followed by an internship placement and a mentor pairing. After the pilot's resounding success, they expanded the program into an e-learning format that allows them to reach a much broader audience by increasing its flexibility and lowering its cost to the students, who have to pay the tuition out-of-pocket. For $40, Godard and Ambrosino provide 100 hours of training in accounting fundamentals and business readiness, which can make a young graduate job-ready. Since the program's February 2019 launch, they have trained over 400 students from Rwanda, Kenya, Uganda, Ghana, and Tanzania and have placed 40 into full-time accounting and finance positions.[52]

The aim of the program is to prepare participants, many of whom don't have a university degree, for an entry-level accounting or finance job. The long-term goal for the top graduates of the program is to become qualified CPAs. In turn, they will be able to train others, spurring a virtuous cycle. With their organization, Godard and Ambrosino are not only helping build more effective finance functions in Rwandan organizations but also contributing in a small but tangible way to the development of Rwanda's middle class by making it possible for young men and women to become accountants.

The Corporate Governance Agitators: Nicholas Benes and David Webb

Professions that attract mission-driven individuals whose objective is primarily to serve society – think of public school teachers, nurses, and NGO employees, to name a few – tend to be associated with low levels of compensation. For those who have had experience as finance professionals, the trade-offs of pursuing that path can be both greater and smaller: Greater because the opportunity cost can be more significant when considering the financial compensation they would forgo; smaller because a successful finance professional may have earned enough money to lead a comfortable life without worrying about the next paycheck, opening up career choices which may be more difficult to pursue without the safety net provided by substantial savings. In previous chapters, we have encountered examples of those in finance who resisted the temptation to continuously pursue greater wealth because they are driven by a higher calling. David Swensen has stuck with the Yale University endowment for decades despite having the opportunity to move to a large hedge fund and make multiples of what he makes today (which, to be fair, already constitutes rich compensation by any measure). John Bogle founded Vanguard as a cooperative, forgoing any equity ownership in the asset management firm he successfully built over decades, in order to reduce further the cost of intermediation to his customers.

A few finance professionals have moved on from the traditional money-making path in order to contribute to better market dynamics. Nicholas (Nick) Benes stands out for his commitment to building a more productive corporate sector in Japan. As a freshman at Stanford University, he became fascinated by Japan's ability to catch up so quickly to Western nations from the ruins of World War II.[53] With a taste for adventure, he spent much of his undergraduate years studying at Japanese universities, before it became fashionable for Americans to obsess over Japan as an object of fear and admiration. A fighter by instinct, he quickly became fluent after having been told that foreigners can't learn Japanese. He and his Japanese wife established an English language school in Hokkaido, at a time when Japanese interest in learning English was much greater than it is today. After he had come back to earn a JD-MBA from UCLA, one of his academic mentors suggested he look into Morgan Guaranty (now JP Morgan) in Tokyo, being impressed by the quality of Japanese talent the bank had attracted. Benes joined the firm, spending the next eleven years working in investment banking, followed by a stint heading his own middle-market M&A advisory firm. By that point, he had become a Japan lifer, raising bicultural children.

Japan is a challenging country for expatriates. Many Japanese executives don't speak English and cultural norms in the corporate sector defy logic for many executives trained in a Western country. Well-networked foreigners like Benes who can master the nuances of life in Japan possess a tremendous edge. They can deftly navigate the corporate culture, engage with colleagues and customers the way a Japanese professional would, yet be exempted, up to a point, from abiding by the rigid hierarchy and unstated taboos that can stultify

Japanese corporate executives. They have more leeway to think outside of traditional Japanese norms. They can act as river guides to foreign newcomers who invariably feel like lost toddlers in the midst of Japan's assortment of unspoken rules. Even though this implies great commercial opportunities for a local finance expert, Benes has chosen an idiosyncratic path, devoting himself entirely at the prime of his career to improving corporate governance in Japan.

The corporate governance field tends to be populated by technocrats and academics. Corporate governance addresses the system of checks and balances that guide how a firm is controlled. Its objective is to balance the interests of a company's various stakeholders, including its shareholders, management, employees, customers, suppliers, bondholders, and other funders. The field sits at the confluence of economics, law, business ethics, and political economy – the latter because the way in which a corporate governance structure prioritizes the interests of one group of stakeholders relative to another has deep roots in the type of social contract to which a country adheres.

In the United States, corporate governance has tended to prioritize the interests of shareholders, as the owners of a business. In Japan, that relationship is skewed differently, as discussed in our chapter on social wealth creation. The long-term interests of employees have historically been valued above the interests of shareholders. As an overarching objective in the management of a company, the stability of employment generally takes precedence over performance considerations. While there is much to be admired about the Japanese corporate sector's strongly held values and its relative lack of focus on short-term material gains, the flip side of this philosophy has been a highly unproductive corporate sector. Managers are ensconced in their roles, protected by a web of structural defense mechanisms that historically have prevented minority shareholders from gaining control of a company and thus from exerting any kind of meaningful pressure.

From the mid 1990s onward, Benes started increasingly engaging in public advocacy, publishing some forty op-eds in the *Wall Street Journal Asia* on Japanese governance-related issues. He kept at it despite many false starts. A 2001 piece he wrote heralded the upcoming shareholder revolution in Japan, but no consequential initiative materialized in the following years, despite some hints of change during the Koizumi era in the mid 2000s. Frustrated by the lack of progress, Benes carved for himself an unlikely role in the reform development process, channeling critical, behind-the-scenes input into their eventual design and implementation. For many years, he led the FDI Committee of the American Chamber of Commerce in Japan (ACCJ), which produced more than twenty-five detailed policy memos related to governance improvement and economic reforms to promote investment. In 2010, as a Governor of the ACCJ, he led a growth strategy taskforce white paper project that provided, along with other sources, many of the intellectual foundations underpinning the Abe administration's "Third Arrow," the set of restructuring initiatives whose aim is to boost productivity in the economy and jolt it out of its two-decade-long torpor.[54]

Of particular significance, Benes advocated on behalf of corporate governance reforms as a critical component of any sustainable program to boost productivity. After consulting with the Deputy Governor of the Bank of Japan, he sought out Yasuhisa Shiozaki, a senior member of the Diet who was a close ally to LDP (Japan's ruling party) leader Shinzo Abe, to make specific proposals at an auspicious time, when Abe had just retaken the reins of government on an ambitious economic transformation platform.[55]

In the Harvard-trained Shiozaki, Benes found a sharp mind who was willing to not only engage on the issues, but take quick action as well. At that stage, a stewardship code, to prod domestic asset managers to hold their portfolio companies more accountable, was already in the works. Benes endeavored to convince Shiozaki of the necessity of creating in parallel a corporate governance code, to instill in the senior managers of listed companies a greater shareholder orientation (both codes are discussed earlier in this book). He also advocated on behalf of having the FSA, the finance industry regulatory agency, lead the effort rather than the Ministry of Economy, Trade, and Industry (METI), given its explicit mandate to protect investors and promote market efficiency and its lower propensity to have its work influenced by Japan, Inc. – the established companies which were generally cool to the idea of corporate governance reforms. He was eventually invited by the LDP to formally make his proposals to a committee of its growth strategy council.

Both legs of the reforms were adopted as part of Abe's restructuring reforms.[56] They built on the efforts of many other governance advocates who, over the years, were willing to go against vested interests propping up the status quo, a Herculean task in the context of Japanese culture. But Benes was a particularly significant contributor, even if not all of his recommendations were ultimately taken up – for instance, the promotion of fully independent board committees.[57] Since their launch, the codes have gained traction, spurring noticeable changes in corporate behavior and significant foreign investor enthusiasm. Other reforms he suggested were adopted later, such as disclosures about former CEOs who serve as advisors post-retirement.

As one of the architects of these reforms, Benes was perfectly positioned to benefit from them financially if he so chose, especially given the slew of hedge funds entering the market to engage in strategies motivated by these reforms. Combined with his experience sitting on multiple Japanese corporate boards, a still relatively rare occurrence for a foreigner, he has a depth of expertise that is hard to match. Yet he has chosen to immerse himself in leading the non-profit organization he created in 2009, the Board Director Training Institute (BDTI), which is dedicated to training board members in Japan to be more effective. Pugnacious to a fault, he pushed back four times against official suggestions to give up in the arduous process of certifying BDTI as a "public interest" non-profit, finally securing the designation in 2011. To support the organization, he spent four years working for no salary and donated a substantial amount of his savings.[58] He has had to discipline himself to live on significantly less money than he did when he worked in the private sector. That has implied almost never eating out, few vacations, and limited spending on himself and his family.

And it's hard to argue that he does it for the glory. Japan has a history of explicitly seeking out foreign knowledge for its own improvement, most famously during the Meiji restoration era, when missions were sent to learn from Western institutions. Consistent with that pattern, the Corporate Governance Code draws heavily from the United Kingdom's own corporate governance code and its reliance on a "comply or explain" mechanism rather than hard company law. But Benes' contribution to the reforms' design and his input into the bureaucratic syndication process are largely unheralded, while BDTI gets no support from the government and little mention in the media.

Over time, the corporate governance reforms are likely to be seen as one of the Abe administration's most tangible legacies. So far, the narrative in the media has emphasized the roles of Professor Kunio Ito and those of several other high-profile establishment figures, including Shiozaki, who went on to become the Minister of Health, Labor and Welfare; Motoyuki Yufu, the FSA manager directly in charge of the

Code's drafting; Nobu Mori, the thoughtful and uncompromising driver of financial services reforms as the head of the FSA; and Takeshi Niinami, the CEO of beverage giant Suntory, who was the first public proponent of a Stewardship Code as a member of a CEO advisory group for Abe. Benes was not invited to join the Councils of Experts convened to finalize the Stewardship and Corporate Governance Codes, despite his active involvement in initial phases of development.[59]

While his own role remains overlooked, Benes derives much satisfaction from the corporate governance reforms' progress. Ditto with the main ideas behind Abe's Third Arrow – Professor Kyoji Fukao won the most prestigious economics book prize in Japan for the work he did on behalf of Benes' growth strategy task force, but scant reference can be found to the white paper written by Benes and his team. If anything, he is piqued by the cavalier treatment of the investment professionals and other financial types who benefit from his work but look at him askew for his choice to pursue this cause on a full-time basis.[60]

Benes has become an indefatigable proselytizer, repeatedly advocating for further corporate governance adoption by laggard Japanese companies and for additional actions by the government. He frequently conjures up new ways to move the process forward – whether by creating a unique disclosure search engine for Japanese listed companies made freely available to all, getting the government to prod corporate pension funds to join the Stewardship Code, or writing op-eds to provide a status update on the reforms and introduce new ideas. It isn't a stretch to posit that few other M&A or legal specialists would do so without finding at least some angle to generate a comfortable revenue stream and ensure an adequate retirement. He lives in a modest house deep in the suburbs of Tokyo and is content channeling all of his energy toward helping the Japanese economy become more dynamic.

Like Benes, David Webb is a principled activist who has had outsized impact in his market, Hong Kong. A former investment banker who moved from London to Hong Kong in 1991, he has been for more than two decades a thorn in the side of Hong Kong insiders caught abusing their power or shirking their responsibilities, whether local tycoons, corporate managers, or government officials. After leaving the corporate world in 1998 to concentrate on investing his own capital in small-cap companies, he found himself increasingly publishing opinion pieces advocating for improvements in corporate governance.

In 1998, he created webb-site.com, to post his op-eds. Over the years, his website has grown into a highly potent online platform calling out breaches of corporate and economic governance in Hong Kong, with a particular focus on minority shareholder rights.

His content is freely available to all, with an emphasis on unbiased analysis and unfiltered information via links to source materials. Transparency and the promotion of free markets and democratic principles anchor his crusades. His targets are government cronyism, favoritism, protectionism, anti-competitive behavior and breaches of minority shareholder rights by corporations, and any limitations imposed on the freedom of speech and the democratic process.[61] Out of intellectual honesty, he has never taken down any of his postings over the past two decades.[62]

Webb constructs his cases in details that are often excruciating for the perpetrators, whose misdeeds are laid bare. During a stint as a junior analyst covering Hong Kong stocks, I had a humbling experience crossing paths with Webb. One of the companies whose prospects I found most attractive, a manufacturer of luxury goods named Egana-Goldpfeil, had struck a deal with Geneva-based luxury conglomerate Richemont to manufacture goods on behalf of several of Richemont's brands. Confident in my ability to thoroughly evaluate the company based on "deep" due diligence that included numerous meetings with its CFO, I was comforted by the dramatic rise in Egana's share price as earnings grew robustly and the Richemont deal was announced. I was stunned when one morning in July 2007, Webb posted on his governance site a detailed take-down of Egana.[63] Webb had conducted truly deep due diligence, highlighting red flags that no institutional investors should have missed. The list of suspicious facts I had overlooked was embarrassingly long, including a cozy relationship with an investment bank that turned out to have been a cauldron of fraudulent companies brought to the Hong Kong market over the years, a web of cross-shareholdings that turned out to be related-party transactions (often in completely unrelated businesses), unexplained long-term receivables on the balance sheet, questionable promissory notes that were treated as cash, a dubious acquisition of a distributor in exchange for cancelling accounts receivable, and multiple changes in auditing firms in recent years, including one three days before the end of the fiscal year.

In a hastily arranged call with investors, Egana's management tried to explain itself. Management's contorted answers to Webb's detailed, fact-based allegations further impaired Egana's credibility. Its claim that an investment in the Tonga Group, which had a forestry business in Suriname and a B2B building materials platform, was made for the purpose of supplying wood and building materials to the Beijing Olympic Village left investors unimpressed given that the initial investment was made prior to China winning the Olympic bid (not to mention the fact that Egana's core business of luxury goods was hardly synergistic with a timber business).[64]

Webb's report invited closer scrutiny via a special audit, which revealed that Egana's enterprising CFO had created fake accounts registered in Macau to boost the firm's revenues with non-existent wholesale contracts. The company's shares, which were suspended in the wake of Webb's allegations, never traded again.

Consistent with many of his campaigns targeting egregious breaches in corporate governance, Webb's report read like a mystery novel. After setting some context, Webb invited the reader to "put a big pot of coffee on," before embarking on his narrative, methodically building his case by revealing clues and linking misdeeds. The strength of Webb's reports lies in their analytical rigor, derived from his investment banking experience and investigative flair. Webb fills a gap in the market as few are incentivized to call out corporate misdeeds. Investment banks tend to be conflicted. They either already cover a stock that turns out to be a fraud, in which case they might quietly end coverage before a bombshell surfaces, or they don't cover it, in which case they would stay away from it since they are in the business of drumming up trading activity (and many Hong Kong-listed small and mid-caps are off the exchange's "approved" list of shortable stocks, while being typically difficult to short due to the lack of availability of stock to borrow).

The quality of Webb's research has made him a respected authority to which the Hong Kong market pays attention. In May 2017, he published a report highlighting the vulnerability of a group of fifty Hong Kong-listed small caps, which he dubbed the "Enigma Network" due to their intricate web of cross-shareholdings.[65] It took him years to precisely link these cross-shareholdings via painstaking review of hundreds of filings.[66] Six weeks after the report was published, many of the shares he had highlighted collapsed, some as much as 90%. In the wake of this rout, Webb lambasted the regulatory authorities for letting these types of issues fester, advocating for moving the Hong Kong Exchange's regulatory function to the Securities and

Futures Commission (SFC) by highlighting the inherent conflict of interest of having a for-profit corporation with regulatory authority. Since Webb's report and these stocks' collapse, Hong Kong authorities have conducted the largest financial raid ever, searching multiple premises linked to these companies, and made several arrests of senior corporate officers.

Unsurprisingly, Webb's uncompromising stance has earned him his share of enemies in Hong Kong. Not one to shy away from confrontation, he has taken on some of Hong Kong's biggest tycoons. In a memorable showdown, he excoriated Richard Li, the chairman of Hong Kong's largest telecom company and a son of Li Ka-shing, the dean of Hong Kong tycoons. In 2009, Webb led a one-person vendetta against Li's attempt to take private PCCW, his telecom company. Webb made a complaint to the Hong Kong regulators, publicizing the fact that he had found suspiciously registered new shares prior to the vote to approve the privatization.[67] The deal foundered following a court decision. This was not the first time Webb had taken on Li, having railed in 1999 against the uncompetitive awarding to Li of the right to develop Cyberport, a new IT hub on the island.

On multiple occasions, Webb's nagging criticism has been highly effective in triggering change. In 2003, he launched a campaign to have companies release a vote count at shareholder meetings under the premise of "one share, one vote," rather than "one person, one vote." He adopted a hands-on approach, purchasing ten shares in each of the Hang Seng Index constituent companies and splitting them into five registered names to force each company to adopt poll voting (one person, one vote) by representing enough holders to make a formal demand. After six years of campaign, the change was made mandatory across Hong Kong-listed companies.[68]

Webb has aggressively used the media to put pressure on his targets. Some have found his frequent media presence grating. But he seems to care little about how he might be perceived. Having successfully run for election and re-election to the board of the Hong Kong stock exchange's listed parent, Webb resigned, venting his frustration with the company's governance issues and the slow progress of reforms in a published letter. He believes that in this case he can be most effective as a gadfly commenting from the sidelines.

Taking on abuses by Hong Kong's public authorities has always been a critical piece of Webb's advocacy. Webb has shown no sign of reducing the intensity of his campaigns under Xi Jinping's tightened grip over Hong Kong. Many Hong Kong-based critics have paid a heavy price under the new austerity. As a permanent Hong Kong citizen of British nationality, Webb may feel no more at risk than in the past, although hardly invulnerable, as illustrated by the de facto expulsion in October 2018 of Victor Mallet, a *Financial Times* editor who had hosted an independence activist at an event at Hong Kong's Foreign Correspondent Club.

Webb pursues his governance campaigns in parallel to investing his own money in "undervalued but well governed" companies.[69] He attempts to mitigate conflicts of interest by disclosing the fact that he might own long or short positions in companies he writes about. As an investor, he has performed spectacularly well. He stated having generated about 20% annual returns on his personal portfolio since 1995, building up a fortune of at least $170 million, according to Bloomberg estimates.[70] He ascribes his success to his ability to weed out badly governed companies by going into the details of almost all of a company's regulatory filings, which he does most days in his Hong Kong home office until 2 a.m.[71] For ten years, he published a Christmas stock pick, a recommendation to purchase the stock of a well-run small-cap company, which, as he consistently disclosed, he owned in his portfolio. After drawing some criticism for benefiting from his annual stock recommendation – his picks returned a cumulative 1118% over a ten-year period – he decided to end the practice because it had become too much of a distraction from his main mission of improving economic and corporate governance in Hong Kong.[72]

He divides his time equally between his own investments and his governance activism, expecting no returns from the latter, since he largely highlights governance problems but has never shorted any of the vulnerable stocks he has exposed, even if he reserves the right to do so.[73] As for his motivation, he stated that "I don't want to reach the end of my life and say, 'I was a really good investor, that was fun, but I didn't advance the human condition'."[74]

As illustrated by the individual stories in this chapter, finance professionals are particularly well positioned to contribute to society outside of their customer mandates. Those who have generated wealth can engage in philanthropic activities thoughtfully, as many do. More broadly, the versatility of their skill set can be applied to serve society in many different ways, by serving in public institutions and not-for-profit organizations, or by creating new businesses which target positive social impact.

CONCLUSION

A recurring concern for my first-year undergraduate students contemplating a career in finance is that they will turn into hypocrites: spend several years in college being exhorted to act in the service of humanity, perhaps studying great thinkers, absorbing humanistic values, and devising solutions for a better society, and, as soon as they leave their idealized intellectual community, become cogs in a gigantic machine optimized to generate short-term profits.

For those lucky enough to attend a prestigious university, the window during which they can concentrate on their studies – and ponder humanity's great challenges – has diminished. In a number of top US colleges, investment banks have started recruiting during a student's first undergraduate year. To be sure, this is a first-world problem. In fact, even in the United States and most advanced economies, such concerns are only relevant for those at the top of the pyramid, who will end up populating commercial and investment banks, alternative asset funds, and other financial institutions.

In the preceding pages, we delineated how career paths in these traditional, profit-seeking areas of finance can be informed by humanistic values. We considered a simple framework to evaluate what a virtuous path in finance might look like, inspired by the Aristotelian tradition and its emphasis on moral character, practical wisdom adapted to context, and moderation, as well as by Adam Smith's understanding of human beings as inherently motivated by a combination of self-interest and interest in the welfare of others.

The framework projects simple messages: Serve your customers faithfully. Do not extract value from others. Treat colleagues with dignity. And, as much as possible, apply your finance skills and resources toward the collective interest. This approach embraces certain virtues, in particular that of self-restraint. Jack Bogle – as close to a wise man as the industry will ever have – perhaps said it best by titling one of his most thoughtful books *Enough*.[1] Among the scourges of modern times, he bemoaned the primacy of maximizing wealth, which increasingly trumps other considerations and places business objectives above professional values.

Recognizing that individual behavior is largely driven by incentives, which, in turn, are shaped by market forces and regulation, the framework's aspirations are modest: it seeks to influence the behavior of a subset of finance professionals operating within the industry's existing structure and context. It is unlikely to hold much sway with those who thrive by knowingly gaming others. Rather, it targets well-intentioned individuals who are self-interested, neither altruistic nor greedy, likely ambitious in achieving upward mobility, yet keen to succeed while upholding their values and contributing to society. For all the demonization of finance in popular culture, I suspect that this is a large group within the industry. Moreover, the sharp rise in interest in the use of finance as a tool to address social and economic problems, particularly among students and young professionals, suggests the potential for a generational shift in the approach to finance.

The framework challenges traditional concepts of success, understanding that many industry professionals will continue to enthusiastically play the game by its own rules and be motivated by conventional markers of success such as financial compensation and promotion. It doesn't purport to offer a comprehensive solution to the finance industry's ills. But it aspires to nudge an important group away from self-serving ends toward serving clients and society more earnestly.

Greater awareness of ways in which the industry impacts society could also inform decisions made by institutions – for instance, by explicitly considering the impact of their activities on the collective interest, a national pension fund or a university endowment may decide to no longer allocate capital to certain investment strategies if they determine that those strategies generate excess returns by extracting value from the rest of society.

If individuals targeted by this book are well-intentioned to begin with, why is such a framework necessary? Because the industry, more often than not, is cloaked in complexity and opacity, skewed by information asymmetry, and rife with conflicts of interest, presenting unusually fertile grounds for cultivating cognitive biases. Finance professionals are so deeply embedded in a daily web of short-term objectives, high pressure, and engrossing incentives, that they can all too easily become oblivious to the practical implications of their actions: the casual boosting of hidden fees which surreptitiously shift value from the customer to the financial service provider, the nominal successes on behalf of clients which entail extracting value from other constituents, the asymmetric risk-taking which generates large private gains and negative social returns. While finance has been a critical enabler of prosperity across the world and much of the industry inherently serves society, the opportunities for finance professionals to self-serve remain pervasive. By responding to their financial incentives and echoing the conduct of their successful peers, well-meaning individuals can unwittingly slip into self-serving mode, even when paying heed to the rules of the game.

Is it unrealistic to suggest following guidelines that might clash with systematic short-term profit maximization? It is unlikely to boost anyone's career in the short term. Embracing deeply held values may be helpful in the long term, but that benefit remains speculative.

A theme of the book is that finance professionals have examples to emulate – individuals who are self-interested, ambitious, and successful and yet are able to express their humanistic values as finance professionals. The vast majority of those are anonymous and unheralded. They comprise professionals at all levels of the organization, who, for instance, diligently score credit to extend loans at the appropriate price, guide customers toward the saving instruments that are best suited to their profile and circumstances, oversee the operational minutiae of replicating market indices with virtually no tracking error, or identify the best product to insure a family's assets. By engaging in core financial services which support real economic activities with their clients' interest in mind, they help people achieve their goals and, in doing so, benefit society.

We delved into specific examples – individuals who merit our attention for having deviated from the path of least resistance, the one that would have maximized their own material wealth by simply going along with their peers. At times, they stand out less because of the bravura of their action – diligently penny-pinching expenses on behalf of customers or promoting diversity in the workplace may strike readers as pedestrian – than for the simple fact that so few people in the industry take that path. Being involved in the industry and familiar with the countless pressure points that lead finance professionals to conform, I have found myself inspired by their example.

There are those who exercised self-restraint – a deceptively simple goal made complicated by the fact that it typically entails lower profits in the short-term, often going against the grain of corporate priorities and colleagues' own financial goals. They left money on the table, in an industry where doing so is often perceived by peers as a sign of either incompetence or confused logic. In a reversal of industry practices, Andy Okun and his partner Stephen Modzelewski systematic-ally set up terms for their hedge fund that skew in favor of their clients, even when those terms are not particularly valued or even known by these clients. The Japanese "herbivores" are endeavoring to introduce a low-cost active asset management model to Japan and sway their peers. Highly successful endowment managers such as David Swensen and Andy Golden have stuck with their beloved academic institutions for decades, eschewing the call for greater pay elsewhere.

All of those individuals may have taken their cues from those in past generations who broke ranks during their time. John Whitehead determined that Goldman Sachs wouldn't engage in hostile take-overs at the time they took off, despite heavy demand from clients. Warren Hellman decided to retire from Hellman & Friedman, the firm he co-founded, without "cashing out," to motivate future partners by paying it forward.

Others created new models that simply served customers better, even if it meant lower profits. Jack Bogle revolutionized the asset management industry, slowly at first and then drastically, by introdu-cing index funds and tirelessly advocating on behalf of shifting savings into passive asset management.

Some migrated beyond the industry to apply their skills and resources toward the collective interest. We discussed a broad group of people, comprising statesmen such as Robert Lovett and entrepreneurs such as Michaela Walsh. Most encouragingly, we noted how young professionals can make a considerable difference at an early stage in their career: for instance, Erin Godard, who, at the age of 28 and with only five years of professional accounting experience, created an accounting training institute in Rwanda which can generate outsized social returns.

Finally, there are those who were willing to agitate, mostly on behalf of others, often at a personal cost. They went beyond the baseline expectation of my framework – to work in finance in a self-interested manner while upholding humanistic values and contributing to society. For these professionals, self-interest and collective interest meld, at least in the situations discussed. Nick Benes has long forgone personal wealth creation in order to help Japan move toward better corporate governance. David Webb has assumed the role of governance vigilante in all matters Hong Kong, to great effect. Natasha Lamb has led a relentless shareholder campaign in the United States pressuring large listed companies to abide by contemporary norms of diversity, showing remarkable traction.

Not all of these individuals were successful in balancing the collective good with their personal interest. Alayne Fleischmann's brave intervention at JP Morgan was made at enormous personal cost. She exemplifies the long list of whistleblowers who were willing to put their livelihoods and reputations at risk in order to call out egregious corporate misdeeds that were hurting customers.

Perhaps it is fitting to end this book with the example of the architect of the US financial system, Alexander Hamilton. Of the many virtues that Hamilton exhibited as a public servant, his ability to resist enriching himself is particularly striking in light of his role as the effective founder of the modern US financial system and his recurring struggle throughout his life to provide for his family. He differs from most examples in this book in that he was not trained as a financial professional. His life was devoted to public service, except for stints running a law practice in New York. While he lived in an era whose mores would be foreign to the contemporary professional, the tensions between the public mandate and the private interests of public servants – such as the temptation to benefit from graft, influence peddling, and the revolving door – remain perennial challenges, making this example timeless.

Arguably the most brilliant of the US Founding Fathers, Hamilton left a legacy whose range almost defies reason, against all odds. He distinguished himself first as an agitator in favor of US independence and as a valiant soldier and military leader whose charge at Yorktown contributed to the British defeat. After independence was achieved, he relentlessly advocated in favor of a constitutional convention and then helped promote the Constitution by drafting fifty-one of the eighty-five installments of the Federalist Papers. They are still regarded as the most authoritative source on the original intent of the US Constitution.

In the eyes of historians, his symbiotic partnership with George Washington through the War of Independence and Washington's presidency, his prowess as a military leader, and his critical impact as a constitutional theorist often overshadow the fact that he was the chief architect of the United States' modern financial system. As the nation's first Secretary of Treasury from 1789 to 1795, Hamilton revolutionized the country's financial system. A self-starter and autodidact, he studied financial history with a particular interest in how the Bank of England had managed its large national debt. Recognizing the potential power of sovereign debt, he founded the country's first central bank, restructured the national debt, established the US dollar as the national currency, and launched the Treasury debt market.[2]

Hamilton also understood the necessity for credit flowing to private enterprise and spurred the development of commercial banks. He did so by encouraging state governments to charter banks which would lend to private businesses and individuals. Between 1790 and 1795, the number of commercial banks grew from three local banks with limited connections to twenty, while new branches of the Bank of the United States were established in several cities.[3] He also actively supported the development of securities markets, leading private brokers to establish exchanges in Philadelphia and New York.

Hamilton perceived the modern financial system as an enabler of growth and national power. He was prescient in his vision. Most historians and economists did not systematically make that connection until the end of the twentieth century. His motivation was visceral, having sensed that the war against the British had lasted longer than it should have because the British were much better financed than the Americans.[4]

What was remarkable besides his prodigious achievements was his restraint from deriving any kind of personal financial benefit. He cared about national power and prosperity, but devoted very limited attention to his own material comfort. There would have been no lack of opportunities to personally gain from being at the helm of a rapidly expanding financial system.

He exercised great discipline in averting conflicts of interest, eliminating all outside sources of income when he was in office, in contrast to George Washington, Thomas Jefferson, and James Madison.[5] As a member of Congress, he waived the pension he had been entitled to as an officer because he was deeply involved in the debate on veteran benefits.[6] He also waived his right to "bounty" land that went to officers. In establishing the Treasury Department, he created internal compliance rules that prevented employees from transacting in government securities.[7]

These were not benevolent gestures from a man of means whose lifestyle was assured by substantial assets. On the contrary, he frequently found himself in need of money, not because he spent it but because he made so little of it, and did not take advantage of his exalted status in society or his unique position in finance while he built up the financial system. To his credit, he left office in a much weaker personal financial state than he did entering it. As Treasury Secretary, he made $3,500 a year, much less than he would have made in private law practice.[8] Among his many responsibilities, he oversaw the Customs Service, which meant that he had purview over enormous amounts of cash – yet, he handled transactions with utmost integrity.[9]

Hamilton resigned from the Treasury Department unashamedly invoking his need to make money to support his family. Even then, he refrained from the easy money available to men of his status. A clear opportunity presented itself when an old classmate offered to enroll him in a lucrative real estate project soon after he left office.[10] Hamilton graciously declined, likely because his friend represented foreign capital which might present a conflict of interest in the future. He died leaving his family in a financial bind, prompting a discreet fundraising effort among his friends on behalf of his wife Eliza and their seven surviving children.[11]

The US financial system – the most expansive and powerful in human history – was established by a man who embodies the antithesis of the concept "grab what you can when you can." Of course, the current system would be unrecognizable to Alexander Hamilton, but the moral challenges faced by its participants endure. Even if Hamilton's circumstances were unique, his eagerness to succeed on his own terms and his ability to refrain from self-serving – no matter how common or expected that behavior may be – permeate the individuals we discussed in this book, from this US Founding Father to Erin Godard, who is still in her twenties. Their stories point to a path in finance that may appeal to well-intentioned professionals who are keen to contribute to society and uphold their values, while improving finance from within.

ACKNOWLEDGMENTS

The idea for this book originated in the freshman seminar on ethics in finance I have taught at Princeton University for over ten years. I structure the course so that we devote attention to both the impact of the structural changes that have taken place on Wall Street over the past decades – and how they have created new and more complex conflicts of interest – and the norms, incentives, and cognitive biases that affect the individual behavior of finance professionals, drawing on the major traditions of moral philosophy to frame the discussion. Early on, a student noted the course's implicit focus on bad behavior. Naturally inclined to look at the good in people, I embraced the idea of examining virtuous conduct and searched for literature on ethical role models in the industry. Unable to find any, I set out to write this book.

The project's initial focus was on the people in finance I admired for their moral grounding and professional distinctiveness, particularly those who participated in my seminar, foremost Jack Bogle, John Whitehead, Paul Volcker, Valerie Szczepanik, and Andy Golden (Paul Volcker and Valerie Szczepanik ended up not being in the book because, as lifelong public servants, they didn't precisely fit the book's focus). Following advice from Jay Light, I developed a conceptual framework to delineate what ethical behavior might look like for finance professionals, and to structure learnings from empirical research and anecdotal insights from these exemplars' careers.

I owe particular thanks to my freshman seminar students, as well as to the students in my course on Asian economies and capital markets at both Princeton and the University of Cambridge, for having deepened my thinking on many of the issues addressed in this book. This book is written for them.

I am deeply grateful to the Freshman Seminars Program at Princeton, and in particular to its director Liz Colagiuri and its program coordinator Sha Sanyal, as well as to the John H. Laporte Jr. '67 fund for having supported my seminar for many years (the late Jack Laporte was a participant in the seminar's early years who brought to the classroom insights on conflicts of interest in the asset management industry).

I am also greatly thankful to Markus Brunnermeier and the Bendheim Center for Finance (and Yacine Ait-Sahalia who first hired me) for having supported my courses through the years and for having provided me a home within the economics department at Princeton. I have also benefited from the collaboration with the Julis-Rabinowitz Center for Public Policy and Finance, which, along with the Bendheim Center, have hosted the guest speaker events I have arranged outside of the classroom, helping me share ideas with and learn from a broad group of academics and practitioners.

I owe a great debt to the many who have contributed to the book and helped me sharpen my thinking. Several of them were early supporters who provided me sustained guidance throughout the project. Brent Durbin was the best sounding board, advisor, and friend I could wish for. From the proposal onward, he was consistently helpful. I am also deeply grateful to Bill Janeway, whose vast knowledge of the industry , macro-economic depth, and enthusiasm helped improve the book; John Hendry for his support and sage advice (and whose own book on ethics in finance was an inspiration); and Boudewijn de Bruin for his expert guidance on navigating the waters at the confluence of philosophy and finance. Alan Blinder provided thoughtful guidance at the early and late stages of the book project. Scott Malcomson shared helpful feedback and perspective during the initial phases of the proposal and thereafter.

Many others provided me much-needed "adult supervision" on their areas of expertise. I am thankful to Nick Barberis for his suggestions on my references to behavioral finance and cognitive biases. John Coffee Jr. provided shrewd advice on fiduciary responsibility. Scott Bessent helped improve the sections on macro and derivative strategies with his insights. Richard Sylla made a compelling case that Alexander Hamilton embodied as well as anyone ever could the essence of the book's message and provided helpful input on Hamilton's narrative. Brian Trelstad contributed useful comments on the section on impact investments. Andy Golden provided insights into several sections related to endowments and to alternative assets. Noam Ohana was a helpful sounding board in early stages of the project. Steven Winch provided constructive feedback on several topics, including private equity. The discussion on private equity also benefited from reviews and input from David Bard and Dan Rasmussen. Charley Ellis channeled me early on toward several of the central characters in this book and shared insights on the asset management industry. Trevor Hill shared expert comments on the sections related to Japan.

This book draws from the insights of many others who were generous with their time and advice. I am thankful for their help. Those include Keith Ambachtsheer, Dave Azad, Driss Baloul, Tom Baxter, Tina Bennett, Jon Bergen, John Biggs, Richard Bove, Sue Carter, Antonio Casal, Ron Daniel, Kevin Delaney, Steve Denning, Lisa Di Mona, Seth Ditchik, Chris Douvos, Carl Ferenbach, Dick Foster, Gordon Goldstein, Adam Grant, Kathryn Hall, Ben Hockett, Philip Hammarskjold, Ian Haft, Lea Hansen, Mick Hellman, Henry Kaufman, Richard Kovacevich, Matthew Levine, Steve Levine, Hajime Matsuura, Steven Mandis, Oki Matsumoto, Jack Meyer, Marco Meyer, Chad Myhre, Tom Nicholas, Matthew Nimetz, Susan Ochs, Thomas Philippon, Ellen Rosenman, Clayton Rose, Sachin Rundra, Knut Rostad, Ken Shibusawa, Felix Salmon, Hamid Samandari, Peter Singer, Jonathan Soros, Aaron Tai, Kara Tan Bhala, Simon Taylor, Will Thorndike, Jamie Twiss, Ingo Walter, Robert Wilmers, and Ed Zschau.

Of course, I am thankful to the inspiring individuals I write about, most of whom I connected with to triangulate the narrative I had drawn from research and to test ideas. The underlying premise of this book is that much can be learned from them.

Early research for this book was conducted by Arun Soni, now a highly promising undergraduate at Yale but then a high school sophomore mature beyond his years.

Dividing my time between practicing, teaching, and writing, my great luck has been to find a thoughtful work partner in Jamie Mai, who has embraced my atypical set of activities. He has been a great thought partner through the years and a true friend (and a regular and popular guest speaker in my classes). I am thankful to my other colleagues at Cornwall Capital, from whom I have learned so much over the years.

I had the good fortune to connect early on with Phil Good, my editor at Cambridge University Press. He was supportive from the time I reached out to him, patient, and insightful. I am thankful to his CUP colleagues who have helped the book come to fruition.

My deepest debts are to my family. My wonderful parents, Sol and Michèle de Swaan, brother, Julien de Swaan, and grand-parents, Henri and Suzanne Gehanne, have been a constant source of comfort and support throughout my life. I am immensely fortunate to have at the center of my life my wife, Sun-Sun, and our two girls, Sophie and Alice, who give us so much joy, and showed great patience and affection (in their own way) as I wrote the book over many evenings and weekends at home.

NOTES

Preface

1 Michael Lewis, "Occupational Hazards of Working on Wall Street," *Bloomberg. com*, September 24, 2014, www.bloomberg.com/opinion/articles/2014-09-24/occu pational-hazards-of-working-on-wall-street.

Introduction

1 The information on the Watermark Group was gleaned from a talk I facilitated with co-founder Andy Okun at Princeton University on February 22, 2015, subsequent conversations with Terence Woolf, Watermark's General Counsel and Chief Compliance Officer, on June 23, 2018 and July 16, 2018.

2 Content for the discussion on Frédéric Samama comes from interviews with the author, January 1, 2017, January 1, 2018, and May 19, 2019; Mats Andersson, Patrick Bolton, and Frédéric Samama, "Hedging Climate Risk," *Financial Analysts Journal* 72, no.3 (2016); and Mats Andersson, Patrick Bolton, and Frédéric Samama, "Governance and Climate Change: A Success Story in Mobilizing Investor Support for Corporate Responses to Climate Change," *Journal of Applied Corporate Finance* 28, no.2 (Spring 2016).

3 Content for the discussion on Erin Godard comes from interviews with the author on November 30, 2018 and May 7, 2019; Erin Godard, "My Inspiration," *FinanceYou Blog*, April 15, 2017, http://financeyouinternational.com/my-inspiration/; Jackie March-ildon, "This Global Citizen of Canada Helps NGOs in Rwanda – By Using Her Accounting Skills," *Globalcitizen.org*, December 7, 2017, www.globalcitizen.org/en/content/global-citizen-of-canada-erin-godard/; and Luminari, "These CPAs Left the Big 4, Moved to Rwanda, and Started a Business," *Bizfeed by Luminari*, December 7, 2018, https://bizfeed.luminari.ai/features/cpas-left-big-4-moved-rwanda-started-business/.

4 Andrew Haldane, "Control Rights (and Wrongs)," *Wincott Annual Memorial Lecture*, London, October 24, 2011, www.bankofengland.co.uk/speech/2011/control-rights-and-wrongs-speech-by-andy-haldane.

5 Charles Geisst, *Beggar Thy Neighbor: A History of Usury and Debt* (Philadelphia: University of Pennsylvania Press, 2013), 1–12.

6 Matt Taibbi, "The Great American Bubble Machine," *Rolling Stone*, April 5, 2010, www.rollingstone.com/politics/news/the-great-american-bubble-machine-20100405.

7 See Peter Rousseau and Richard Sylla, "Financial Systems, Economic Growth, and Globalization," in *Globalization in Historical Perspective*, ed. Michael Bordo, Alan Taylor, and Jeffrey Williamson (Chicago: University of Chicago Press, January 2003).

8 For an overview of the state of research, see Philippe Aghion, Peter Howitt, and Ross Levine, "Financial Development and Innovation-Led Growth," in *Handbook of Finance and Development*, ed. Thorsten Beck and Ross Levine (Cheltenham: Edward Elgar, 2018); and Luigi Zingales in "Does Finance Benefit Society?" NBER Working Paper 20894, January 2015, 11. http://faculty.chicagobooth.edu/luigi.zingales/papers/research/finance.pdf.

9 William Cohan, "When Bankers Started Playing with Other People's Money," *The Atlantic*, February 28, 2017, www.theatlantic.com/business/archive/2017/02/how-wall-street-went-public/517419/.

10 For a thoughtful discussion on regulatory arbitrage, see Maureen O'Hara, *Something for Nothing: Arbitrage and Ethics on Wall Street* (New York: W.W. Norton, 2016), 50–54, 101–125.

11 Joe Rennison, "GSO Bought $330m of Protection on Hovnanian Before Controversial Refi Deal," *Financial Times*, January 25, 2018, www.ft.com/content/304902dc-022a-11e8-9650-9c0ad2d7c5b5.

12 See for instance Matthew Levine, "Blackstone May Do Its Cleverest CDS Trade Again," *Bloomberg Opinion*, November 17, 2017, www.bloomberg.com/opinion/articles/2017-11-17/blackstone-may-do-its-cleverest-cds-trade-again.

13 See Ryan Hardy for a discussion on whether GSO breached its contract as a CDS buyer, in "Good Faith Counterparty Dealings in Zero-Sum Contracts," *SpencerFane.com*, January 2, 2014, www.spencerfane.com/publication/good-faith-counterparty-dealings-in-zero-sum-contracts/.

14 Even comedy show host Jon Stewart made that argument on a segment of his show (December 4, 2013) – see www.cc.com/video-clips/og8sum/the-daily-show-with-jon-stewart-blackstone—codere.

15 George Akerlof and Robert Shiller, *Phishing for Phools: The Economics of Manipulation and Deception* (Princeton, NJ: Princeton University Press, 2015).

16 Matthew Levine, "Matt Levine's Money Stuff: Be Careful Wearing Jeans at Goldman," *Bloomberg Opinion*, March 6, 2019, www.bloomberg.com/opinion/articles/2019-03-06/be-careful-wearing-jeans-at-goldman.

17 A different angle into restoring humanistic values into finance is to examine how financial concepts are helpful to society to the extent that finance professionals are true to finance's core ideas. This topic is explored thoughtfully by Mihir Desai, whose approach draws from the humanities, in *The Wisdom of Finance* (New York: Houghton Mifflin Harcourt, 2017).

18 For a helpful overview, see Minette Drumwright, Robert Prentice, and Cara Biasucci, "Behavioral Ethics and Teaching Ethical Decision Making," *Journal of Innovative Education* 13, no.3 (July 2015): 431–458; and Max Bazerman and Ovul Sezer, "Bounded Awareness: Implications for Ethical Decision Making," *Organizational Behavior and Human Decision Processes* 136 (2016): 95–105.

19 John Darley and C. Daniel Batson, "'From Jerusalem to Jericho': A Study of Situational and Dispositional Variables in Helping Behavior," *Journal of Personality and Social Psychology* 27, no.1 (1973): 100–108.

20 Ann Tenbrunsel and David Messik, "Ethical Fading: The Role of Self-Deception in Unethical Behavior," *Social Justice Research* 17, no.2 (June 2004): 223–236.

21 Catherine Schrand and Sarah Zechman, "Executive Overconfidence and the Slippery Slope to Financial Misreporting," *Journal of Accounting and Economics* 53, no.1–2 (February–April 2012): 311–329.

22 Max Bazerman and Ann Tenbrunsel, *Blind Spots: Why We Fail to Do What's Right and What to Do About It* (Princeton, NJ: Princeton University Press, 2011), 79–83.

23 Bazerman and Sezer, "Bounded Awareness," 95.

24 Robert Innes and Arnab Mitra, "Is Dishonesty Contagious? An Experiment," *SSRN* (June 26, 2009), http://dx.doi.org/10.2139/ssrn.1426002.

25 Max Bazerman and Dolly Chugh, "Decisions Without Blinders," *Harvard Business Review* (January 2006), https://hbr.org/2006/01/decisions-without-blinders.

26 Richard Thaler, Cass Sunstein, and John Balz, "Choice Architecture" (April 2, 2010), *SSRN*, http://dx.doi.org/10.2139/ssrn.1583509.

27 Bazerman and Sezer, "Bounded Awareness," 103.

28 Jeffrey Pfeffer, "Why the Assholes Are Winning: Money Trumps All," *Journal of Management Studies* 53, no.4 (January 2016): 663–669.

29 John Hendry, *Ethics and Finance* (Cambridge: Cambridge University Press, 2013), 36.

30 Jesse Norman, *Adam Smith: What He Thought and Why It Matters* (London: Allen Lane, 2018), 154–159.

31 Adam Grant, *Give and Take: Why Helping Others Drives Our Success* (New York: Viking, 2013).

32 Amartya Sen, *On Ethics and Economics* (Oxford: Oxford University Press, 1987), 1–2.

33 Patricia Werhane, *Adam Smith and His Legacy for Modern Capitalism* (Oxford: Oxford University Press, 1991), 27–31.

34 Kimura Masato, "Shibusawa Eiichi's View of Business Morality in Global Society," in *Ethical Capitalism: Shibusawa Eiichi and Business Leadership in Global Perspective*, ed. Patrick Fridenson and Kikkawa Takeo (Toronto: University of Toronto Press, 2017), 127.

35 Kikkawa Takeo, "Introduction," in *Ethical Capitalism*, 7.

36 Tanaka Kazuhiro, "Harmony between Morality and the Economy," in *Ethical Capitalism,* 39.

37 Kazuhiro, "Harmony Between Morality and the Economy," 37.

38 Aristotle, *Nicomachean Ethics*, ed. Roger Crisp (Cambridge: Cambridge University Press, 2000), x–xiv, 3–22.

39 Edith Hall, "Why Read Aristotle Today?" *Aeon*, May 29, 2018, https://aeon.co/essays/what-can-aristotle-teach-us-about-the-routes-to-happiness.

40 On the link between morality and skill-based excellence, see John Dobson, *Finance Ethics: The Rationality of Virtue* (Lanham, MD: Rowman & Littlefield, 1997), 89–114.

41 John Cornwell, "MacIntyre on Money," *Prospect Magazine*, November 2010, www.prospectmagazine.co.uk/magazine/alasdair-macintyre-on-money.

42 Aristotle, *Nicomachean Ethics*, 23–31.

43 Hendry, *Ethics and Finance*, 71.

44 Justin Oakley and Dean Cocking, *Virtue Ethics and Professional Roles* (Cambridge: Cambridge University Press, 2001), 75.

45 Hendry, *Ethics and Finance*, 70.

46 Aristotle, *Nicomachean Ethics*, 79–100.

47 Werhane, *Adam Smith*, viii, 20, 43.

48 Vivian Hunt, Sara Prince, Sundiatu Dixon-Fyle, and Lareina Yee, "Diversity Matters," McKinsey & Company, January 2018.

49 Walter Isaacson and Evan Thomas, *The Wise Men: Six Friends and the World They Made* (New York: Simon & Schuster, 1986).

Chapter 1

1 Maria Aspan, "Wells Fargo's John Stumpf, the 2013 Banker of the Year," *American Banker*, November 21, 2013, www.americanbanker.com/news/wells-fargos-john-stumpf-the-2013-banker-of-the-year.

2 Vito Racanelli, "Apple Tops Barron's List of Respected Companies," *Barron's*, June 27, 2015, www.barrons.com/articles/apple-tops-barrons-list-of-respected-com panies-1435372737.

3 E. Scott Reckard, "Wells Fargo's Pressure-Cooker Sales Culture Comes at a Cost," *Los Angeles Times*, December 21, 2013, www.latimes.com/business/la-fi-wells-fargo-sale-pressure-20131222-story.html.

4 The People of the State of California versus Wells Fargo & Company, BC 580778, Filed May 4, 2015, 3, https://assets.bwbx.io/documents/users/iqjWHBFdfxIU/rPxi_pVaKx2Y/v0; Michael Hiltzik, "Wells Fargo CEO John Stumpf Offers a Clinic in How to Weasel Out of Real Accountability," *Los Angeles Times*, September 20, 2016, www.latimes.com/business/hiltzik/la-fi-hiltzik-stumpf-senate-20160920-snap-story.html.

5 Wells Fargo Annual Report, 2015, https://www08.wellsfargomedia.com/assets/pdf/about/investor-relations/annual-reports/2015-annual-report.pdf.

6 James Rufus Koren, "It's Been a Year Since the Wells Fargo Scandal Broke – and New Problems Are Still Surfacing," *Los Angeles Times*, September 8, 2017, www .latimes.com/business/la-fi-wells-fargo-one-year-20170908-story.html.

7 Renae Merle, "Wells Fargo's Profits Tumble as Mega Bank Struggles to Rebound from Sales Scandal," *The Washington Post*, October 13, 2017, www .washingtonpost.com/news/business/wp/2017/10/13/wells-fargos-profits-tumble-as-mega-bank-struggles-to-rebound-from-sales-scandal/.

8 Emily Glazer and Christina Rexrode, "Wells Fargo CEO Defends Bank Culture, Lays Blame with Bad Employees," *The Wall Street Journal*, September 13, 2016, www.wsj.com/articles/wells-fargo-ceo-defends-bank-culture-lays-blame-with-bad-employees-1473784452.

9 Jason Silverstein, "Wells Fargo Ignored Petition from Thousands of Employees Protesting Unethical Culture, Lawsuit Says," *Daily News*, October 2, 2016, www .nydailynews.com/news/national/wells-fargo-employee-petition-protesting-ethics-suit-article-1.2814693.

10 Emily Glazer, "From 'Gr-Eight' to 'Gaming', a Short History of Wells Fargo and Cross-Selling," *The Wall Street Journal*, September 16, 2016, https://blogs.wsj.com/moneybeat/2016/09/16/from-gr-eight-to-gaming-a-short-history-of-wells-fargo-and-cross-selling/.

11 James Rufus Koren, "How Wells Fargo's Rivals Make It Harder for Employees to Create Fake Accounts," *Los Angeles Times*, October 8, 2016, www.latimes.com/business/la-fi-wells-fargo-incentives-20161005-snap-story.html.

12 The People of the State of California versus Wells Fargo & Company, BC 580778, Filed May 4, 2015, 2, https://assets.bwbx.io/documents/users/iqjWHBFdfxIU/rPxi_pVaKx2Y/v0.

13 Stacy Cowley, "Voices from Wells Fargo: 'I Thought I Was Having a Heart Attack,'" *The New York Times Dealbook*, October 20, 2016, www.nytimes.com/2016/10/21/business/dealbook/voices-from-wells-fargo-i-thought-i-was-having-a-heart-attack.html.

14 "Independent Directors of the Board of Wells Fargo & Company Sales Practices Investigation Report," Four Director Oversight Committee, assisted by independent counsel Shearman & Sterling, April 10, 2017, 22–23.

15 Matt Egan, "Wells Fargo Admits to Signs of Worker Retaliation," *CNN Money*, January 24, 2017, http://money.cnn.com/2017/01/23/investing/wells-fargo-retaliation-ethics-line/index.html.

16 The People of the State of California versus Wells Fargo & Company, BC 580778, Filed May 4, 2015, 1, https://assets.bwbx.io/documents/users/iqjWHBFdfxIU/rPxi_pVaKx2Y/v0.

17 Susan Ochs, "The Leadership Blind Spots at Wells Fargo," *Harvard Business Review*, October 6, 2016, https://hbr.org/2016/10/the-leadership-blind-spots-at-wells-fargo.

18 United States Consumer Financial Protection Bureau, Administrative Proceeding 2016-CFPB-0015 in the Matter of Wells Fargo Bank, filed September 8, 2016, 5–7, http://files.consumerfinance.gov/f/documents/092016_cfpb_WFBconsentorder.pdf.

19 Matt Levine, "Wells Fargo Opened a Couple Million Fake Accounts," *Bloomberg Opinion*, September 9, 2016, www.bloomberg.com/view/articles/2016-09-09/wells-fargo-opened-a-couple-million-fake-accounts.

20 Barry Staw and Richard Boettger, "Task Revision: A Neglected Form of Work Performance," *Academy of Management Journal* 333, no.3 (September 1990): 534–559.

21 Bazerman and Tenbrunsel, *Blind Spots*, 106.

22 Lisa Ordonez, Maurice Schweitzer, Adam Galinsky, and Max Bazerman, "Goals Gone Wild: The Systematic Side Effects of Over-Prescribing Goal Setting," *Harvard Business School Working Paper*, #09-083 (2009), www.hbs.edu/faculty/Publication%20Files/09-083.pdf.

23 Bazerman and Tenbrunsel, *Blind Spots*, 29.

24 Hendry, *Ethics and Finance*, 36.

25 Bazerman and Tenbrunsel, *Blind Spots*, 79–86.

26 Bazerman and Tenbrunsel, *Blind Spots*, 117–127.

27 John Stumpf, "The Vision & Values of Wells Fargo," Wells Fargo, 2015, 4.

28 Andris Zoltners, P. K. Sinha, and Sally Lorimer, "Wells Fargo and the Slippery Slope of Sales Incentives," *Harvard Business Review*, September 20, 2016, https://hbr.org/2016/09/wells-fargo-and-the-slippery-slope-of-sales-incentives.

29 *2020 Edelman Trust Barometer*, Global Report, Edelman, www.edelman.com/trustbarometer.

30 Defined as "quite a lot" or "a great deal" of confidence, in Lydia Saad, "Military, Small Business, Police Still Stir Most Confidence," *Gallup News*, June 28, 2018, https://news.gallup.com/poll/236243/military-small-business-police-stir-confidence.aspx.

31 Blaine Aikin and Kristina Fausti, "Fiduciary: A Historically Significant Standard," *Review of Banking and Financial Law* 30, Boston University School of Law (2010): 157.

32 Ibid., 158.

33 Fiduciary, *Black's Law Dictionary* 702 (9th edn. 2009) (quoting D. W. M Waters, *The Constructive Trust: The Case for a New Approach in English Law* 4 (1964)).

34 Vivek Bhattacharya, Gaston Illanes, and Manisha Padi, "Fiduciary Duty and the Market for Financial Advice," *Sixth Annual Conference on Financial Market Regulation* (May 1, 2019). https://ssrn.com/abstract=3281345.

35 J. Robert Smith, "Are You a Fiduciary?" *Fiduciary Law Blog*, Holland & Hart LLP, August 20, 2014, www.fiduciarylawblog.com/2014/08/are-you-a-fiduciary.html.

36 John Kay, *The Kay Review of UK Equity Markets and Long-Term Decision Making Final Report*, United Kingdom Government, July 2012, www.gov.uk/government/uploads/system/uploads/attachment_data/file/253454/bis-12-917-kay-review-of-equity-markets-final-report.pdf.

37 Benjamin Bain and Robert Schmidt, "Wall Street Sees a Win in SEC Crackdown on Broker Conflicts," *Bloomberg*, May 30, 2019, www.bloomberg.com/news/articles/2019-05-30/wall-street-sees-a-win-in-sec-s-crackdown-on-broker-conflicts; Barry Ritholtz, "SEC's New 'Best Interest' Rule Is Only Good for Laughs," *Bloomberg Opinion*, June 24, 2019, www.bloomberg.com/opinion/articles/2019-06-24/sec-s-new-best-interest-rule-is-only-good-for-laughs.

38 Wells Fargo Annual Report, 2015, 4–10.

39 John Stumpf, *The Vision and Values of Wells Fargo*, Wells Fargo, 2010, 10.

40 Erin El Issa, "2017 American Household Credit Card Debt Study," Nerdwallet, 2017, www.nerdwallet.com/blog/average-credit-card-debt-household/.

41 Ibid.

42 Paul O'Neill, "A Little Gift from Your Friendly Banker," *Life Magazine*, April 27, 1970.

43 John Boatright, *Ethics in Finance* (Malden, MA: Wiley Blackwell, 2014), 89.

44 "Despite US Campaign for Simplicity, Contracts Remain Lengthy, Complex, Unread," CreditCards.com, September 16, 2016, www.creditcards.com/credit-card-news/unreadable-card-agreements-study.php.

45 Akerlof and Shiller, *Phishing for Phools*.

46 Yuliya Demyanyk, Elena Loutskina, and Daniel Kolliner, "Three Myths about Peer-to-Peer Loans," *Economic Commentary*, Federal Reserve Bank of Cleveland, no. 2017–18, November 9, 2017, www.clevelandfed.org/en/newsroom-and-events/publications/economic-commentary/2017-economic-commentaries/ec-201718-3-myths-about-peer-to-peer-loans.aspx.

47 Claire Celerier and Boris Vallee, "What Drives Financial Complexity? A Look into the Retail Market for Structured Products," *Les Cahiers de Recherche*, HEC Paris, (2013): 4.

48 Celerier and Vallee, "What Drives Financial Complexity?" 2–4.

49 Celerier and Vallee, "What Drives Financial Complexity?" 7.

50 The used-car dealer analogy was drawn from Matt Levine, "Used-Car Salesmen Are Just Like Bond Traders," *Bloomberg Opinion*, March 21, 2018, www.bloomberg.com/view/articles/2018-03-21/used-car-salesmen-are-just-like-bond-traders.

51 Patrick Radden Keefe, "The Family That Built an Empire of Pain," *The New Yorker*, October 30, 2017, www.newyorker.com/magazine/2017/10/30/the-family-that-built-an-empire-of-pain.

52 Aikin and Fausti, "Fiduciary," 158.

53 Boatright, *Ethics in Finance*, 41.

54 United States Senate Permanent Subcommittee on Investigations, "Failing to Manage Conflicts of Interest: Case Study of Goldman Sachs," *Wall Street and the Financial Crisis: Anatomy of a Financial Collapse*, April 13, 2011, 396.

55 United States Senate Permanent Subcommittee on Investigations, "Failing to Manage Conflicts of Interest," 397.

56 Testimony from Lloyd C. Blankfein, Chairman and CEO, The Goldman Sachs Group Inc., Permanent Senate Subcommittee on Investigations, April 27, 2010.

57 Testimony from Fabrice Tourre, Executive Director of Structured Products Group Trading, The Goldman Sachs Group Inc., Permanent Senate Subcommittee on Investigations, April 27, 2010.

58 See the head of Goldman Sachs' mortgage department's admission under oath that the firm had acted as a placement agent rather than a market maker; United States Senate Permanent Subcommittee on Investigations, "Failing to Manage Conflicts of Interest," 612.

59 United States Senate Permanent Subcommittee on Investigations, "Failing to Manage Conflicts of Interest," 382–386.

60 United States Senate Permanent Subcommittee on Investigations, "Failing to Manage Conflicts of Interest," 602.

61 Securities and Exchange Commission v. Goldman, Sachs & Co. and Fabrice Tourre, Case No. 10-CV-3229, Consent of Goldman Sachs (July 14, 2010).

62 Marco di Maggio, Francesco Franzoni, Amir Kermani, and Carlo Sommavilla, "The Relevance of Broker Networks for Information Diffusion in the Stock Market," Swiss Finance Institute Research Paper No. 16–63 (June 2017).

63 Andrea Barbon, Marco di Maggio, Francesco Franzoni, and Augustin Landier, "Broker and Order Flow Leakage: Evidence from Fire Sales," Harvard Business School Working Paper 18-046 (November 2017).

64 *Principles for Customer-Oriented Business Conduct*, Working Group on Financial Markets, Japan Financial Services Agency of Japan, January 19, 2017, www.fsa.go.jp/news/28/sonota/20170119-1/01.pdf.

65 Christopher Wells and Tomoko Fuminaga, "Japan Releases Draft Principles for Customer-Oriented Business Conduct," Morgan Lewis, February 17, 2017, www.morganlewis.com/pubs/japan-releases-draft-principles-for-customer-oriented-business-conduct.

66 Mid-2019 SPIVA US Scorecard, *S&P Dow Jones Indices*, https://us.spindices.com/documents/spiva/spiva-us-mid-year-2019.pdf.

67 Aye Soe and Ryan Poirier, "Does Past Performance Matter? The Persistence Scorecard," *S&P Dow Jones Indices*, June 2017, https://us.spindices.com/documents/spiva/persistence-scorecard-june-2017.pdf.

68 Russel Kinnel, "Fund Fees Predict Future Success or Failure," *Morningstar.com*, May 5, 2016, www.morningstar.com/articles/752485/fund-fees-predict-future-success-or-failure.html.

69 A version of this piece on John Bogle was published by the author as "Vanguard's John Bogle Created More Social Good Than Any Contemporary in Finance," *Quartz.com*, January 18, 2019, https://qz.com/1527689/vanguards-john-bogle-created-more-social-good-than-any-contemporary-in-finance/.

70 Paul A. Samuelson, "Challenge to Judgment," *The Journal of Portfolio Management* 1 (Fall 1974): 17–19.

71 Charles D. Ellis, "The Loser's Game," *Financial Analysts Journal* 31 (July–August 1975): 19–26.

72 Burton G. Malkiel, *A Random Walk Down Wall Street* (New York: W.W. Norton, 1973).

73 Thomas Philippon and Ariell Reshef, "Wages and Human Capital in the US Finance Industry: 1909–2006," *The Quarterly Journal of Economics* 127, no.4 (November 2012).

74 Landon Thomas Jr., "An Old-School Investment Manager That Builds Wealth Quietly," *The New York Times*, October 13, 2017, www.nytimes.com/2017/10/13/business/mutfund/dodge-cox-mutual-funds.html.

75 Daniel Ben-Ami, "Strategically Speaking: Dodge & Cox," *IPE Magazine*, February 2017, www.ipe.com/investment/strategically-speaking/strategically-speaking-dodge-and-cox/10017408.fullarticle.

76 Ibid.

77 Antoine Gara, "The Future of Stock Picking: Meet the Investors Good Enough to Offer Refunds," *Forbes Online*, May 22, 2018, www.forbes.com/sites/antoinegara/2018/05/22/the-future-of-stockpicking-meet-the-investors-good-enough-to-offer-refunds/#1ab1cb005786.

78 Jason Zweig, "It's Time for Investors to Go Even Lower," *The Wall Street Journal*, January 6, 2017, www.wsj.com/articles/its-time-for-investor-fees-to-go-even-lower-1483739505.

79 Tom Redmond, Yuko Takeo, and Nao Sano, "One Man's Fight Against the Lions of Japanese Investing" *Bloomberg.com*, February 6, 2018, www.bloomberg.com/news/features/2018-02-06/one-man-s-fight-against-the-lions-of-japanese-investing.

80 Ibid.

81 Ibid.

82 Ibid.

83 Tom Redmond, Yuko Takeo, and Nao Sano, "Demoralized Hedge Fund Trader Finds Success on Ancestor's Path" *Bloomberg.com*, November 16, 2016, www.bloomberg.com/news/articles/2016-11-15/demoralized-hedge-fund-trader-finds-success-on-ancestor-s-path.

84 Ibid.

85 Nobuchika Mori, "Toward a Virtuous Cycle of Finance and Economy," Speech, 10th Japan Securities Summit, SIFMA, February 7, 2018.

86 Nobuchika Mori, "The Next Evolution in Asset Management in Japan," Speech, 8th International Seminar of the Securities Analysts Association of Japan, April 7, 2017.

87 Mori, "Toward a Virtuous Cycle."

88 Mori, "The Next Evolution."

89 "One-and-Ten," *The Economist*, January 29, 2009, www.economist.com/finance-and-economics/2009/01/29/one-and-ten; Ted Seides, "The Hedge Fund Fee Conundrum," *Institutional Investor*, June 1, 2018, www.institutionalinvestor.com/article/b18g7tfmmmjvj7/the-hedge-fund-fee-conundrum.

90 Roger G. Ibbotson, Peng Chen, and Kevin X. Zhu, "The ABC's of Hedge Funds: Alphas, Betas, & Costs," *Financial Analysts Journal* 67, no.1 (2011), www.cfapubs.org/doi/pdf/10.2469/faj.v67.n1.6.

91 The information on the Watermark Group was gleaned from a talk I facilitated with co-founder Andy Okun at Princeton University on February 22, 2015, subsequent conversations with Terence Woolf, Watermark's General Counsel and Chief Compliance Officer, on June 23, 2018 and July 16, 2018, and with Andy Okun.

92 Saijel Kishan and Bei Hu, "A Hedge Fund That Shares the Risk," *Bloomberg Businessweek*, May 20, 2019.

93 Note that some investors prefer to see a gating provision, as gates protect from endemic redemptions not only the investment manager but also the more resilient investors.

94 "Counting the Cost: A Commonfund Viewpoint," Commonfund Institute, March 2017, www.commonfund.org/wp-content/uploads/2017/03/Viewpoint-Counting-the-Cost.pdf.

95 Charles Skorina, "Endowment Costs: The Secret History," The Skorina Letter, October 18, 2017, www.charlesskorina.com/?p=5211.

96 The Yale Investments Office, retrieved on June 30, 2018 at http://investments.yale.edu/.

97 Chrystia Freeland, "Lunch with the FT: David Swensen," *Financial Times*, October 12, 2009, www.ft.com/content/dd91a3ec-b461-11de-bec8-00144feab49a.

98 David Swensen interview with the author, New Haven, CT, February 10, 2015.

99 "Yale's Team," Yale Investments Office, retrieved on June 30, 2018 at http://investments.yale.edu/team

100 Geraldine Fabrikant, "For Yale's Money Man, a Higher Calling," *The New York Times*, February 18, 2007, www.nytimes.com/2007/02/18/business/yourmoney/18swensen.html.

101 Robert Frank, "Why Yale Shouldn't Lionize a Money Manager," *The Wall Street Journal*, April 21, 2008, https://blogs.wsj.com/wealth/2008/04/21/why-yale-shouldnt-lionize-a-money-manager/.

102 David Swensen interview with author.

103 Ibid.

104 University of Notre Dame 2018 Annual Report (2018), https://controller.nd.edu/assets/302174/2018_university_annual_report_singlepages.pdf.

105 Frances Denmark, "25 Years Later, Scott Malpass Is Still Notre Dame MVP," *Institutional Investor*, February 18, 2014, www.institutionalinvestor.com/article/b14zbl458mxjmj/25-years-later-scott-malpass-is-still-notre-dame-mvp.

106 "Admission & Aid," Princeton University, retrieved on January 21, 2019. www.princeton.edu/admission-aid.

107 Ludovic Phalippou, Christian Rauch, and Marc Umber, "Private Equity Portfolio Company Fees," April 5, 2016, *Said Business School Working Paper 2015–22*.

108 Phalippou, "Private Equity Portfolio Company Fees," 1, 6–7.

109 Phalippou, "Private Equity Portfolio Company Fees," 20.

110 John Gittelson, "Calpers Pushes to Buy Like Buffett, Reduce PE Fees," *Reuters*, July 17, 2017, https://news.bloomberglaw.com/corporate-law/calpers-pushes-to-buy-like-buffett-reduce-private-equity-fees.

111 Randy Diamond, "Calpers Studies Ways to Keep Private Equity Afloat," *Pensions & Investments*, December 12, 2016.

112 Roger Berkowitz, "An Interview with Vincent Mai," in *The Intellectual Origins of the Global Financial Crisis*, ed. Roger Berkowitz and Taun N. Toay (New York: Fordham University Press, 2012).

113 "Global Private Equity Report 2018," Bain & Company, 21, http://go.bain.com/rs/545-OFW-044/images/BAIN_REPORT_2018_Private_Equity_Report.pdf?aliId=16898857.

114 Interview of Vincent Mai by the author, June 26, 2015.

115 Interview of Vincent Mai by the author, August 16, 2018.

116 Taylor Majewksi, "How This 50-Person Startup Is Planning to Completely Transform the Real Estate Industry," *Builtinnyc*, April 5, 2017, www.builtinnyc.com/2017/04/05/cadre-disrupting-real-estate-nyc.

117 Interview of Ryan Williams by the author, July 7, 2018.

118 Private Equity Enforcement, Andrew Ceresney, Director, Division of Enforcement, SEC, May 12, 2016.

119 "2016-2017 PE/VC Partnership Agreements Study," *Buyouts Insider*, New York.

120 Matt Taibbi, "The $9 Billion Witness: Meet JP Morgan Chase's Worst Nightmare," *RollingStone*, November 6, 2014, www.rollingstone.com/politics/politics-news/the-9-billion-witness-meet-jpmorgan-chases-worst-nightmare-242414/.

121 Ibid.

122 Ibid.

123 Michael Winston, "A Whistleblower's Tainted Defeat: CA Appellate Reversal Paves Way for Continued Bank Retaliation," *Naked Capitalism*, May 20, 2014, www.nakedcapitalism.com/2014/05/whistleblowers-tainted-defeat-ca-appellate-reversal-paves-way-continued-bank-retaliation.html.

124 Paul Moore, *Crash, Bank, Wallop: The Memoirs of the HBOS Whistleblower* (York, UK: New Wilberforce Media, 2015).

125 Alexander Dick, Adair Morse, and Luigi Singales, "Who Blows the Whistle on Corporate Fraud?" *The Journal of Finance* 65, no.6 (December 2010): 2213–2253.

126 Adam Waytz, James Dungan, and Liane Young, "The Whistleblower's Dilemma and the Fairness–Loyalty Tradeoff," *Journal of Experimental Social Psychology* 49, no.6 (November 2013): 1027–1033.

127 "Small Town Canadian Values versus JP Morgan Chase," *Corporate Crime Reporter*, November 25, 2014, www.corporatecrimereporter.com/news/200/small-town-canadian-values-versus-jpmorgan-chase/.

128 "SEC Awards Whistleblowers Whose Information Helped Stop Fraud," SEC Press Release, January 22, 2020, https://www.sec.gov/news/press-release/2020-15.

129 Aaron Kesselheim, David Studdert, and Michelle Mello, "Whistle-Blowers' Experiences in Fraud Litigation against Pharmaceutical Companies," *The New England Journal of Medicine* 362 (2010): 1832–1839.

130 Guy Rolnik, "SEC and Revolving Doors: Q&A with Eric Ben-Artzi, the Deutsche Bank Whistleblower Who Rejected a Multimillion Dollar Award," *ProMarket*, August 29, 2016, https://promarket.org/sec-revolving-doors-qa-eric-ben-artzi-12-billion-dollar-deutsche-whistleblower/.

131 Eric Ben-Artzi, "We Must Protect Shareholders from Executive Wrongdoing," *Financial Times*, August 18, 2016, www.ft.com/content/b43d2d96-652a-11e6-8310-ecfobddad227.

132 Matthew Levine, "Deutsche Bank Ignored Some 'Losses' Until They Went Away," *Dealbreaker*, December 6, 2012 updated on January 14, 2019, https://dealbreaker.com/2012/12/deutsche-bank-ignored-some-losses-until-they-went-away.

133 Christine Parrish, "The Saint of Wall Street: Whistle-Blower Turns Down $8.25 Million Award, Says Crooked Bankers Groomed to Oversee SEC," *The Free Press*, October 27, 2016, https://freepressonline.com/Content/Home/Homepage-Rotator/Article/PopTech-The-Saint-of-Wall-Street-Whistle-Blower-Turns-Down-8-25-Million-Award-Says-Crooked-Bankers-Groomed-to-Oversee-SEC/78/720/48824.

Chapter 2

1 This argument has been made by others in the past. In particular, John Cassidy made a similar argument in "What Good Is Wall Street?" *New Yorker*, November 29, 2010, www.newyorker.com/magazine/2010/11/29/what-good-is-wall-street. See also Roger Bootle, *The Trouble with Markets* (London: Nicholas Brealey Publishing, 2009), 115–117; and John Kay, *Other People's Money* (New York: PublicAffairs, 2015).

2 John Cornwell, "MacIntyre on Money," *Prospect Magazine*, November 2010, www.prospectmagazine.co.uk/magazine/alasdair-macintyre-on-money.

3 Gustavo Piga, "Derivatives in Public Debt Management, Committee on Economic Affairs and Development," November 29, 2010, www.gustavopiga.it/wordpress/wp-content/uploads/2012/03/discussion.pdf; Satyajit Das, "Greek Window Dressing Puts Derivatives' Role on Full Display," *Financial Times*, February 18, 2010; Nicholas Dunbar and Elisa Martinuzzi, "Goldman Secret Greece Loan Shows Two Sinners as Client Unravels," *Bloomberg*, March 6, 2012, www.bloomberg.com/news/articles/2012-03-06/goldman-secret-greece-loan-shows-two-sinners-as-client-unravels.

4 "Goldman Sachs Transaction with Greece," Goldman Sachs Media Relations, February 21, 2010, accessed September 25, 2017, www.goldmansachs.com/media-relations/in-the-news/archive/greece.html.

5 Note that some argue that Greece was fleeced by Goldman Sachs, which pocketed a reported $500 million profit from the deal – see for instance Jim Armitage, "Greek Debt Crisis: Goldman Sachs Could Be Sued for Helping Hide Debts When It Joined Euro," *Independent*, July 10, 2015, www.independent.co.uk/news/world/europe/greek-debt-crisis-goldman-sachs-could-be-sued-for-helping-country-hide-debts-when-it-joined-euro-10381926.html.

6 See in particular O'Hara, *Something for Nothing*, 153–157, and William D. Cohan, "Plenty Deserve Blame for Greece's Woes, but Maybe Not Goldman Sachs," *New York Times*, July 13, 2015, www.nytimes.com/2015/07/14/business/dealbook/plenty-deserve-blame-for-greeces-woes-but-maybe-not-goldman-sachs.html?mcubz=3.

7 Mariana Mazzucato, *The Value of Everything: Making and Taking in the Global Economy* (London: Allen Lane, 2018), 12.

8 Mazzucato, *Value of Everything*, 9.

9 J. E. King and Michael McLure, "Value: History of the Concept" in *International Encyclopedia of the Social & Behavioral Sciences,* ed. J. Wright (New York: Elsevier, 2015), 2nd edn., 7–13.

10 Mazzucato, *Value of Everything*, 15, 60–62.

11 Mazzucato, *Value of Everything*, xix.

12 Mazzucato, *Value of Everything*, 12, 272.

13 Thomas Piketty, *Capital in the Twenty-First Century* (Cambridge, MA: The Belknap Press of Harvard University Press, 2014), 298–317.

14 William H. Janeway, *Doing Capitalism in the Innovation Economy* (Cambridge, UK: Cambridge University Press, 2012), 325.

15 Adair Turner, *Economics after the Crisis: Objectives and Means* (Cambridge, MA: MIT University Press, 2012), xi–xii, 1–17.

16 Michael Sandel, *What Money Can't Buy* (New York: Farrar, Straus and Giroux, April 2012).

17 Bootle, *Trouble with Markets*, 115–117

18 Mazzucato, *Value of Everything*, 6.

19 See Rousseau and Sylla, "Financial Systems, Economic Growth, and Globalization"; Asli Demirguc-Kunt and Ross Levine, "Finance, Financial Sector Policies, and Long-Run Growth," *World Bank Policy Research Paper* #4469 (January 2008), https://elibrary.worldbank.org/doi/abs/10.1596/1813-9450-4469; Thorsten Beck, *The Role of Finance in Economic Development: Benefits, Risks, and Politics*, European Banking Center Discussion Paper # 2011-038 (December 2011).

20 Luigi Guiso, Paola Sapienza, and Luigi Zingales, "Does Local Financial Development Matter?" *Quarterly Journal of Economics* 119; M. Mollica and Luigi Zingales, "The Impact of Venture Capital on Innovation and the Creation of New Businesses," Working Paper, University of Chicago.

21 Thorsten Beck, A. Demirguc-Kunt, and Ross Levine, "Finance, Inequality, and the Poor," *Journal of Economic Growth* 12, no.1, (2007); Ross Levine and Yona Rubinstein, "Liberty for More: Finance and Educational Opportunities," *Cato Papers on Public Policy*, Volume 3 (2014).

22 Stephen Cecchetti and Enisse Kharroubi, "Reassessing the Impact of Finance on Growth," BIS Working Paper no.381 (July 2012); Jean-Louis Arcand, Enrico Berkes, and Ugo Panizza, *Too Much Finance?*, IMF Working Paper 12/161 (June 2012).

23 Cecchetti and Kharroubi, "Reassessing the Impact of Finance on Growth."

24 Turner, *Economics after the Crisis*, 18–19.

25 Luigi Zingales in "Does Finance Benefit Society?" Working Paper, January 2015, 11, http://faculty.chicagobooth.edu/luigi.zingales/papers/research/finance.pdf.

26 This argument has been made by Robert Shiller in "The Best, Brightest, and Least Productive?" *Project Syndicate*, September 20, 2013, www.project-syndicate.org/commentary/the-rent-seeking-problem-in-contemporary-finance-by-robert-j–shiller?barrier=accessreg.

27 That argument has been prominently made by George Akerlof and Robert Shiller in *Phishing for Phools: The Economics of Manipulation and Deception* (Princeton, NJ: Princeton University Press, 2015).

28 Thomas Philippon and Ariell Reshef, "Wages and Human Capital in the US Finance Industry: 1909–2006," *The Quarterly Journal of Economics* 127, no.4 (November 2012).

29 Mazzucato, *Value of Everything*, 109, 147.

30 Hans-Martin von Gaudecker, "How Does Household Portfolio Diversification Vary with Financial Literacy and Financial Advice?" *The Journal of Finance* 70, no.2 (April 2015): 489–507.

31 Mid-2019 SPIVA US Scorecard, *S&P Dow Jones Indices*, https://us.spindices.com/documents/spiva/spiva-us-mid-year-2019.pdf.

32 Andrew Haldane, Simon Brennan, and Vasileios Madouros, "The Contribution of the Financial Sector – Miracle or Mirage?" in *The Future of Finance: The LSE Report* (London: July 14, 2010): 97–102.

33 Paul Woolley, "Why Are Financial Markets so Inefficient and Exploitative – and a Suggested Remedy," in *The Future of Finance: The LSE Report* (London: July 14, 2010): 129.

34 Ing-Haw Cheng, Sahil Raina, and Wei Xiong, "Wall Street and the Housing Bubble," *American Economic Review* 104, no.9 (2014).

35 Nicholas Barberis, "Psychology and the Financial Crisis of 2007–2008," in *Financial Innovation and Crisis* (Cambridge, MA: MIT Press, 2011); Boudewijn de Bruin, *Ethics and the Global Financial Crisis* (Cambridge: Cambridge University Press, 2015); Roland Benabou, "Groupthink: Collective Delusions in Organizations and Markets," *Review of Economic Studies* 80 (2013).

36 Boudewijn de Bruin, "Ethics Management in Banking and Finance," in *Capital Failure: Rebuilding Trust in Financial Services*, ed. Nicholas Morris and David Vines (Oxford: Oxford University Press, 2014), 268.

37 US Senate Report, "Failing to Manage Conflicts of Interest: Case Study of Goldman Sachs" in *Wall Street and the Financial Crisis: Anatomy of a Financial Collapse* (April 13, 2011), 499.

38 Adair Turner, "What Do Banks Do? Why Do Credit Booms and Busts Occur and What Can Public Policy Do About It?" in *The Future of Finance: The LSE Report* (London: July 14, 2010): 13.

39 Turner, "What Do Banks Do?" 15, 33.

40 Turner, "What Do Banks Do?" 34.

41 Piketty, *Capital in the Twenty-First Century*, 48.

42 It is worth noting that there are linkages between the risks associated with promoting inequality and financial instability. For instance, Piketty points out that rising inequality and the quasi-stagnation of purchasing power for the lower and middle classes in the United States may have contributed to financial instability by pushing many of these households to take on more debt than they should have; Piketty, *Capital in the Twenty-First Century*, 297.

43 William J. Baumol, "Productive, Unproductive, and Destructive," *Journal of Political Economy* 98, no.5 (October 1990), part 1.

44 Tom Nicholas and David Chen, "Georges Doriot and American Venture Capital," *Harvard Business School Note* #9-812-110, January 2012; "Done Deals: Venture Capitalists Tell Their Story: Featured HBS Arthur Rock," *Harvard Business School Working Knowledge*, December 4, 2000.

45 For an excellent overview of innovative finance targeting economic and social problems, see Georgia Levenson Keohane, *Capital and the Common Good* (New York: Columbia Business School Press, 2016).

46 Levenson Keohane, *Capital and the Common Good*, 89–92.

47 Grameen Bank, *Performance Indicators and Ratio Analysis*, December 2015.

48 Alison Beard, "Leadership: Muhammad Yunus Interview," *Harvard Business Review*, December 2012, https://hbr.org/2012/12/muhammad-yunus.

49 Grameen Bank Web Site, Retrieved on September 17, 2017, www.grameen-info.org/grameen-founder-muhammad-yunus/

50 Levenson Keohane, *Capital and the Common Good*, 91.

51 Amy Kazmin, "Access All Areas," in *Impact Investing Financial Times Report*, September 2018, 34–41.

52 Abhijit Banerjee, Dean Karlan, and Jonathan Zinman, "Six Randomized Evaluations of Microcredit: Introduction and Further Steps," *American Economic Journal: Applied Economics* 7, no.1 (2015); Kentaro Toyama, "Lies, Hype, and Profit: The Truth about Microfinance," *The Atlantic*, January 28, 2011, www.theatlantic.com/business/archive/2011/01/lies-hype-and-profit-the-truth-about-microfinance/70405/.

53 *Does Microfinance Still Hold Promise for Reaching the Poor?* The World Bank, March 30, 2015.

54 Abhijit Banerjee, Esther Duflo, Nathanael Goldberg, Dean Karlan, Robert Osei, William Pariente, Jeremy Shapiro, Bram Thuysbaert, and Christopher Udry, "A Multifaceted Program Causes Lasting Progress for the Very Poor: Evidence from Six Countries," *Science*, May 15, 2015, https://science.sciencemag.org/content/348/6236/1260799; Microfinance Pioneer Sir Fazle Hasan Abed, Founder of BRAC, Advances "Business in a Box" Strategy, BRAC web site, November 15, 2011.

55 The term was initially coined at the International Conference on Financing for Development in 2002 and has been popularized by several leaders and academics, including Georgia Levenson Keohane in *Capital and the Common Good*.

56 Conor Reynolds, "UK Start-Up Wagestream Wants to See the End of Pay Day Loans," *Computer Business Review*, November 2, 2018, www.cbronline.com/feature/pay-day-loans.

57 Hannah Williams, "Fintech Startup Wagestream Wants to Tackle Britain's 'Poverty Premium'," *Techworld*, October 10, 2018, www.techworld.com/startups/fintech-startup-wagestream-tackle-uk-poverty-premium-3684812/.

58 Levenson Keohane, *Capital and the Common Good*, 1–3.

59 IFFIm website, Overview, www.iffim.org/about/overview/, retrieved September 16, 2017.

60 Climate Bonds Initiative History, Climate Bonds Initiative web site, retrieved on January 11, 2019, www.climatebonds.net

61 Levenson Keohane, *Capital and the Common Good*, 43–49; Chris Floods, "Green Bonds Need Global Standards," *Financial Times*, May 7, 2017, www.ft.com/content/ef9a02d6-28fe-11e7-bc4b-5528796fe35c.

62 John Maxfield, "US Bancorp CEO Richard Davis to Step Down at the Top of His Game," *The Motley Fool*, January 18, 2017, www.fool.com/investing/2017/01/18/us-bancorp-ceo-richard-davis-to-step-down-at-the-t.aspx.

63 "US Bank CEO Richard Davis Stepping Down; St. Paul-reared COO Taking Over," Dow Jones News Service for *Twin City Pioneer Press*, January 17, 2017, www.twincities.com/2017/01/17/u-s-bank-ceo-richard-davis-stepping-down/.

64 Boatright, *Ethics in Finance*.

65 Most prominently, this argument has been made by Joanne Hill from Goldman Sachs, in "Alpha as a Net Zero-Sum Game," *The Journal of Portfolio Management* 32, no.4 (Summer 2006): 24–32.

66 William Sharpe, "The Arithmetic of Active Management," *Financial Analysts Journal* 47, no.1 (1991): 7–9. www.jstor.org/stable/4479386.

67 Eugene Fama and Kenneth French, "Why Active Investing Is a Negative Sum Game," *Fama/French Forum*, Dimensional.com, June 3, 2009, https://famafrench.dimensional.com/essays/why-active-investing-is-a-negative-sum-game.aspx.

68 Thomas Helbling, "What Are Externalities?" *Finance & Development* 47, no.4 (December 2010), www.imf.org/external/pubs/ft/fandd/2010/12/basics.htm.

69 JC de Swaan, "Japan Is Counting on Shareholder Activism to Improve Its Economy," *Harvard Business Review Online*, September 20, 2017, https://hbr.org/2017/09/japan-is-counting-on-shareholder-activism-to-improve-its-economy

70 As of August 22, 2017.

71 Will Gornall and Ilya Strebulaev, "The Economic Impact of Venture Capital: Evidence from Public Companies," *Stanford University Graduate School of Business Research Paper* #15–55 (November 2015), www.gsb.stanford.edu/faculty-research/working-papers/economic-impact-venture-capital-evidence-public-companies.

72 Manju Puri and Rebecca Zarutskie, "On the Life Cycle Dynamics of Venture-Capital and Non-Venture Capital Finance Firms," *The Journal of Finance* 67, no.6 (November 2012), www.nber.org/papers/w14250.

73 Nicholas and Chen, "Georges Doriot and American Venture Capital," 5.

74 Ibid.; Spencer Ante, *Creative Capital: Georges Doriot and the Birth of Venture Capital* (Cambridge, MA: Harvard Business Press, 2008).

75 Georges Doriot, "Closing Statements by General Georges F. Doriot to Manufacturing Class," May 17, 1966, GFD-HBS, cited in Georges F. Doriot, Educating Leaders, Building Companies, Harvard Business School Baker Library Historical Collections, www.library.hbs.edu/hc/doriot/.

76 Nicholas and Chen, "Georges Doriot and American Venture Capital," 9.

77 Ibid., 9–10.

78 Doriot, "Closing Statements by General Georges F. Doriot."

79 Felda Hardymon, Tom Nicholas, and David Lane, "Greylock Partners," *Harvard Business School Note* 9-813-002, April 26, 2013, 1–2.

80 Ibid., 3.

81 2019, Pitchbook data, National Venture Capital Association, Washington D.C.

82 CrunchBase, "The Crunchbase Unicorn Leaderboard," May 29, 2019, https://techcrunch.com/2019/05/29/the-crunchbase-unicorn-leaderboard-is-back-now-with-a-record-herd-of-452-unicorns/.

83 Based on OECD data, in Gilles Durufle, Thomas Hellman, and Karen Wilson, "From Start-up to Scale-up: Examining Public Policies for the Financing of High-Growth Ventures," *Said Business School Research Papers* (January 2017).

84 Ernst & Young, "Back to Reality: EY Global Venture Capital Trends 2015."

85 Cambridge Associates, *Q2 2018 Private Equity and Venture Capital Performance*, June 30, 2018.

86 Steven Kaplan and Antoinette Schoar, "Private Equity Performance: Returns, Persistence, and Capital Flows," *The Journal of Finance* 60, no.4 (August 2005).

87 Michael McKenzie and William Janeway, "Venture Capital Funds and the Public Equity Market," *Accounting and Finance* 51, no.3 (2011).

88 Janeway, *Doing Capitalism in the Innovation Economy*, 85.

89 Marc Andreessen, "What Kinds of Returns Are Limited Partners Seeking from a VC Fund?" *Quora*, February 4, 2011, www.quora.com/What-kinds-of-returns-are-limited-partners-seeking-from-a-VC-fund-Are-there-term-sheets-agreements-between-LPs-and-VC-general-partners-On-what-terms.

90 Rolfe Winkler, "Andreessen Horowitz's Returns Trail Venture-Capital Elite," *Wall Street Journal*, September 1, 2016, www.wsj.com/articles/andreessen-horowitzs-returns-trail-venture-capital-elite-1472722381.

91 Benchmark Capital LinkedIn site, accessed on June 27, 2019, www.linkedin.com/company/benchmark-vc.

92 Kleiner Perkins Caufield & Byers China website, accessed on June 27, 2019, https://kpcb.com/china.

93 Puri and Zarutskie, "Life Cycle Dynamics."

94 Thomas Hellmann and Manju Puri, "Venture Capital and the Professionalization of Start-up Firms: Empirical Evidence," *Journal of Finance* 57, no.1 (February 2002): 169–197.

95 Samuel Kortum and Josh Lerner, "Assessing the Contribution of Venture Capital to Innovation," *RAND Journal of Economics* 31, no.4 (2000); Masayuki Hirukawa and Masako Ueda, "Venture Capital and Industrial Innovation," Working Paper (September 2008), http://dx.doi.org/10.2139/ssrn.1242693.

96 For a good survey, see Marco Da Rin, Thomas Hellmann, and Manju Puri, "A Survey of Venture Capital Research," *NBER Working Paper* 17523, 2011; and "State of the Field: Venture Capital," *Kauffman Foundation*, June 2016, www.kauffman.org/microsites/state-of-the-field/topics/finance/equity/venture-capital.

97 David Blanchflower and Andrew Oswald, "What Makes an Entrepreneur?" *Journal of Labor Economics* 16, no.1 (1998).

98 Marcos Mollinca and Luigi Zingales, "The Impact of Venture Capital on Innovation and the Creation of New Business," unpublished working paper, University of Chicago, 2007.

99 Sampsa Samila and Olav Sorenson, "Venture Capital, Entrepreneurship, and Economic Growth," *The Review of Economics and Statistics* 93, no.10 (February 2011).

100 Samila and Sorenson, "Venture Capital, Entrepreneurship, and Economic Growth."

101 Janeway, *Doing Capitalism*, 86.

102 Samila and Sorenson, "Venture Capital, Entrepreneurship, and Economic Growth."

103 *2019 Preqin Global Private Equity & Venture Capital Report*, http://docs.preqin.com/reports/2019-Preqin-Global-Private-Equity-Report-Sample-Pages.pdf.

104 Pitchbook.

105 Although there is little evidence of persistence for private equity funds, as opposed to venture capital; see Robert Harris, Tim Jenkinson, Steven Kaplan, and Ruediger

Stucke, "Has Persistence Persisted in Private Equity? Evidence from Buyout and Venture Capital Funds," *SSRN Working Paper* (August 2014), https://papers.ssrn.com/sol3/papers.cfm?abstract_id=2304808.

106 2017 Preqin Global Private Equity & Venture Capital Report.

107 Amy Whyte, "Survey: Endowments and Foundations Unfazed by Private Equity Valuations," *Institutional Investor*, November 14, 2017, www.institutionalinvestor.com/article/b15lszg3l63vv6/survey-endowments-and-foundations-unfazed-by-private-equity-valuations.

108 Cambridge Associates, Buy-Out & Growth Equity Index and Selected Benchmark Statistics, September 2019, www.cambridgeassociates.com/wp-content/uploads/2020/02/WEB-2019-Q3-USPE-Benchmark-Book.pdf

109 See Jean-Francois L'Her, Rossitsa Stoyanova, Kathryn Shaw, William Scott, and Charissa Lai, "A Bottom-up Approach to the Risk-Adjusted Performance of the Buyout Fund Market," *Financial Analysts Journal* 72, no.4 (2016), www.cfapubs.org/doi/pdf/10.2469/faj.v72.n4.10; Ludovic Phalippou, "Performance of Buyout Funds Revisited," *Review of Finance* 18, no.1 (2014): 189–218; Robert Harris, Tim Jenkinson, and Steven Kaplan, "Private Equity Performance: What Do We Know?" *Journal of Finance* 69, no.5 (2013), https://doi.org/10.1111/jofi.12154; Erik Stafford, "Replicating Private Equity with Value Investing, Homemade Leverage, and Hold-to-Maturity Accounting," *Harvard Business School Working Paper*, January 2016, www.hbs.edu/faculty/Pages/item.aspx?num=50433; Brian Chingono and Daniel Rasmussen, "Leveraged Small Value Equities," *SSRN*, August 1, 2015, https://papers.ssrn.com/sol3/papers.cfm?abstract_id=2639647; Brian Boyer, Taylor Nadauld, Keith Vorkink, and Michael Weisbach, "Private Equity Indices Based on Secondary Market Transactions," *NBER Working Paper No. 25207* (November 2018), https://www.nber.org/papers/w25207.

110 Erik Stafford, "Replicating Private Equity," 28.

111 Bernard Condon and Nathan Vardi, "How Harvard's Investing Superstars Crashed," *Forbes*, February 20, 2009, www.forbes.com/2009/02/20/harvard-endowment-failed-business_harvard.html.

112 2018 Preqin Global Private Equity & Venture Capital Report.

113 Q3 2015 Earnings Call, The Blackstone Group.

114 Julie Creswell, "Profits for Buyout Firms as Company Debt Soared," *New York Times*, October 4, 2009, www.nytimes.com/2009/10/05/business/economy/05simmons.html

115 "How the Twinkie Made the Super-Rich Even Richer," *New York Times*, December 10, 2016, http://nyti.ms/2h8Vlfo.

116 Natalie Harrison and Mariana Santibanez, "Refile-Platinum's Rapid LBO Exit Stuns High-Yield Market," *Reuters*, February 14, 2014, www.reuters.com/article/platinum-pik-highyield/refile-platinums-rapid-lbo-exit-stuns-high-yield-market-idUSL5N0LH4Q020140214.

117 Nabila Ahmed and Sridhar Natarajan, "Private Equity Wins Even When It Loses, Thanks to Debt Markets," *Bloomberg*, March 20, 2017, www.bloomberg.com/news/articles/2017-03-20/private-equity-wins-even-when-it-loses-thanks-to-debt-markets.

118 LCD, S&P Global Market Intelligence, quoted in Tom Metcalf, "This Billionaire Made His Fortune on $50 Chainsaws," *Bloomberg*, February 14, 2017.

119 Pitchbook.

120 Henny Sender, "Private Equity Turns to Early Loans to Boost Returns," *Financial Times*, January 1, 2018, www.ft.com/content/5a4c68fe-e573-11e7-97e2-916d4fbacoda.

121 "Unilever Was a Deal Too Far for Kraft Heinz," *Financial Times Editorial*, February 20, 2017, www.ft.com/content/820fe386-f76a-11e6-bd4e-68d53499ed71.

122 "Barbarians at the Plate," *The Economist*, February 25, 2017, www.economist.com/business/2017/02/25/3g-missed-unilever-but-its-methods-are-spreading.

123 Craig Giammona and Katherine Chiglinsky, "Kraft Heinz Couldn't Stomach 3G's Relentless Cost-Cutting," *Bloomberg*, February 28, 2019, www.bloomberg.com/news/articles/2019-02-28/kraft-heinz-couldn-t-stomach-3g-s-relentless-cost-cutting.

124 Steven Kaplan, "The Effects of Management Buyouts on Operating Performance and Value," *Journal of Financial Economics* 24 (October): 217–254.

125 Steven J. Davis, John Haltiwanger, Kyle Handley, Ron Jarmin, Josh Lerner, and Javier Miranda, "Private Equity, Jobs and Productivity," *American Economic Review* 104, no.12 (2014), https://papers.ssrn.com/sol3/papers.cfm?abstract_id=2460790.

126 Quentin Boucly, David Sraer, and David Thesmar, "Growth LBOs," *Journal of Financial Economics* 102, no.2 (September 2012): 432–453, https://papers.ssrn.com/sol3/papers.cfm?abstract_id=1354087.

127 Richard Harris, Donald Siegel, and Mike Wright, "Assessing the Impact of Management Buyouts on Economic Efficiency: Plant-Level Evidence from the United Kingdom," *Review of Economics and Statistics* 87, no.1 (February 2005): 148–153, https://econpapers.repec.org/paper/rpirpiwpe/0304.htm.

128 Morten Sorensen, Per Stromberg, and Josh Lerner, "Private Equity and Long-Run Investment: The Case for Innovation," *The Journal of Finance* 66, no.2 (2010): 445–477, https://papers.ssrn.com/sol3/papers.cfm?abstract_id=1949337.

129 Tereza Tykvova and Mariela Borell, "Do Private Equity Owners Increase the Risk of Financial Distress and Bankruptcy?" *Journal of Corporate Finance* 18, no.1 (February 2012): 138–150, https://papers.ssrn.com/sol3/papers.cfm?abstract_id=2334073.

130 Steven Kaplan and Per Stromberg, "Leveraged Buyouts and Private Equity," *Journal of Economic Perspectives* 23, no.1 (Winter 2009): 121–46, https://econpapers.repec.org/article/aeajecper/v_3a23_3ay_3a2009_3ai_3a1_3ap_3a121-46.htm.

131 Steven J. Davis, John Haltiwanger, Kyle Handley, Ron Jarmin, Josh Lerner, and Javier Miranda, "Private Equity, Jobs and Productivity," *American Economic Review* 104, no.12 (December 2014): 3956–3990, www.jstor.org/stable/43495362?seq=1#page_scan_tab_contents.

132 Nick Wilson, Mike Wright, Donald Siegel, and Louise Scholes, "Private Equity Portfolio Company Performance during the Global Recession," *Journal of Corporate Finance* 18, no.1 (2012): 193–205, https://econpapers.repec.org/article/eeecorfin/v_3a18_3ay_3a2012_3ai_3a1_3ap_3a193-205.htm.

133 Kevin Amess and Mike Wright, "The Wage and Employment Effects of Leveraged Buyouts in the UK," *International Journal of the Economics of Business* 14, no.2 (2007): 179–195, https://papers.ssrn.com/sol3/papers.cfm?abstract_id=1043081.

134 Michael C. Jensen, "Eclipse of the Public Corporation," *Harvard Business Review*, September–October 1989, https://hbr.org/1989/09/eclipse-of-the-public-corporation.

135 Serdar Aldatmaz and Gregory Brown, "Private Equity in the Global Economy: Evidence on Industry Spillovers," *UNC Kenan-Flagler Research Paper no. 2013–9* (August 9, 2016), https://papers.ssrn.com/sol3/papers.cfm?abstract_id=2189707.

136 Jarrad Harford, Jared Stanfield, and Feng Zhang, "How Does an LBO Impact the Target's Industry?" *SSRN*, September 2016, https://papers.ssrn.com/sol3/papers.cfm?abstract_id=2489300.

137 Andrew Ross Sorkin, "Is Private Equity Giving Hertz a Boost?" *New York Times*, September 23, 2007; Aldatmaz and Brown, "Private Equity in the Global Economy."

138 John C. Coffee and Darius Palia, "The Wolf at the Door: The Impact of Hedge Fund Activism on Corporate Governance," *Columbia Law School Working Paper no.521* (September 4, 2015), 100, https://papers.ssrn.com/sol3/papers.cfm?abstract_id=2656325.

139 Francesco Guerrera, "Welch Condemns Share Price Focus," *Financial Times*, March 12, 2009, www.ft.com/content/294ff1f2-0f27-11de-ba10-0000779fd2ac.

140 Benjamin Graham and David Dodd, *Security Analysis: Principles and Technique* (New York: McGraw-Hill, 1934); Benjamin Graham, *The Intelligent Investor: A Book of Practical Counsel* (New York: Harper).

141 Jeff Gramm, *Dear Chairman: Boardroom Battles and the Rise of Shareholder Activism* (New York: HarperBusiness, 2016), 1–11.

142 Coffee and Palia, "The Wolf at the Door."

143 Sullivan & Cromwell, "Review and Analysis of 2018 U.S. Shareholder Activism," March 14, 2019, www.sullcrom.com/files/upload/SC-Publication-SandC-MnA-2018-US-Shareholder-Activism-Analysis.pdf.

144 Eric Rosenbaum, "A Big Climate Change Vote against Exxon Mobil, with Some Heavyweight Investors behind It," *CNBC*, May 31, 2017, www.cnbc.com/2017/05/31/index-giant-vanguard-does-about-face-on-big-investing-position-report.html?view=story&%24DEVICE%24=native-android-mobile.

145 JP Morgan, *The 2017 Proxy Season*, July 2017, www.jpmorgan.com/jpmpdf/1320739681811.pdf.

146 Nelson Schwartz, "How Wall Street Bent Steel," *New York Times,* December 6, 2014, www.nytimes.com/2014/12/07/business/timken-bows-to-investors-and-splits-in-two.html.

147 Nathan Vardi, "Hedge Fund ValueAct Capital's Valeant Legacy," *Forbes*, June 6, 2016, www.forbes.com/sites/nathanvardi/2016/06/06/hedge-fund-valueact-capitals-valeant-legacy/#5e2b3af9203a.

148 Tom Buerkle, "On Succession, ValueAct Hedge Fund Practices What It Preaches," *The New York Times DealBook*, May 16, 2017, www.nytimes.com/2017/05/16/business/dealbook/valueact-hedge-fund-succession.html.

149 FactSet.

150 Ram Charan, Michael Useem, and Dennis Carey, "Your Board Should Think Like Activists," *Harvard Business Review*, February 9, 2015, https://hbr.org/2015/02/your-board-should-be-full-of-activists.

151 Coffee and Palia, "The Wolf at the Door," 57.

152 Ibid., 18–21.

153 Ibid., 28–42.

154 Owen Walker, *Barbarians in the Boardroom* (London: FT Publishing, 2016), 212.

155 FactSet, June 30, 2017.

156 Alexandra Stevenson and Michael de la Merced, "With Crowding in US Market, Activist Investors Look to Europe," *Dealbook, The New York Times*, June 26, 2017, www.nytimes.com/2017/06/26/business/dealbook/activist-investors-after-saturating-us-market-look-to-europe.html.

157 Walker, *Barbarians*, 213.

158 Ibid., 216.

159 Jen Wieczner, "Meet Europe's Best Activist Investor," *Fortune*, August 27, 2015, http://fortune.com/2015/08/27/christer-gardell-activist-investor-europe/.

160 "Leading from Behind," *The Economist*, June 17, 2017.

161 Yvon Allaire and Francois Dauphin, "Hedge Fund Activism: Preliminary Results and Some New Empirical Evidence," *Institute for the Governance of Public and Private Organizations*, April 1, 2015, www.shareholderforum.com/access/Library/20150401_Allaire.pdf.

162 "An Investor Calls," *The Economist*, February 5, 2015, www.economist.com/briefing/2015/02/05/an-investor-calls.

163 Alon Brav, Wei Jiang, Song Ma, and Xuan Tian, "How Does Hedge Fund Activism Reshape Corporate Innovation?" *NBER Working Paper* #22273, May 24, 2016, www.nber.org/papers/w22273.

164 Lucian Bebchuk, Alan Brav, and Wei Jiang, "The Long-Term Effects of Hedge Fund Activism," *Columbia Law Review* 115 (2015), https://columbialawreview.org/content/the-long-term-effects-of-hedge-fund-activism/.

165 April Klein and Emanuel Zur, "The Impact of Hedge Funds on the Target Firm's Existing Bondholders," *Review of Financial Studies* 24, no.5 (2011): 1735–1771, https://papers.ssrn.com/sol3/papers.cfm?abstract_id=1291605.

166 Bebchuk, Brav, and Jiang, "How Does Hedge Fund Activism Reshape Corporate Innovation?"

167 Coffee and Palia, "The Wolf at the Door."

168 Martin Lipton, Theodore Mirvis, and Jay Lorsch, "The Proposed Shareholder Bill of Rights Act of 2009," *Harvard Law School Forum on Corporate Governance & Financial Regulation*, May 12, 2009, https://corpgov.law.harvard.edu/2009/05/12/the-proposed-shareholder-bill-of-rights-act-of-2009/.

169 Yvan Allaire and Francois Dauphin, "The Game of 'Activist' Hedge Funds: Cui Bono?" *International Journal of Disclosure and Governance*, November 2015, http://clsbluesky.law.columbia.edu/2015/10/14/the-game-of-activist-hedge-funds-cui-bono/; Coffee and Palia, "The Wolf at the Door," 85.

170 Klein and Zur, "The Impact of Hedge Funds."

171 Alon Brav, Wei Jiang, and Hyunseob Kim, "The Real Effects of Hedge Fund Activism: Productivity, Asset Allocation, and Industry Concentration," SSRN, May 2013, https://papers.ssrn.com/sol3/papers.cfm?abstract_id=2022904.

172 Steven Davidoff Solomon, "In Allergan Fight, a Focus on Clever Strategy Overshadows Goals," *New York Times*, August 13, 2014 – highlighted in Coffee and Palia, "The Wolf at the Door," 56.

173 Joseph Walker and Liz Hoffman, "Allergan's Defense: Be Like Valeant," *The Wall Street Journal*, July 22, 2014, highlighted in Coffee and Palia, "The Wolf at the Door," 56.

174 Coffee and Palia, "The Wolf at the Door," 57.

175 Joseph Walker, "Botox Itself Aims Not to Age," *Wall Street Journal*, May 19, 2014, highlighted by Coffee and Palia, "The Wolf at the Door," p. 56.

176 Walker, *Barbarians in the Boardroom*, 104–105.

177 Ibid., 117.

178 Ibid., 119.

179 Matthew Levine, "Bill Ackman Is Done Losing Money on Valeant," *Bloomberg Opinion*, March 14, 2017, www.bloomberg.com/opinion/articles/2017-03-14/bill-ackman-is-done-losing-money-on-valeant.

180 Anders Melin and Jenn Zhao, "Perks for American CEOs Aren't What They Used to Be," *Bloomberg*, July 21, 2017, www.bloomberg.com/news/articles/2017-07-21/ski-eat-pizza-and-dress-on-the-cheap-perks-of-america-s-ceos.

181 John Buchanan, Dominic Heesang Chai, and Simon Deakin, *Hedge Fund Activism in Japan* (Cambridge: Cambridge University Press, 2012), 107–110, 119.

182 Communication with Trevor Hill, June 21, 2019.

183 In 2019, investor roundtable discussion dinners hosted by SMBC in Tokyo have jokingly featured a bottle of Bull-Dog sauce by each place setting for guests to take home, as a "shout-out" to the dark days of confrontational activism. Sourced from Trevor Hill, Global Head of Equity, SMBC Nikko Securities, June 21, 2019.

184 "Appointment of Independent Directors/Auditors: Ratio of 1st Section Companies with Two or More Independent Directors," Japan Exchange Group, Retrieved on June 19, 2019, www.jpx.co.jp/english/listing/others/ind-executive/index.html.

185 Board of Governors of the Federal Reserve System, Federal Reserve Statistical Release Z.1, "Financial Accounts of the United States: Flow of Funds, Balance Sheets, and Integrated Macroeconomic Accounts," Table F-223: Corporate Equities, March 2017.

186 John Kay, *The Kay Review of UK Equity Markets and Long-Term Decision Making*, Department for Business, Innovation, and Skills, United Kingdom government, September 2011, 23, www.gov.uk/government/consultations/the-kay-review-of-uk-equity-markets-and-long-term-decision-making

187 Kay, *Kay Review*, 28.

188 William Lazonick, "The Functions of the Stock Market and the Fallacies of Shareholder Value," Working Paper #58, *Institute for New Economic Thinking*, June 3, 2017, www.ineteconomics.org/research/research-papers/the-functions-of-the-stock-market-and-the-fallacies-of-shareholder-value.

189 Matthijs Breugem and Adrian Buss, "Institutional Investors and Information Acquisition: Implications for Asset Prices and Informational Efficiency," *National Bureau of Economic Research Working Paper* #23561 (June 2017), https://papers.ssrn.com/sol3/papers.cfm?abstract_id=2999540.

190 For a useful discussion on value creation versus values alignment, see Matthew Weatherley-White, "You Didn't Build That," Part 2, *Medium*, May 18, 2016, https://medium.com/@i3impact/you-didnt-build-that-part-2-94701f183b4b.

191 *Adapting Portfolios to Climate Change*, Blackrock Investment Institute, September 2016, 10.

192 Ibid., 9.

193 "Sustainable Reality: Understanding the Performance of Sustainable Investment Strategies," *Morgan Stanley*, March 2015, www.morganstanley.com/assets/pdfs/sustainableinvesting/sustainable-reality.pdf.

194 "LO Funds Generation Global Sustainability Report," *Lombard Odier Investment Managers*, First quarter 2019. www.lombardodier.com/modules/documents/QR/QR_1038_CH_EN.PDF

195 Gillian Tett, "Ethical Investing Has Reached a Tipping Point," *Financial Times*, June 18, 2019, www.ft.com/content/7d64d1d8-91a6-11e9-b7ea-60e35ef678d2.

196 "Swiss Re Among First in the Re/insurance Industry to Integrate ESG Benchmarks into Its Investment Decisions," Swiss Re corporate website, July 6, 2017, www.swissre.com/media/news-releases/2017/nr20170706_MSCI_ESG_investing.html.

197 Junko Fujita, "Japan's GPIF Expects to Raise ESG Allocations to 10 Percent: FTSE Russell CEO," *Reuters*, July 14, 2017, www.reuters.com/article/us-japan-

gpif-esg/japans-gpif-expects-to-raise-esg-allocations-to-10-percent-ftse-russell-ceo-idUSKBN19Z11Y.

198 Frédéric Samama interviews with the author, January 1, 2017, January 1, 2018, and May 19, 2019.

199 Andersson, Bolton, and Samama, "Hedging Climate Risk."

200 Mats Andersson, Patrick Bolton, and Frédéric Samama, "Governance and Climate Change: A Success Story."

201 Siew Hong Teoh, Ivo Welch, and C. Paul Wazzan, "The Effect of Socially Activist Investment Policies on the Financial Markets: Evidence from the South African Boycott," *Journal of Business* 72, no.1 (1999), https://papers.ssrn.com/sol3/papers.cfm?abstract_id=10203.

202 For a good example of this argument, see Paul Brest, Ronald Gilson, and Mark Wolfson, "How Investors Can (and Can't) Create Social Value," *Stanford Social Innovation Review,* December 8, 2016, https://papers.ssrn.com/sol3/papers.cfm?abstract_id=3150347.

203 Finnegan Schick, "Yale to Partially Divest from Fossil Fuels," *Yale Daily News*, April 12, 2016, https://yaledailynews.com/blog/2016/04/12/yale-begins-divestment-from-fossil-fuels/.

204 "The Long View: US Proxy Voting Trends on E&S Issues from 2000 to 2018," Harvard Law School Forum on Corporate Governance, January 31, 2019, https://corpgov.law.harvard.edu/2019/01/31/the-long-view-us-proxy-voting-trends-on-es-issues-from-2000-to-2018/.

205 Based on Proxy Monitor data, in Mary-Hunter McDonnell, Brayden King, and Sarah Soule, "A Dynamic Process Model of Private Politics: Activist Targeting and Corporate Receptivity to Social Challenges," *American Sociological Review*, April 2015, https://journals.sagepub.com/doi/abs/10.1177/0003122415581335?journalCode=asra.

206 Grewal, Serafeim, and Yoon, "Shareholder Activism on Sustainability Issues."

207 "How Does Activism Drive Corporate Change?," *Kellogg Insight*, June 2, 2015, https://insight.kellogg.northwestern.edu/article/how-do-activists-create-change.

208 McDonnell, King, and Soule, "A Dynamic Process Model of Private Politics."

209 Keith Griffin, "Why PETA Buys Stock in Companies," *TheStreet*, August 4, 2016.

210 "How Does Activism Drive Corporate Change?" *Kellogg Insight*.

211 Tom Redmond, Anna Kitanaka, and Toshiro Hasegawa, "How a Novice Quant Developed an Index for Changing Japan," *Bloomberg*, August 27, 2014, www.bloomberg.com/news/articles/2014-08-26/how-a-novice-quant-developed-an-index-for-changing-japan.

212 Communication between Trevor Hill and the author, June 24, 2019.

213 Larry Elliott, "Black Wednesday, 20 Years on: A Bad Day for the Tories but Not for Britain," *The Guardian*, September 13, 2012, www.theguardian.com/business/2012/sep/13/black-wednesday-bad-day-conservatives.

214 Ibid.

215 Niall Ferguson and Jonathan Schlefer, "Who Broke the Bank of England?" *Harvard Business School Case* #9-709-026, September 9, 2009, www.hbs.edu/faculty/Pages/item.aspx?num=36754; Philip Stephens, "The Road from Black Wednesday to Brexit," *Financial Times*, September 13, 2017, www.ft.com/content/a331a3ca-96d8-11e7-a652-cde3f882dd7b; Elliott, "Black Wednesday, 20 Years On."

216 Anatole Kaletsky, "How Mr. Soros Made a Billion by Betting against the Pound – George Soros," *The London Times*, October 26, 1992, cited in Ferguson and Schlefer, "Who Broke the Bank of England?"

217 Ferguson and Schlefer, "Who Broke the Bank of England?"

218 Norman Lamont, *In Office*, Little, Brown, and Co., 1999, p.259, as cited in Ferguson and Schlefer, "Who Broke the Bank of England?"

219 George Soros, *Soros on Soros: Staying Ahead of the Curve* (London: John Wiley, 1995), 82.

220 George Soros, "Fallibility, Reflexivity, and the Human Uncertainty Principle," *Journal of Economic Methodology*, January 13, 2014, www.georgesoros.com/2014/01/13/fallibility-reflexivity-and-the-human-uncertainty-principle-2/.

221 This section draws from input by Scott Bessent.

222 Lynn Stout, "Does Wall Street Do 'God's Work'? Or Even Anything Useful?" *Pro-Market Blog*, University of Chicago Booth School of Business, August 31, 2016, https://promarket.org/wall-street-gods-work-even-anything-useful/.

223 Jack Hirshleifer, "The Private and Social Value of Information and the Reward to Inventive Activity," *The American Economic Review* 61, no.4, September 1971, https://econpapers.repec.org/article/aeaaecrev/v_3a61_3ay_3a1971_3ai_3a4_3ap_3a561-74.htm.

224 Communication with Scott Bessent, June 25, 2019.

225 "From Mr. Copper to Choc Finger: Past Attempts to Corner Commodity Markets," *The Telegraph*, December 3, 2010, www.telegraph.co.uk/finance/newsbysector/industry/mining/8178976/From-Mr-Copper-to-Choc-Finger-Past-attempts-to-corner-commodity-markets.html.

226 Jonathan Hoenig, "Why Cornering a Market Doesn't Work," *MarketWatch*, December 16, 2010, www.marketwatch.com/story/why-cornering-a-market-doesnt-work-1292524790364.

227 Lynn Stout, "Does Wall Street Do 'God's Work'?"

228 John Kay, "Wind Down the Market in Five-Legged Dogs," *Financial Times*, January 20, 2009, www.ft.com/content/c08a764a-e70f-11dd-8407-0000779fd2ac.

229 Communication with Scott Bessent, June 25, 2019.

230 For a clear discussion of this topic, see O'Hara, *Something for Nothing*, 132–138.

231 O'Hara, *Something for Nothing*, 133.

232 Brian Trelstad, "Impact Investing: A Brief History," *Capitalism and Society* 11, no.2, article 4 (2016), https://papers.ssrn.com/sol3/papers.cfm?abstract_id=2886088.

233 Ibid.

234 Ibid.

235 Ibid.

236 Jonathan Godsall and Aditya Sanghvi, "How Impact Investing Can Reach the Mainstream," McKinsey & Company, November 2016.

237 Ibid.

238 Ibid.

239 "About DBL Partners," DBL Partners website, www.dblpartners.vc/about/, accessed on October 3, 2017.

240 Beth Kowitt, "This Start-Up Has a Plan to Take on Big Food," *Fortune*, November 15, 2016, http://fortune.com/2016/11/15/revolution-foods-product-launch/.

241 Nancy Pfund and Lisa Hagerman, "Response to 'How Investors Can (and Can't) Create Social Value'," *Stanford Social Innovation Review*, December 8, 2016, https://ssir.org/up_for_debate/how_investors_can_and_cant_create_social_value/pfund_hagerman; PitchBook data accessed on February 18, 2020.

242 Melissa Mittelman, "TPG Seals Record $2 Billion for Fund Co-Led by Bono," *Bloomberg*, October 3, 2017, www.bloomberg.com/news/articles/2017-10-03/tpg-seals-record-2-billion-for-rise-impact-fund-co-led-by-bono.

243 See in particular Cambridge Associates and Global Impact Investing Initiative (GIIN), Introducing the Impact Investing Benchmark 2015, www.thegiin.org/assets/documents/pub/Introducing_the_Impact_Investing_Benchmark.pdf and Jacob Gray, Nick Ashburn, Harry Douglas, and Jessica Jeffers, "Great Expectations: Mission Preservation and Financial Performance in Impact Investing," *Wharton Social Impact Initiative*, https://socialimpact.wharton.upenn.edu/wp-content/uploads/2016/09/Great-Expectations-Mission-Preservation-and-Financial-Performance-in-Impact-Investing.pdf.

244 "PE/VC Impact Investing Index & Benchmark Statistics," Cambridge Associates, September 2019, www.cambridgeassociates.com/wp-content/uploads/2020/02/PEVC-Impact-Investing-Benchmark-Statistics-2019-Q3.pdf.

245 Owen Walker, "Changing Mindsets," *Impact Investing Financial Times Report*, September 2018, 6–9.

246 Sasha Dichter, "Quantitative Social Metrics for Impact Investing," *Acumen Blog*, February 12, 2014, https://acumen.org/blog/quantitative-social-metrics-for-impact-investing/.

247 Acumen and Root Capital, "Innovations in Impact Measurement," November 2015, http://acumen.org/wp-content/uploads/2015/11/Innovations-in-Impact-Measurement-Report.pdf.

Chapter 3

1 Michael Pirson, *Humanistic Management: Protecting Dignity and Promoting Well-Being* (Cambridge: Cambridge University Press, 2017), 89, 127.

2 Pirson, *Humanistic Management*, 45.

3 Robert Greenleaf, *The Servant as Leader* (Indianapolis, IN: The Greenleaf Center for Servant Leadership, 1991).

4 Charles D. Ellis, *What It Takes: Seven Secrets of Success from the World's Greatest Professional Firms* (Hoboken, NJ: John Wiley & Sons, 2013), 153.

5 Max Bazerman and Ann Tenbrunsel, *Blind Spots: Why We Fail to Do What's Right and What to Do About It* (Princeton, NJ: Princeton University Press, 2011), 49.

6 Jeffrey Pfeffer, "Why the Assholes Are Winning: Money Trumps All," *Journal of Management Studies* 53, no.4 (January 2016): 663–669, www.gsb.stanford.edu/faculty-research/publications/why-assholes-are-winning-money-trumps-all.

7 Katherine Chiglinsky and Laura Keller, "Junk-Bond Star Is a Bully Who Terrified Subordinates, Peers Say," *Bloomberg*, August 14, 2018, www.bloomberg.com/news/articles/2018-08-14/junk-bond-star-is-a-bully-peers-say-who-terrified-subordinates.

8 Bazerman and Tenbrunsel, *Blind Spots*, 81–83.

9 Simon Mundy, "PwC Hit With 2-Year India Audit Ban for Satyam Case," *Financial Times*, January 11, 2018, www.ft.com/content/c1231f40-f695-11e7-88f7-5465a6ce1a00.

10 Jeffrey Pfeffer, *Leadership BS: Fixing Workplaces and Careers One Truth at a Time* (New York: HarperBusiness, 2015), 38.

11 David Brooks, *The Road to Character* (New York: Random House, 2015).

12 Adam Grant, *Give and Take: Why Helping Others Drives Our Success* (New York: Viking, 2013).

13 Grant, *Give and Take*, 17.

14 Grant, *Give and Take*, 23–25.

15 Leena Rao, "Sand Hill Consiglieres: August Capital," *Techcrunch.com*, June 14, 2014, https://techcrunch.com/2014/06/14/sand-hill-roads-consiglieres-august-capital/.

16 Marvin Bower, *Perspective on McKinsey* (privately published by McKinsey & Company, 1979), 173.

17 Bernard Ferrari, *Power Listening: Mastering the Most Critical Business Skill of All* (New York: Portfolio/Penguin, 2012), 3.

18 Susan Ochs, "Inside the Banker's Brain: Mental Models in the Financial Services Industry and Implications for Consumers, Practitioners and Regulators," *Initiative on Financial Security*, The Aspen Institute (2014), https://assets.aspeninstitute.org/content/uploads/files/content/upload/IFSBankersBrainPaper_FINAL_6–9-14.pdf.

19 Ellis, *What It Takes*, 12.

20 Quoted in Ellis, *What It Takes,* 36.

21 Ellis, *What It Takes*, 112–115.

22 John Gittelsohn, "Capital Group Has a Crazy Idea It Should Know the Stocks It Owns," *Bloomberg*, May 14, 2019. www.bloomberg.com/news/features/2019-05-14/the-1-9-trillion-fund-giant-with-a-crazy-idea-about-investing.

23 Warren Hellman in Robert Finkel and David Greising, *The Masters of Private Equity and Venture Capital: Management Lessons from the Pioneers of Private Investing* (New York: McGraw-Hill Education, December 2009), 53.

24 Hellman in Finkel and Greising, *Masters of Private Equity*, 54–55.

25 Hellman in Finkel and Greising, *Masters of Private Equity*, 60.

26 Interview by the author of Mick Hellman (son of Warren Hellman), September 22, 2015.

27 Interview by the author of Philip Hammarskjold, co-CEO of Hellman & Friedman, September 3, 2015.

28 Ryan Mac, "Warren Hellman, San Francisco Private Equity Pioneer, Dies at 77," *Forbes*, December 18, 2011, www.forbes.com/sites/ryanmac/2011/12/18/san-francisco-private-equity-pioneer-dies-at-77/#2ff6564695a1.

29 Hellman in Finkel and Greising, *Masters of Private Equity*, 55.

30 *CEO Pay Ratio Survey*, Equilar, February 2018, https://marketing.equilar.com/31-2018-ceo-pay-ratio-survey.

31 While Bridgeway stands out for the way in which the founder's values inform its structure, its path hasn't always been seamless. The firm agreed in 2004 to a $5 million settlement with the SEC for overcharging performance fees on three mutual funds between 1995 and 2004. "Bridgeway Capital Management and Its President, John Montgomery," *Pensions & Investments*, September 15, 2004, www.pionline.com/article/20040915/ONLINE/409150704/bridgeway-capital-management-and-its-president-john-montgomery.

32 Bridgeway Capital Management website, retrieved on February 14, 2020, www.bridgeway.com/giving-back/our-commitment/.

33 Stephanie Klein, "Why Bridgeway Capital Gives Away 50% of Profits to Charity," *Knowledge@Wharton*, March 19, 2015, https://knowledge.wharton.upenn.edu/article/why-bridgeway-capital-gives-away-half-of-its-profits-to-charity/.

34 Bridgeway Capital Management website, retrieved on August 20, 2018, www.bridgeway.com/giving-back/our-commitment/.

35 *Cure for the Common Culture: How to Build a Healthy Risk Culture*, PwC (October 2014), www.pwc.com/us/en/financial-services/publications/viewpoints/assets/bank-financial-services-sustainable-risk-culture-pwc.pdf.

36 Tim Loughran, Bill McDonald, and Hayong Yun, "A Wolf in Sheep's Clothing: The Use of Ethics-Related Terms in 10-K Reports,." *Journal of Business Ethics* 89, no.1 (2008): 39–49, https://papers.ssrn.com/sol3/papers.cfm?abstract_id=1007727.

37 Luigi Guiso, Paola Sapienza, and Luigi Zingales, "The Value of Corporate Culture," *NBER Working Paper* 19557 (October 2013), www.nber.org/papers/w19557.pdf.

38 Joe Garner, "A Duty or a Culture of Care?" in *Transforming Culture in Financial Services*, Discussion Paper DP18/2, Financial Conduct Authority (March 2018), 27–29, http://business-school.exeter.ac.uk/media/universityofexeter/businessschool/documents/centres/cls/FCA_dp18–02.pdf.

39 Steven G. Mandis, *What Happened to Goldman Sachs?* (Boston, MA: Harvard Business Review Press, 2013), 17.

40 Ellis, *What It Takes*, 41–45, 163.

41 John C. Whitehead, *A Life in Leadership: From D-Day to Ground Zero* (New York: Basic Books, 2005), 107.

42 Ellis, *What It Takes*, 99–101.

43 Whitehead, *A Life in Leadership*, 276.

44 John Whitehead interview with the author, New York, November 13, 2014.

45 Charles D. Ellis, *The Partnership: The Making of Goldman Sachs* (New York: Penguin, 2008), 195.

46 Whitehead, *A Life in Leadership*, 118.

47 Mandis, *What Happened to Goldman Sachs?* 93–116.

48 John Whitehead interview with the author, New York, May 16, 2014.

49 Mandis, *What Happened to Goldman Sachs?* 40.

50 Brian Nosek, Mahzain Banaji, and Anthony Greenwald, "Math = Male, Me = Female, Therefore Math ≠ Me," *Journal of Personality and Social Psychology* 83, no. 1, 44–59, http://projectimplicit.net/nosek/papers/nosek.math.JPSP.2002.pdf.

51 "When Women Thrive: Financial Services Perspective," Mercer (October 2016), www.mercer.com/our-thinking/gender-diversity-financial-services-industry-report.html.

52 "Making Diversity a Reality," PwC (2015), www.pwc.com/gx/en/industries/financial-services/publications/making-diversity-reality.html, 7.

53 "Making Diversity a Reality," PwC, 7.

54 "Making Diversity a Reality," PwC, 3.

55 "Gender Pay: Fewer Than Half of UK Firms Narrow Gap," *BBC News*, April 5, 2019. www.bbc.com/news/business-47822291.

56 Phone interview of Natasha Lamb by the author, May 6, 2019.

57 Jane Meggitt, "The Warrior Woman of Arjuna Capital," *Advisors Magazine*, June 29, 2018, www.advisorsmagazine.com/component/content/article/242-fp-slideshow/23208-the-warrior-woman-of-arjuna-capital.

58 Morten Bennedsen, Elena Simintzi, Margarita Tsoutsoura, and Daniel Wolfenzon, "Research: Gender Pay Gaps Shrink When Companies Are Required to Disclose Them," *Harvard Business Review*, January 23, 2019, https://hbr.org/2019/01/research-gender-pay-gaps-shrink-when-companies-are-required-to-disclose-them.

59 Natasha Lamb, "The Median Gender Pay Gap: It's Time to Tell the Whole Story," *Quartz*, February 13, 2019, https://qz.com/work/1549162/the-median-gender-pay-gap-arjuna-capital-wants-the-data-revealed/.

60 Sara Wechter, "Global Pay Equity at Citi," *Citigroup Blog*, January 16, 2019. https://blog.citigroup.com/2019/01/global-pay-equity-at-citi.

61 Vivian Hunt, Sara Prince, Sundiatu Dixon-Fyle, and Lareina Yee, "Diversity Matters," *McKinsey & Company*, January 2018, 8, www.mckinsey.com/business-functions/organization/our-insights/delivering-through-diversity.

62 Katherine Phillips, "How Diversity Makes Us Smarter," *Scientific American*, October 1, 2014, www.scientificamerican.com/article/how-diversity-makes-us-smarter/; David Rock and Heidi Grant, "Why Diverse Teams Are Smarter," *Harvard Business Review*, November 4, 2016, https://hbr.org/2016/11/why-diverse-teams-are-smarter.

63 "When Women Thrive," Mercer, 4.

64 "Making Diversity a Reality," PwC, 4.

65 Laura Pavlenko Lutton, "Fund Managers by Gender," *Morningstar Research Report*, June 2015, 1, http://corporate.morningstar.com/US/documents/ResearchPapers/Fund-Managers-by-Gender.pdf.

66 Barry Ritholtz, "Why Don't More Women Hold Top Jobs in Finance?" *Bloomberg View*, February 24, 2016, www.bloomberg.com/view/articles/2016-02-24/why-dont-more-women-hold-top-jobs-in-finance.

67 Laura Pavlenko Lutton, "Fund Managers by Gender: Through the Performance Lens," *Morningstar Research Report*, March 8, 2018, 5–14.

68 Rob Copeland, "At Hedge Funds, Where Are the Women?" *Wall Street Journal*, August 23, 2018, www.wsj.com/articles/at-hedge-funds-where-are-the-women-1535030899.

69 Helena Morrissey, *A Good Time to Be a Girl: Don't Lean in, Change the System* (Glasgow: William Collins, 2018), 14.

70 Chris Newlands "Schroders Responds to Helena Morrissey Discrimination Claims," *Financial News*, February 19, 2018, www.fnlondon.com/articles/schroders-responds-to-helena-morrissey-discrimination-claims-20180219.

71 Charlie Bibby, "Boldness in Business Person of the Year: Helena Morrissey," *Financial Times*, March 16, 2017, www.ft.com/content/556912de-d830-11e6-944b-e7eb37a6aa8e.

72 Kalyeena Makortoff, "L&G Steps up Action against Firms with Few Female Board Members," *The Guardian*, April 15, 2019, www.theguardian.com/business/2019/apr/16/lg-steps-up-action-against-firms-with-few-female-board-members.

73 Brad Barber and Terrance Odean, "Boys Will Be Boys: Gender, Overconfidence, and Common Stock Investment," *The Quarterly Journal of Economics* 116, no.1 (February 2001): 261–292, https://papers.ssrn.com/sol3/papers.cfm?abstract_id=139415.

74 John Coates, Mark Gurnell, and Zoltan Sarnyai, "From Molecule to Market," in *The Leadership Hubris Epidemic: Biological Roots and Strategies for Prevention*, ed. Peter Garrard (London: Palgrave Macmillan, 2018), 25–56.

75 Sigridur Benediktsdottir, Gauti Bergdoruson Eggertsson, and Eggert Dorarinsson, "The Rise, Fall, and Resurrection of Iceland: A Postmortem Analysis of the 2008 Financial Crisis," in *Brookings Papers on Economic Activity* (Fall 2017), 198, www.brookings.edu/wp-content/uploads/2018/02/benediktsdottirtextfa17bpea.pdf.

76 Michael Lewis, "Wall Street on the Tundra," *Vanity Fair*, March 3, 2009, www.vanityfair.com/culture/2009/04/iceland200904-2.

77 Benediktsdottir et al., "The Rise, Fall, and Resurrection of Iceland," 228.

78 Lewis, "Wall Street on the Tundra."

79 Janet Elise Johnson, "Iceland's Government Has Collapsed Because the Prime Minister's Father Wanted to 'Restore' a Child Molester's 'Honor.' What Is Going on?" *The Washington Post*, September 26, 2017.

80 Solomon Teaguel, "Can Feminine Values Fix Finance?" *CNBC*, October 14, 2011, www.cnbc.com/id/44860469.

81 Lewis, "Wall Street on the Tundra."

82 "The Women Who Want to Save Banking," *BBC News*, May 18, 2009, http://news.bbc.co.uk/2/hi/business/8048488.stm.

83 Ruth Sunderland, "After the Crash, Iceland's Women Lead the Rescue," *theguardian.com*, February 21, 2009, www.theguardian.com/world/2009/feb/22/iceland-women.

84 John Taft, *Stewardship: Lessons Learned from the Lost Culture of Wall Street* (Hoboken, NJ: Wiley, 2012), 37.

85 Taft, *Stewardship*, 40–43.

86 Taft, *Stewardship*, 43–49, citing Thelma Beam and Hugh Oddie, *Americans Are from Mars, Canadians Are from Venus*, presentation for Royal Bank of Canada (Canadian Cultural Research/Oddities Inc., 2010).

87 John Dobson, *Finance Ethics: The Rationality of Virtue* (Lanham, MD: Rowman & Littlefield, 1997), 136–137.

88 Jessica Kennedy, Laura Kray, and Gillian Ku, "A Social-Cognitive Approach to Understanding Gender Differences in Negotiator Ethics: The Role of Moral Identity," *Organizational Behavior and Human Decision Processes* 138 (January 2017): 28–44, http://gap.hks.harvard.edu/social-cognitive-approach-understanding-gender-differences-negotiator-ethics-role-moral-identity.

Chapter 4

1 William MacAskill, "Replaceability, Career Choice, and Making a Difference," *Ethical Theory and Moral Practice* 17, no.2 (April 2014): 269–283, www.academia.edu/1557895/Replaceability_Career_Choice_and_Making_a_Difference.

2 Eui Young Kim, "Effective Altruism Leader Shares Philosophy," *Yale Daily News*, February 5, 2018, https://yaledailynews.com/blog/2018/02/05/effective-altruism-leader-shares-philosophy/.

3 William MacAskill, *Doing Good Better* (New York: Avery, 2015), 12.

4 MacAskill, *Doing Good Better*, 156.

5 Philip Shenon, "America's Worst Credit Card: First Premier Bank's Dubious Distinction," *Dailybeast.com*, October 19, 2010, www.thedailybeast.com/americas-worst-credit-card-first-premier-banks-dubious-distinction.

6 Ben Luthi, "First Premier Credit Card Review: Bad Option for Bad Credit," www.nerdwallet.com, April 7, 2017, www.nerdwallet.com/blog/credit-cards/first-premier-bank-credit-card-review/.

7 "About T. Denny Sanford," *Sanford Institute of Philanthropy*, retrieved on December 7, 2018, www.sanfordinstituteofphilanthropy.org/our-mission-vision-history-impact/about-t-denny-sanford/.

8 Michael Gentilucci, "The 18 Most Generous Philanthropists in Finance," *Inside Philanthropy*, August 13, 2014, www.insidephilanthropy.com/home/2014/8/13/the-18-most-generous-philanthropists-in-finance.html.

9 David Whelan, "Dying Broke," *The Forbes 400, Forbes Magazine*, October 8, 2007, www.forbes.com/free_forbes/2007/1008/232.html.

10 Anatole Kaletsky, "How Mr. Soros Made a Billion by Betting against the Pound – George Soros," *The London Times*, October 26, 1992, cited in Ferguson and Schlefer, "Who Broke the Bank of England?"

11 Juliet Chung and Anupreeta Das, "George Soros Transfers $18 Billion to His Foundation, Creating an Instant Giant," *Wall Street Journal*, October 17, 2017, www.wsj.com/articles/george-soros-transfers-18-billion-to-his-foundation-creating-an-instant-giant-1508252926.

12 Chung and Das, "George Soros Transfers $18 Billion."

13 Lauren Debter, "How George Soros Became One of America's Biggest Philanthropists and a Right-Wing Target," *Forbes.com*, October 23, 2018, www.forbes.com/sites/laurengensler/2018/10/23/how-george-soros-became-one-of-americas-biggest-philanthropists-and-a-right-wing-target/#15349d9e39ba.

14 "Members," Giving What We Can, Retrieved on December 11, 2018, www.givingwhatwecan.org/about-us/members/.

15 Center for Effective Altruism, retrieved on December 11, 2018, www.centreforeffectivealtruism.org/.

16 Zachary Mider, "The $13 Billion Mystery Angels," *Bloomberg*, May 14, 2014, www.bloomberg.com/news/articles/2014-05-08/three-mysterious-philanthropists-fund-fourth-largest-u-dot-s-dot-charity.

17 Kenneth Weiss, "The Man Behind the Land," *Los Angeles Times*, October 27, 2004, http://articles.latimes.com/2004/oct/27/local/me-donor27.

18 Bloomberg Harvard City Leadership, Harvard Kennedy School, accessed on December 4, 2018, https://ash.harvard.edu/cityleadership.

19 Jim Tankersley, "Wall Street Veteran Heads New Federal Office Tasked with Making Better Economic Forecasts," *The Washington Post*, April 5, 2013.

20 Walter Isaacson and Evan Thomas, *The Wise Men: Six Friends and the World They Made* (New York: Simon & Schuster, 1986).

21 Isaacson and Thomas, *The Wise Men*, 28–29.

22 Isaacson and Thomas, *The Wise Men*, 90–91.

23 Isaacson and Thomas, *The Wise Men*, 108–111.

24 Isaacson and Thomas, *The Wise Men*, 183.

25 Alvin Krebs, "R.A. Lovett, ex-Chief of Defense Who Pressed Build-Up in 50's, Dies," *The New York Times*, May 8, 1986, www.nytimes.com/1986/05/08/obituaries/ra-lovett-ex-chief-of-defense-who-pressed-buildup-in-50-s-dies.html.

26 Isaacson and Thomas, *The Wise Men*, 194, 555–556.

27 Isaacson and Thomas, *The Wise Men*, 192

28 Isaacson and Thomas, *The Wise Men*, 593–594.

29 Isaacson and Thomas, *The Wise Men*, 117.

30 Richard McKinzie and Theodore Wilson, "Oral History Interview with Robert A. Lovett," Harry S. Truman Presidential Library and Museum, July 7, 1971, www.trumanlibrary.org/oralhist/lovett.htm.

31 Joseph Lawler, "Why Goldman Sachs Thrives in Government," *Washington Examiner*, December 31, 2016, www.washingtonexaminer.com/why-goldman-sachs-thrives-in-government.

32 Josh Gerstein, "How Obama Failed to Shut Washington's Revolving Door," *Politico*, December 31, 2015, www.politico.com/story/2015/12/barack-obama-revolving-door-lobbying-217042.

33 "Riddle Solved: Why It Pays to Become America's Treasury Secretary," *The Economist*, June 15, 2006, www.economist.com/finance-and-economics/2006/06/15/riddle-solved.

34 Steven Mandis, *What Happened to Goldman Sachs?* (Boston: Harvard Business Review Press, 2013), 232–234.

35 Michaela Walsh with Shamina de Gonzaga and Lilia Clemente, *Founding a Movement: Women's World Banking 1975–1990* (New York: Cosimo, 2012), 2.

36 Walsh, de Gonzaga, and Clemente, *Founding a Movement*, 1.

37 Walsh, de Gonzaga, and Clemente, *Founding a Movement*, 2.

38 Michaela Walsh interviewed by Dr. Judy Kuriansky, *The Light Millennium*, May 3, 2006, www.lightmillennium.org/2006_18th/drjudyk_mwalsh_interview.html.

39 Interview with the author, New York, January 28, 2019.

40 Walsh, de Gonzaga, and Clemente, *Founding a Movement*, 6.

41 Communication with the author, June 18, 2019.

42 Walsh, de Gonzaga, and Clemente, *Founding a Movement*, 10.

43 Zohreh Tabatalai, in Walsh, de Gonzaga, and Clemente, *Founding a Movement*, 9.

44 Amy Duffuor, "In Conversation with Michaela Walsh, Women's World Banking," IIX Foundation, October 13, 2014, https://iixfoundation.org/2014/10/13/conversation-michaela-walsh-womens-world-banking/.

45 Phone interview with the author, New York, May 7, 2019.

46 *The Global Findex Database 2017: Measuring Financial Inclusion and the Fintech Revolution*, World Bank Group, https://globalfindex.worldbank.org/.

47 Erin Rogers, "How a Global Mindset Inspired Two Next-Gen Accountants," *EY Our Alumni, ey.com*, www.ey.com/ca/en/alumni/connect-2018-03-01-godard-ambrosino.

48 Erin Godard, "My Inspiration," *FinanceYou Blog*, April 15, 2017, http://financeyouinternational.com/my-inspiration/.

49 Jackie Marchildon, "This Global Citizen of Canada Helps NGOs in Rwanda – By Using Her Accounting Skills," *Globalcitizen.org*, December 7, 2017, www.globalcitizen.org/en/content/global-citizen-of-canada-erin-godard/.

50 Luminari, "These CPAs Left the Big 4, Moved to Rwanda, and Started a Business," *Bizfeed by Luminari*, December 7, 2018, https://bizfeed.luminari.ai/features/cpas-left-big-4-moved-rwanda-started-business/.

51 Erin Godard phone interview with the author, November 30, 2018.

52 Erin Godard phone interview with the author, May 7, 2019 and communication on February 15, 2020.

53 Nick Benes phone interview with the author, November 12, 2018.

54 Nicholas Benes ed., *Charting a New Course for Growth*, American Chamber in Japan White Paper, American Chamber in Japan, 2010, www.accj.or.jp/uploads/4/9/3/4/49349571/accj_charting_a_new_course_for_growth.pdf; Nicholas Smith and Nicholas Benes, *Serving Notice – Corporate Governance Interplay: Returns Spark Rallies*, CLSA University Blue Books, CLSA, November 20, 2017.

55 Nick Benes, "How the Corporate Governance Code Was Born," BDTI, https://bdti.or.jp/en/blog/en/cgcodejapanbirth/.

56 Nick Benes phone interview with the author, November 12, 2018.

57 Benes, "How the Corporate Governance Code Was Born."

58 Nick Benes phone interview with the author, November 9, 2018.

59 Eleanor Warnock (former WSJ Tokyo correspondent present at some of the initial LDP working group meetings) interview with the author, December 7, 2018.

60 Nick Benes phone interview with the author, November 9, 2018.

61 David Webb, "About Us," *Webb-Site*, Retrieved on November 9, 2018, https://webb-site.com/pages/aboutus.asp.

62 David Webb video interview with the author, December 5, 2018.

63 David Webb, "Egana and Upbest," *Webb-site.com*, July 26, 2007, https://webb-site.com/articles/eganaupbest.asp.

64 David Webb, "Egana Update," *Webb-site.com*, August 6, 2007, https://webb-site.com/articles/egana2.asp.

65 David Webb, "The Enigma Network: 50 Stocks Not to Own," *Webb-site.com*, May 15, 2017, https://webb-site.com/articles/enigma.asp.

66 Leslie Shaffer, "This Investor Called a Rout in Hong Kong Stocks. Now He Has a Message for Regulators," *CNBC*, June 29, 2017, https://ca.finance.yahoo.com/news/investor-called-rout-hong-kong-031754778.html.

67 Charles Lee, "David Webb: Tireless Champion of Shareholder's Rights," *Financial Times*, October 13, 2009, www.ft.com/content/9d7a49c6-b790-11de-9812-00144feab49a.

68 Charles Lee, "David Webb: Tireless Champion."

69 Parvathy Ullatil and James Pomfret, "David Webb, a Fly in HK's Corporate Ointment," *Reuters*, April 23, 2009, www.reuters.com/article/us-hongkong-webb-idUSTRE53M4LN20090423.

70 Sam Mamudi, Benjamin Robertson, and Kana Nishizawa, "The 20%-a-Year Stock Picker Who Wishes His Edge Would Disappear," *Bloomberg*, January 2, 2019, www.bloomberg.com/news/articles/2019-01-02/the-20-a-year-stock-picker-who-wishes-his-edge-would-disappear.

71 Mamudi, Robertson, and Nishizawa, "The 20%-a-Year Stock Picker."

72 David Webb, "The Christmas Pick," *Webb-site.com*, December 18, 2009, https://webb-site.com/articles/pick2009.asp.

73 David Webb video interview with the author, December 5, 2018.

74 Charles Lee, "David Webb: Tireless Champion."

Conclusion

1 John Bogle, *Enough: True Measures of Money, Business and Life* (Hoboken, NJ: Wiley, 2009).

2 Richard Sylla and David Cowen, *Alexander Hamilton on Finance, Credit, and Debt* (New York: Columbia University Press, 2018), 3–5.

3 Sylla and Cowen, *Alexander Hamilton on Finance*, 6.

4 Sylla and Cowen, *Alexander Hamilton on Finance*, 317.

5 Ron Chernow, *Alexander Hamilton* (New York: Penguin Press, 2004), 287.

6 Chernow, *Alexander Hamilton*, 725.

7 Chernow, *Alexander Hamilton*, 293.

8 Chernow, *Alexander Hamilton*, 483.

9 Chernow, *Alexander Hamilton*, 341.

10 Chernow, *Alexander Hamilton*, 484.

11 Chernow, *Alexander Hamilton*, 725.

INDEX